MONOPOLIES, MERGERS AND COMPETITION POLICY

Monopolies, Mergers and Competition Policy

F.M. Scherer

Professor of Public Policy and Corporate Management in the Aetna Chair, Emeritus
Harvard Kennedy School of Government, USA

EE Edward **Elgar**
PUBLISHING

Cheltenham, UK • Northampton, MA, USA

Published by
Edward Elgar Publishing Limited
The Lypiatts
15 Lansdown Road
Cheltenham
Glos GL50 2JA
UK

Edward Elgar Publishing, Inc.
William Pratt House
9 Dewey Court
Northampton
Massachusetts 01060
USA

A catalogue record for this book
is available from the British Library

Library of Congress Control Number: 2017953164

ISBN 978 1 78536 247 7

Printed and bound by CPI Group (UK) Ltd, Croydon, CR0 4YY

Contents

PART IV   POLICY FOR DEVELOPING COUNTRIES

Acknowledgements

The editor and publishers wish to thank the authors and the following publishers who have kindly given permission for the use of copyright material.

American Antitrust Institute for paper: F.M. Scherer (2009), 'On the Paternity of a Market Delineation Approach', *American Antitrust Institute Working Paper #09-01*, January, 2–10.

American Bar Association via the Copyright Clearance Center for excerpt: F.M. Scherer (2008), 'Technological Innovation and Monopolization', in Wayne D. Collins and Joseph Angland (eds), *Issues in Competition Law and Policy, Volume II*, Chapter 44, 1033–68.

Robert Anderson, Jayashree Watal and Cambridge University Press for paper: F.M. Scherer and Jayashree Watal (2014), 'Competition Policy and Intellectual Property: Insights from Developed Country Experience', *John F. Kennedy School of Government Faculty Research Working Paper RWP14-013*, title page, 1–31.

The Bureau of National Affairs, Inc. for paper: F.M. Scherer (2003), 'Microsoft and IBM in Europe', *Antitrust and Trade Regulation Report*, **84** (2090), January 24th, 65–6.

Elsevier Ltd for article: William S. Comanor and F.M. Scherer (2013), 'Mergers and Innovation in the Pharmaceutical Industry', *Journal of Health Economics*, **32** (1), January, 106–13.

Organisation for Economic Co-operation and Development for the paper: F.M. Scherer (2012), 'Merger Efficiencies and Competition Policy', *Organisation for Economic Co-operation and Development Note DAF/COMP/WD(2012)47*, October, 2–9.

Oxford University Press for excerpt: F.M. Scherer (2004), 'Retailer-Instigated Restraints on Suppliers' Sales: Toys "R" Us (2000)', in John Kwoka and L.J. White (eds), *The Antritrust Revolution*, 4th edn, Case 16, 441–55.

SAGE Publications, Inc. for article: F.M. Scherer (2004), 'Vertical Relations in Antitrust: Some Intellectual History', *Antitrust Bulletin*, **49**, Winter, 841–58.

Springer Science and Business Media for articles: F.M. Scherer (2006), 'A New Retrospective on Mergers', *Review of Industrial Organization*, **28** (4), June, 327–41; F.M. Scherer (2011), 'Standard Oil as a Technological Innovator', *Review of Industrial Organization*, **38** (1), May, 225–33; Frederic M. Scherer (2011), 'Abuse of Dominance by High Technology Enterprises: A Comparison of U.S. and E.C. Approaches', *Economia e Politica Industriale – Journal of Industrial and Business Economics*, **38** (1), March, 39–62; F.M. Scherer (2015), 'The Federal Trade Commission, Oligopoly, and Shared Monopoly', *Review of Industrial Organization*, **46** (1), February, 5–23.

Every effort has been made to trace all the copyright holders but if any have been inadvertently overlooked the publishers will be pleased to make the necessary arrangement at the first opportunity.

Introduction

F.M. Scherer

This volume collects 14 papers on competition policy written by me during the first 15 years of the 21st century. It augments an earlier collection on the same theme published by Edward Elgar in 2000 under the title, *Competition Policy, Domestic and International*. The new papers date from 2003 to 2015, including one that was still working its way through the publication process.

Statutory laws with an express pro-competition slant had their clearest origins in the United States, first in several states and then with the enactment of the federal Sherman Antitrust Act in 1890. Diffusion to other nations was at first slow, but adoption of pro-competition statutes and the creation of enforcement agencies spread after World War II, initially gradually but then rapidly.[1] By 2015, representatives of some 40 nations and supra-national groups had compiled reports on their domestic policies, among other things for discussion at fora conducted regularly by the Organisation for Economic Co-operation and Development (OECD) at its Paris headquarters. On the whole, with notable exceptions, national policies evolved away from the toleration or even overt encouragement of monopolistic industry structures and toward emphasizing competition as an allocator of economic resources.

Competition policy is all about structure and conduct in economic markets, and economics has from the early years played an important role in illuminating the issues, staking out the metes and bounds of desirable behavior, and assisting in the prosecution (usually by lawyers) of formal complaints alleging the infringement of national or supranational rules. An early role for formal economic analysis was recognized when US President Theodore Roosevelt established in 1903 an independent Bureau of Corporations, whose analytic and report-publishing functions were absorbed into the Federal Trade Commission in 1914. Among other things, the directorate general for Competition Policy at the European Commission headquarters in Brussels employs a substantial staff of economists to support review and enforcement activities. Staff economists sometimes testify in formal enforcement actions. On other occasions, they are supplemented by academic economists serving as consultants to the responsible government agencies. Academic economists have also represented the companies responding to enforcement agency complaints so that both sides (or all sides!) of an argument are presented. In 1961 a new for-profit enterprise, National Economic Research Associates Inc., was created to provide full-time support staffs and retain academic experts, usually working on behalf of enterprises charged with competition policy violations or needing to navigate other regulatory shoals. Since then many similar organizations have emerged. Indeed, economic analysis for competition policy enforcement activities has been a vigorous growth industry.

The essays in this volume were written by the author partly as an independent academic observer of competition policy issues and partly as a result of participating as an actual or potential witness in formal proceedings. None of the latter was an advocacy piece per se; all attempt to take a more balanced view. The essays are oriented around three main themes:

monopolization, that is, the achievement or attempt to achieve something approximating a monopoly position in relevant markets; merger policy, which is a common route toward the attainment of monopoly-like market positions (and also, although not always, toward the realization of desirable efficiencies); and other practices that reflect or enhance the attainment of monopoly power in some markets. Most are focused on the conditions that prevail in highly developed markets such as the United States and Europe. A final chapter, however, assesses the role of competition policy and its interactions with intellectual property (mostly patents) in less-developed nations.

Monopolies and monopolization

Monopoly positions often result from successful acts of technological or marketing innovation, and once monopoly positions are attained, one might ask, does vigorous innovation continue? The author's curiosity on these matters was fired when, as an undergraduate at the University of Michigan in the 1950s, I read Joseph Schumpeter's classic 1942 book, *Capitalism, Socialism, and Democracy*. Two compelling themes advanced by Schumpeter in that book (as well as others) were (1) that technological innovation has been the main fount of improvement in citizens' economic well-being since at least the onset of the industrial revolution; and (2) that large, even monopolistic, corporations had become a particularly fertile source of continuing technological innovations. On the second of these themes, Schumpeter criticized contemporary anti-monopoly policies as counter-productive, arguing (p. 103) that:

> What we have got to accept is that [the large-scale establishment or unit of control] has come to be the most powerful engine of ... progress and ... long-run expansion not only in spite of, but to a considerable extent through, this strategy which looks so restrictive when viewed ... from the individual point in time. In this respect, perfect competition is not only impossible but inferior, and has no title to being set up as a model of ideal efficiency.

Since that time, the questions raised by Schumpeter were an important focus of my intellectual forays. Chapter 1 responded to an invitation by the American Bar Association to address the issues. It reviews the histories of seven 'great' monopolization challenges in US history: Standard Oil, the electric lamp cartel, several cases involving telephone giant AT&T, DuPont's cellophane near-monopoly, Xerox, IBM, and Microsoft. In all seven cases, technological and organizational innovations did sow the seeds for powerful monopoly positions. But in most of the cases, the rise to monopoly was accompanied by practices such as predatory pricing, cartel and other restrictive agreements (often in conjunction with patent conflict settlements), price discrimination, mergers, and other actionable competition policy infringements. And in many cases, once monopoly positions were achieved, the monopolist often rested on its technological oars, blocked access to complementary technologies needed by others to develop superior products, or failed to introduce on a timely basis improvements that were either overlooked or that were seen as 'cannibalizing' existing monopoly rents. In several prominent cases, the weakening of monopoly positions through antitrust action opened the door to important new technological advances. Perhaps most striking in this respect was the response of Xerox, when its huge patent portfolio was required under an antitrust settlement to be opened for licensing by others. Xerox's management found it necessary to 'reinvent' the company, reducing its costs and introducing new and more advantageous products.

I was particularly surprised and captivated by the evidence compiled for my American Bar Association analysis of Standard Oil, broken up in 1911 following an antitrust case that set precedents for much subsequent competition policy enforcement in America. Especially striking were the retardation of invention patent growth once Standard achieved industry dominance, the resurgence when Standard was broken up, and the delay in implementing an extremely important petroleum cracking technology until after the breakup. These findings were reviewed again in Chapter 2. However, the main impetus for that article was the assertion in Standard's defense against monopolization charges that it had shown special innovative flair in introducing the Frasch–Burton process for refining high-sulfur oil. Pulling the widely scattered facts together, I realized that the key invention had in fact been made by a former employee of Standard whose inventive genius had been overlooked while he was an employee. Only by buying out Hermann Frasch and his patents did Standard belatedly enable utilization of its rich Lima, Ohio, oil deposits. Again, the evidence failed to support Schumpeter's assertion of innovative superiority for ongoing monopolistic enterprises.

When the US government commenced a monopolization case against Microsoft in the late 1990s, I collaborated with three other scholars in writing an *amici curiae* brief for the action's presiding judge, Judge Thomas Jackson.[2] We recommended *inter alia* the divestiture of Microsoft into separate operating system and applications units – a remedy ordered by Judge Jackson but overturned when the government defended its position ineptly before an appellate court. The European Commission then marched into the breach with its own complaint. When this action was announced, a friend suggested to me that the experience from the Commission's previous monopolization case against another high-technology giant – IBM – be reviewed and brought back to public notice. I reviewed documentation from the EC's action and interviewed two companies deemed most likely to have been affected positively by the Commission's order that IBM make timely disclosure of technical data required by manufacturers of peripheral equipment (so-called PCMs) designed to achieve plug-compatibility with IBM mainframes. Chapter 3 briefly reports my findings. One PCM considered the mandated disclosures important to the success of its own efforts; another believed that even without the disclosures, it could achieve the desired interfaces. My article at least served to inform skeptics that the European Commission's charges against Microsoft had an efficacious prior history in another computer-intensive realm.

I had been heavily involved as a witness, first for competitor Advanced Micro Devices and then for the Federal Trade Commission, in early US legal actions against Intel, and I testified before a European appellate court in Luxembourg on one facet of the European Commission's case against Microsoft. I was therefore closely acquainted with both the US and European records involving Microsoft and Intel. When the European judgments proved to be much tougher than those effected in the United States, I decided to review the historical evidence critically. Chapter 4 was the result. It infers that the monopolization abuse complaints on both sides of the Atlantic Ocean had substantial factual and analytic support. It finds, however, that the Commission had a hard time forcing Microsoft to disclose relevant interface information until very substantial fines were levied, and that the order compelling Microsoft to 'unbundle' its Windows Media Player was an abject failure because of Microsoft's strategic pricing responses. Insufficient evidence had accumulated to determine whether Intel significantly changed the pricing policies that put its main rival at the time, Advanced Micro Devices, at a serious disadvantage. However, it has since become clear that AMD's fortunes waned nevertheless. Also, Intel lost market share because demand shifted away from personal computer microprocessors, in which Intel's principal advantage lay, to smart phone chips, for whose supply Intel was poorly positioned. There, the inexorable advance of technology – Schumpeter's 'creative destruction' – did more to undermine Intel's monopoly power than competition agency action. Chapter 4 also criticizes the European Commission for its tendency to serve as a complaint bureau for aggrieved competitors rather than initiating cases through the analytic work of its own economists. In effect, the Commission renders itself vulnerable to the complaint that it is protecting 'competitors rather than competition'.

Merger policy

Mergers can unify previously-competing firms, enhancing their power to charge monopoly-like prices. The US Clayton Act of 1914 singled out for antitrust sanctions corporate acquisitions whose effect 'may be to substantially lessen competition ... or tend to create a monopoly'. Judicial interpretations of the law opened up many loopholes, however, and in the Celler–Kefauver Act of 1950, the US Congress reiterated its intent to stop mergers whose effect 'may be substantially to lessen competition, or to tend to create a monopoly'. In addition to reversing a split infinitive, the new law goaded the antitrust enforcement agencies and the courts to take a tough line, and many strong precedents followed.

Mergers are undertaken, however, for many reasons other than simply to enhance monopoly power. They may displace ineffective management, permit operational reorganizations that enhance operating efficiency, help participants capture speculative gains, entrench management, and much else. Competition laws and their enforcement have weighed these disparate effects in varying ways as additional precedents and rules have emerged.

Chapter 5 presents the author's most recent synthesis of the evidence on merger effects other than straight monopoly power. It advances several points. For one, it clarifies why random stock price fluctuations, shown by finance specialists to be an important market reality, set the stage for mergers yielding essentially speculative gains. Second, it shows that making mergers has come to be an increasingly significant component of corporate management skills, augmented *inter alia* by the emphasis business schools place on it in their curricula. Third, it complements a substantial received literature revealing that most mergers yield at best disappointing efficiency gains by showing that at the economy-wide level, periodic waves of merger-making and changes in productivity growth were essentially uncorrelated.

Since mergers can in principle have both bad effects such as enhancing monopoly power and good effects, e.g., facilitating efficiencies, one might suppose that law-makers and enforcers would attempt to balance the two in judging actual situations. This approach was rejected in early US Supreme Court interpretations of the 1950 Celler–Kefauver Act. The Court said, for example, in a seminal bank merger decision:[3]

> Congress ... proscribed anticompetitive mergers, the benign and the malignant alike, fully aware, we must presume, that some price might have to be paid.

This approach was widely debated in the scholarly literature on competition policy, with strong criticisms coming among others from economists. In 1968 Oliver Williamson, fresh from an assignment as economic adviser to the head of antitrust enforcement at the US

Department of Justice and later (2009) Nobel laureate in economic science, castigated competition policy enforcers' aversion to making tradeoffs.[4] He showed *inter alia* that when a merger led both to cost reductions and monopoly price-raising, the increase in economic welfare from the cost savings could easily outweigh the negative effects of price increases. At first the notion of an explicit tradeoff was rejected by US enforcement agencies.[5] However, in 1984, when revised *Merger Guidelines* were published by the US Department of Justice, a policy reversal was announced, with a statement on p. 22 that:

> Some mergers that the Department otherwise might challenge may be reasonably necessary to achieve significant net efficiencies. If the parties to the merger establish by clear and convincing evidence that a merger will achieve such efficiencies, the Department will consider those efficiencies in deciding whether to challenge the merger.

Efficiency tradeoff analyses began to evolve in merger case selection and adjudication. Shortly after the 1984 *Guidelines* were issued, I was asked to participate in what was expected to be the first formally litigated merger efficiencies defense – on a merger between two high-fructose corn syrup producers. However, the case dragged on for years procedurally, so that the formal trial was only an early, and probably not the first, contest.[6]

How competition agencies should undertake such merger efficiency tradeoffs came to the attention of a much broader multinational forum, the Competition Policy unit of the OECD. In 2012, I was commissioned by OECD to prepare an analytic report on the issue. Chapter 6 was the result.[7] It illustrates the standard Williamson price raising vs. efficiency tradeoff and supports tradeoff analysis in cases (perhaps atypical) where there are substantial indications of probable efficiency effects. But it raises a caveat. At the time, many nations, especially in Europe, were still experiencing high rates of unemployment following the 2008 macroeconomic crisis. Taking a general equilibrium perspective, my contribution suggests that cost savings may not increase overall economic welfare much because they lead mainly to higher unemployment rather than increased output (utilizing freed labor resources) in other industries. It also addresses from my own experience the difficulties of predicting before a merger actually occurs the likelihood and magnitude of merger-induced efficiencies. Alternative approaches to implementing merger-based efficiencies tradeoffs are explored.

One of the challenges addressed by economists serving as expert witnesses in anti-merger actions is defining the relevant market in which the would-be merger parties operate, and hence in which the fusion is said to reduce competition. If the market is defined too narrowly, meaningful substitute products may be overlooked, leading to over-estimation of the merging parties' market shares and hence to an exaggeration of their potential monopoly power. Too broad a definition can conversely include providers of substitutes that have little influence on the merging parties' pricing. Market definitions tended in the early days of Celler–Kefauver Act enforcement to be made more or less ad hoc, with little or no strong rationale in relevant economic theory. In 1982 the Department of Justice issued its first formal *Merger Guidelines*, suggesting (p. 4) that additional products be added to the market being defined if 'a *s*ignificant percentage of the buyers of products already included would be likely to shift to those other products in response to a *S*mall but *S*ignificant and *N*on-transitory *I*ncrease in *P*rice'. Combining the italicized letters yields SSNIP, and so the test became known, in a city famous for its use of acronyms, as the SSNIP test. When the *Guidelines* were published, my placid reaction was, 'Hmmm. I've already used that test – as an expert witness in three previous cases'. But later, when retrospective articles were published suggesting that at the time no prior usages were known to the *Guidelines* drafters, my ire over the neglect of a previous 'discovery' was aroused.[8] Chapter 7, which was rejected by the editor of the most relevant economics journal outlet, was the result. In it I observe that not only had I used the SSNIP approach in three prior antitrust actions, but a prior literature citation on a different point by one of the *Guidelines* co-authors was taken from my own new statement of market definition principles only one page away in the 1980 edition of my textbook.[9] The 1980 version, it should be noted, departed from the more traditional market definition approaches reviewed in my 1970 (first) edition as a result of the location theory I had utilized in a 1975 book on *The Economics of Multi-Plant Operation*.

Chapter 8, written with William S. Comanor, explores an issue raised much less frequently in the application of competition law to mergers. Traditional merger analysis seldom deals with the question of how mergers might affect firms' virtuosity in effecting technological innovations. But in some industries – pharmaceuticals is a prime example – innovation is perhaps the most important single facet of firms' performance. Since at least the onset of the 21st century, traditional 'Big Pharma' companies have experienced a slowdown in their ability to discover, develop, and introduce new, therapeutically pioneering molecules. Many have turned to merger as a means of sustaining their prior growth. Concurrently, an important new source of pharmaceutical innovations – companies exploiting techniques of gene splicing and DNA analysis – have risen to prominence. Such companies often lack the financial resources needed to test their new molecules clinically and to market them to all likely prescribers. 'Big Pharma' companies have therefore tended often to license and commercialize the discoveries of smaller and more innovative companies, but sometimes also to take them over lock stock and barrel through merger, embedding them into their more bureaucratic innovative cultures. Or in one of the most egregious cases, industry leader Merck acquired in 2015 a small firm, Cubist, that had experienced a rare success developing a new antibiotic effective against highly resistant bacteria. Merck added the drug, Cubicin, to its product line and shortly thereafter fired all 120 researchers in Cubist's Lexington, Massachusetts, laboratories – researchers who were working on four prospective future drugs.[10] On this and other acquisitions of small, research-oriented biotech companies, US antitrust authorities stood by and sucked their thumbs.[11] In Chapter 8,[12] Comanor and I review the evidence on pharmaceutical mergers and tap relevant 'parallel paths' theory showing that, given the large technological uncertainties confronting new drug discovery, progress is best sustained by maintaining many independent sources of R&D initiative. As Linda Loman lamented in Arthur Miller's *Death of a Salesman*, attention must be paid.

Other monopolistic practices

There is, of course, much more to competition policy than mergers and monopolization. The competition laws of virtually every nation prohibit overt agreements to fix prices. But what if the number of rivals is small and each rival refrains from active price competition because it recognizes that all will realize higher profits if all behave similarly? This is the classic problem of oligopoly pricing theory, singled out for attention by a host of early economists ranging from Augustin Cournot (1838) to Edward Chamberlin (1933). Chapter 9 was written for a Festschrift honoring the 100th anniversary of the US Federal Trade Commission (FTC)'s establishment. In it I review the FTC's two most famous attempts to deal with oligopolies charging high prices when there was little or no evidence of overt collusion: in providing the 'wonder drug' tetracycline (during the 1950s) and in ready-to-eat breakfast cereals (1970s). In both cases, frustration was the order of the day. Recognizing the difficulties, US antitrust agencies have emphasized merger control to inhibit the formation of tight oligopoly market structures before they facilitate tacit collusion.

Monopolization, mergers, and oligopoly pricing issues mostly involve the quest for or exercise of monopoly power in a particular market. Competition policy also deals, however, with questions of *vertical* power – that is, when a powerful firm influences the pricing and other policies of its suppliers, or of firms that serve as wholesale or retail intermediaries in the progression of the power-holder's products or services to final consumers. Chapter 10 surveys the most interesting vertical power relationships and how they have been treated in US antitrust policy. Three main nexuses are analysed. *Monopsony power* exists when a buyer is so powerful that it can influence – usually depress – the prices at which its upstream suppliers provide their offerings. The original Standard Oil monopoly was an early example. It controlled not only the prices at which its kerosene was made available to consumers, but also took actions that reduced the prices it had to pay crude oil extractors. Second, monopoly power may appear at multiple stages of a vertical chain – e.g., when railroads, each the sole provider on some length of track, must 'interchange' the goods they carry with other railroads similarly positioned on origin and destination segments over which traffic flows. From seminal work by Charles Ellet Jr. (in 1839) it was known that the stacking of monopolized railroad segments vertically could lead to more restriction of output than having a single line carry goods over the full distance. Vertical integration in this case tends to permit lower overall prices and higher outputs. Analogous problems emerge when the royalty-seeking actions of diverse patent holders impair attempts to introduce new technologies requiring an array of patented 'prior art'.[13] And third, powerful actors may act to increase their own profits by imposing diverse restrictions – so-called vertical restraints – on their suppliers or on the merchants who channel their goods to ultimate consumers.

One classic example of a vertical restraint is resale price maintenance (RPM), under which, for example, manufacturers require their retailers to charge a prescribed and usually uniform price to their customers. Its legality under US antitrust statutes varied over the years between permissiveness and outright prohibition. The legal developments were accompanied by a fierce debate among economists as to whether resale price maintenance should be curbed because of its tendency to raise prices or encouraged because it might induce retailers to offer a richer array of pre-sale services ranging from advertising to on-site product demonstration. A key test case came before the US Supreme Court in the 2007.[14] Chapter 11 reproduces the *amicus curiae* brief presented to the Court by William Comanor, my longest-standing friend from graduate school in economics, and me. In it we adopted the stance of President Truman's hated two-armed economist – 'on the one hand, but on the other hand...' We rejected some economists' demand for per se illegality of RPM, but also argued against other economists' argument favoring blanket legality. Instead, we tried to provide the foundations for a rule of reason analysis distinguishing the good applications from the bad – the latter occurring when retailers agreed among themselves to enforce RPM or when most of the goods traded under a relevant line of commerce were subjected to RPM. Our brief was cited seven times in the Court's majority and minority opinions. But unfortunately, the majority failed to rule on our 'quantitative substantiality' test, leaving to the lower courts the task of working out rule of reason guidelines.

Chapter 12 recounts another of my forays into the complex world of vertical restraints. In the 1990s, Toys 'R' Us (TRU) was the leading retail supplier of toys in the United States. It was worried, however, by encroaching low-price competition from recently expanding 'warehouse clubs' – i.e., retail chains that collected membership fees and then offered merchandise to their members at sharply discounted prices. TRU was concerned not only with the direct loss of sales to warehouse clubs, but also by the fear that the clubs' pricing would undermine consumers' belief that it was the lowest-price toy retailer. To combat this development, it pressured toy manufacturers not to supply their most popular toys to warehouse clubs and encouraged the manufacturers to agree among themselves in supporting such a boycott. The FTC charged TRU with violating the antitrust laws. I was principal economics witness for the FTC, matched against Dennis Carlton of the University of Chicago, who advanced typical Chicago-school permissiveness toward all kinds of vertical restraints. Chapter 12 summarizes the facts and the outcome. In a word, the FTC found TRU's activities to violate antitrust law. TRU appealed, choosing as a venue the Seventh Circuit Court of Appeals in Chicago, on which sat *inter alia* three University of Chicago professors who, TRU's lawyers supposed, would support their home team's favorable inclinations. They were wrong. The presiding judge, a University of Chicago Law School faculty member, came down strongly in favor of the FTC's finding of illegality.

Chapter 13 summarizes my reflections from personal experience with still another facet of US antitrust law – allowing individuals and firms that have been harmed by competition law violations to sue as a group (i.e., in so-called 'class actions') for recovery of damages (in the US, trebled relative to the court's accepted assessment of actual damages sustained through price-fixing actions). It was presented at a workshop in Italy anticipating the passage (which eventually occurred) of similar damages recoupment policies in the European Community. My views were largely cautionary, in part because the threat of paying treble damages if apprehended had clearly not dried up price-fixing activities in the United States, because the law firms specialized in bringing treble damages suits often pursued their targets with blackmail motives in mind, and partly because of a defect in US law that allowed only the first purchasers of a good whose price had been fixed through illegal conspiracy to obtain restitution.

Policy for developing countries

Concluding Chapter 14 shifts its emphasis from industrialized nations, which were the first to implement active pro-competition policies, to developing nations. The principal context is the abuse of patent positions – i.e., actions that go beyond the legitimate innovation-inducing function of the patent system.[15] Beginning in 1994, many nations, and especially LDCs, were required to increase the scope and strength of their patent laws under the so-called TRIPS (Trade-Related Aspects of Intellectual Property Rights) treaty culminating one facet of the Uruguay Round of international trade negotiations.[16] However, Article 40 provided an escape clause, stating that nations could take legal action against abuses of patent or copyright protection having an adverse effect on competition in their home markets. Article 31(k) authorized compulsory licensing of patents – i.e., taking away the presumption of exclusive use – in cases where such licensing practices were ruled administratively or judicially to be anti-competitive. The treaty probably accelerated the diffusion of formal competition policy laws to less-developed nations, but exactly how those new laws would be enforced in cases of intellectual property abuse was yet to be determined. Chapter 14 was written by Jayashree Watal of the World Trade Organization and myself to provide guidance. It reviews the history of competition policy interventions triggered by alleged abuse of intellectual property positions in the most developed nations and suggests how those precedents might be applied by LDCs. Needless to say, most of the relevant history remains to unfold.

Notes

1. For a succinct history, see F.M. Scherer, *Competition Policies for an Integrated World Economy* (Brookings Institution: 1994), Chapter 3.
2. Robert Litan, Roger Noll, William Nordhaus, and F.M. Scherer, *Remedies Brief of Amici Curiae in re U.S. v. Microsoft Corporation* (2000; available online).
3. *U.S. v. Philadelphia National Bank*, 374 U.S. 321, 371 (1963).
4. 'Economies as an Antitrust Defense: The Welfare Tradeoffs', *American Economic Review*, March 1968, pp. 18–36.
5. As chief economist of the U.S. Federal Trade Commission in 1976, the author proposed a formal test in considering a merger believed from prior research to offer substantial efficiencies. Incorporating an efficiencies analysis was approved by the full Commission, but it was opposed by enforcement staff attorneys and eventually subverted.
6. *U.S. v. Archer-Daniels-Midland Co. et al.*, 781 F. Supp. 1400 (1991). An affidavit I submitted in 1987 for the case suggesting guidelines for an efficiencies defense is reproduced in F.M. Scherer, *Competition Policy, Domestic and International* (Edward Elgar: 2000), pp. 259–69.
7. It originally appeared in OECD, *Policy Roundtable: The Role of Efficiency Claims in Antitrust Proceedings* (2012), pp. 257–64. Found at www.oecd.org/competition/EfficiencyClaims2013.pdf.
8. In this I followed a great scientific tradition. See the presidential address by Robert Merton, 'Priorities in Scientific Discovery: A Chapter in the Sociology of Science', *American Sociological Review*, vol. 22 (1957), pp. 635–59.
9. *Industrial Market Structure and Economic Performance*, 2nd ed. (Rand-McNally: 1980), p. 60.
10. 'Merck Dumps 120 Cubist Researchers After Its $9.5B Merger', *Fierce Biotech*, March 5, 2015.
11. In a few previous cases, where each of the merger partners had directly competing drug candidates in development or production, the US authorities have required spin-off or compulsory licensing of one candidate to an independent entity.
12. The reader is cautioned that Table 1 omits the acquisition of Schering AG by Bayer in 2006. Also, on that table's entry 8, second line, 'Beckham' should be 'Beecham'.
13. See Robert P. Merges and Richard R. Nelson, 'On the Complex Economics of Patent Scope', *Columbia Law Review*, May 1990, pp. 839–916.
14. *Leegin Creative Leather Products Inc. v. PSKS Inc.*, 551 U.S. 877 (2007).
15. Abuses of copyright are also covered.
16. On the interest group activities that underlay the treaty and the propagandistic origins of the term 'intellectual property', see F.M. Scherer, 'The Political Economy of Patent Policy Reform in the United States', *Journal on Telecommunications & High Technology Law*, vol. 7 (Spring 2009), pp. 201–10.

PART I

MONOPOLIES AND MONOPOLIZATION

Chapter 44

TECHNOLOGICAL INNOVATION AND MONOPOLIZATION

F. M. Scherer[*]

This chapter explores the role Section 2 of the Sherman Act can play in promoting innovation by examining seven seminal cases, ranging from *Standard Oil* to *Microsoft*. Finding that antitrust authorities were relatively unsuccessful in resolving disputed issues on a timely basis, the chapter proposes three prescriptions: (1) judges should be able to retain technical expert as a clerk, (2) Section 2 review should be conducted swiftly and in favor of minimizing barriers to innovative new entry, and (3) even natural monopolies should not be allowed to outlive the 20-year shelf life of their patents.

1. Introduction

Especially in industrial product markets, dominant positions are often achieved as a consequence of innovation. In passing the Sherman Act, Congress used without precise definition the word "monopolize" to indicate in Section 2 how the new law would be violated. From the congressional debates, it is clear that more was required than merely possessing a monopoly market share. Some antitrust scholars have argued along with economist Joseph A. Schumpeter that when a monopoly position follows from or is accompanied by technological innovation, all Sherman Act bets should be off, in part because temporary monopoly is a natural concomitant of innovation and also because the "creative destruction" associated with innovation inexorably threatens existing monopolies and forces them to behave competitively:

> But in capitalist reality as distinguished from its textbook picture . . . the kind of competition which counts [is] the competition from the new commodity, the new technology, the new source of supply, the new type of organization (the large-scale unit of control for instance)—competition which commands a decisive cost or quality advantage and which strikes not at the margins of the profits and the outputs of the existing firms but at their foundations and their very lives . . . . [Such] competition . . . acts not only when in being but also when it is merely an ever-present threat. It disciplines before it attacks. The businessman feels himself to be in a competitive situation even if he is alone in his field or if, though not alone, he holds a position such that investigating government experts fail to see any effective competition . . . .[1]

This chapter traces the nonlinear path over which Sherman Act Section 2 adjudication has evolved for situations in which technological innovation played a prominent role. Ignoring Justice Oliver Wendell Holmes's admonition that "[g]reat cases like hard cases make bad law,"[2] it addresses the issues by reviewing the history of several "great" U.S.

---

*   John F. Kennedy School of Government, Harvard University.
1.   JOSEPH A. SCHUMPETER, CAPITALISM, SOCIALISM AND DEMOCRACY 84-85 (1942).
2.   N. Sec. Co. v. United States, 193 U.S. 197, 400 (1904) (Holmes, J., dissenting).

monopolization cases: *Standard Oil* (1911), the various electric lamp cases, the diverse antitrust actions involving AT&T, the *Cellophane* case, the *Xerox* case, the IBM cases, and the various Microsoft cases.

The emphasis is on questions explored at a more abstract and general level in the extensive economic literature on dynamic relationships between market structure and incentives for innovation.[3]   Thus, did dominant positions result from acts of unambiguous technological leadership? Or did the seminal inventive activities originate in a wider array of enterprises, from which one firm emerged dominant by dint of either technical superiority or other less clearly laudable courses of conduct? Once dominance was achieved, did innovation continue at high levels of vigor?

The intrinsic difficulty of these questions forces us to ask whether the adjudicating courts can cope effectively with the factual issues arising in innovation-plus-monopolization cases. Can they weigh on a timely basis the causal role of technical superiority as compared to practices that by themselves would support an inference of monopolistic intent? And can they devise remedies that restore competition without jeopardizing incentives for innovation?

This is an ambitious agenda. It is too ambitious to expect final, definitive answers. The author has struggled with some of the issues for four decades, only to conclude that the most favorable environment for technological progress depends upon nuanced circumstances. The most we can hope for is an indication of general tendencies, some suggestions for improvement, and clarification of issues that will continue to be debated. We proceed in rough chronological order.

2. Standard Oil

To the twenty-first century reader, characterizing petroleum refining as high-technology might seem strange. But in its early days, the industry indeed pressed the frontiers of technology. And Standard Oil defended itself, arguing inter alia in its attorneys' brief to the Missouri circuit court that it had innovated both technologically and in the scale economies-enhancing investments by which it aggressively expanded its business:

> They have been unremitting in their efforts to improve the processes of refining, to diversify the useful by-products to be obtained from the refining of petroleum and to introduce them into general use, and these efforts have resulted to their great advantage as well as to the general benefit of the industry and the public at large . . . . They have made great efforts to solve the problem of refining refractory oils and through the success of these efforts they have been able to utilize to their great advantage oils that otherwise were useless except for fuel purposes.[4]

---

3.   For surveys, see JENNIFER F. REINGANUM, *The Timing of Innovation: Research, Development, and Diffusion, in* 1 HANDBOOK OF INDUSTRIAL ORGANIZATION 849 (1989); WESLEY M. COHEN & RICHARD C. LEVIN, *Empirical Studies of Innovation and Market Structure, in* 2 HANDBOOK OF INDUSTRIAL ORGANIZATION 1059 (1989); and WILLIAM M. BALDWIN & JOHN T. SCOTT, MARKET STRUCTURE AND TECHNOLOGICAL CHANGE (1987).

4.   Brief for Defendants on the Facts at 109, United States v. Standard Oil Co., 173 F. 177, 196 (E.D. Mo. 1909) (No. 5371).

Emphasized among Standard's innovative accomplishments was the Frasch-Burton process for deriving satisfactory illuminating oil (kerosene) from the high-sulphur oil found in the fields around Lima, Ohio.[5]

One of America's most eminent business historians, Alfred Chandler, argues in an early book that Standard Oil was a leader in the "mass production revolution" and that "the high speed of throughput and the resulting lowered unit cost gave John D. Rockefeller his initial advantage in the competitive battles . . . during the 1870s."[6] In a later elaboration, stressing the "unprecedented cost advantages of the economies of scale and scope," he attributes a decline in unit refining costs from 1.5 cents per gallon, observed in 1885 for independent refineries having a daily processing capacity of 1,500 to 2,000 barrels per day, to 0.452 cents, realized in Standard's much larger refineries, with capacities of 5,000 to 6,500 barrels.[7]

Reconsidering the *Standard Oil* case, economist Dominick Armentano stresses that refined petroleum prices fell significantly between 1880 and 1897 while Standard's output expanded strongly. From this he concludes that "[i]n short, there was no restriction of supply, and monopoly prices were never realized, even during periods of relatively high market share. Standard was a large, competitive firm in an open, competitive market."[8] In this, however, he commits a fallacy repeated by other scholars. It is easy to show using economic theory that even the tightest of monopolies will expand output over time if the demand it is facing shifts to the right, when, for example, consumers learn the advantages of kerosene as an illuminant, as population grows, and as new geographic markets are reached. And with rightward-shifting demand, prices can fall even under complete monopoly conditions if economies of larger scale are realized and/or technological changes shift cost curves downward.[9] The key questions therefore are factual: how great were the scale economies realized by Standard vis-à-vis rivals, and to what extent did its innovative efforts contribute uniquely to the decrease in refining and transportation costs?

In adjudicating the *Standard Oil* case, the courts could not ignore Standard's claims of superior entrepreneurship. The Supreme Court observed, for example, that

> in a powerful analysis of the facts, it is insisted [by Standard] that they demonstrate that the origin and development of the vast business which the defendants control was but the result of lawful competitive methods, guided by economic genius of the highest order,

---

5. Hermann Frasch emigrated to the United States in 1868 at the age of 17 and was employed thereafter by diverse Cleveland area companies. His first patent assigned to Solar Refining, a Cleveland-based Standard affiliate, appears to have been issued in 1891. He previously invented a more famous process for mining sulphur. William Burton later invented the first successful thermal cracking apparatus.

6. ALFRED D. CHANDLER JR., THE VISIBLE HAND: THE MANAGERIAL REVOLUTION IN AMERICAN BUSINESS 256 (1977).

7. ALFRED D. CHANDLER JR., SCALE AND SCOPE: THE DYNAMICS OF INDUSTRIAL CAPITALISM 21, 25 (1990). For my argument that such cost savings were too great to stem from scale economies alone and Chandler's rebuttal, see Colloquium, 64 BUS. HIST. REV. 694-95, 737-38 (1990).

8. DOMINICK ARMENTANO, ANTITRUST AND MONOPOLY: ANATOMY OF A POLICY FAILURE 66 (2d ed. 1990).

9. This is most uniformly true when demand curve shifts are isoelastic, i.e., when the quantity demanded at any price is multiplied by a constant. Exceptions can readily arise when the shift is parallel—a case common in textbook analyses but less common in the real world than isoelastic shifts.

sustained by courage, by a keen insight into commercial situations, resulting in the acquisition of great wealth, but at the same time serving to stimulate and increase production, to widely extend the distribution of the products of petroleum at a cost largely below that which would have otherwise prevailed, thus proving to be at one and the same time a benefaction to the general public as well as of enormous advantage to individuals.[10]

Nevertheless, both the circuit court of first instance and the Supreme Court manifestly failed to address and resolve the contending claims. The Supreme Court at least admitted the task's difficulty:

> [T]o discover and state the truth concerning these contentions both arguments call for the analysis and weighing . . . of a jungle of conflicting testimony covering a period of forty years, a duty difficult to rightly perform and, even if satisfactorily accomplished, almost impossible to state with any reasonable regard to brevity.[11]

Instead, asserting from historical and legal reasoning "an obvious truth" that individuals should not be allowed to secure monopolies by wrongful means, the circuit court concluded summarily, "nor can arguments of reduced prices of product, economy in operation, and the like have weight," commencing its remedial order only two paragraphs later.[12] Similarly, without engaging in the kind of balancing a modern rule of reason analysis might entail, the Supreme Court found that

> [Standard's] very genius for commercial development and organization which . . . was manifested from the beginning soon begot an intent and purpose to exclude others which was frequently manifested by acts and dealings wholly inconsistent with the theory that they were made with the single conception of advancing the development of business power by usual methods, but which on the contrary necessarily involved the intent to drive others from the field and to exclude them from their right to trade and thus accomplish the mastery which was the end in view.[13]

As a result, Standard Oil was broken into 34 fragments, partly delineated by function (e.g., crude oil production, transportation, or refining) and partly geographically.

One might speculate that the courts in *Standard Oil* attempted no balancing of the evidence on innovation and cost reduction because the job had been done for them, despite the evident lack of judicial gratitude, in a massive study the Bureau of Corporations completed two years before the circuit court delivered its opinion. The Bureau's staff observed inter alia that by far the largest declines in the margin between crude petroleum prices and refined product prices occurred between 1866 and 1872, "before the Standard can be said to have exercised any influence,"[14] that in the first decade of the 20th Century there was very little difference between the unit costs of Standard refineries and those of its larger rivals (who, it argued, would have been even

---

10. Standard Oil Co. v. United States, 221 U.S. 1, 48 (1911).
11. *Id.*
12. United States v. Standard Oil Co., 173 F. 177, 196 (E.D. Mo. 1909).
13. *Standard Oil Co.,* 221 U.S. at 76. In his dissent, Justice John Marshall Harlan criticized the majority for articulating its "rule of reason" to adjudicate monopolization cases without any evident basis in congressional intent.
14. 2 REPORT OF THE COMMISSIONER OF CORPORATIONS ON THE PETROLEUM INDUSTRY, PRICES AND PROFITS 625 (1907).

larger and joined by others but for Standard's restrictive practices),[15] and, on technological innovation:

> It is a familiar fact that whenever any absolutely new industry springs up, particularly one of a complex character, the costs at the outset are exceedingly high and are rapidly reduced with the first few succeeding years . . . . It is doubtless true that the Standard Oil Company . . . was able to secure economies somewhat greater than could have been secured by a number of smaller concerns. It is, however, absurd to contend that no further economies in the industry would have been brought about after 1873 in the absence of the Standard or a similar combination . . . . The reduction of cost, even by small concerns, has been due to the natural development of the industry and to the general progress of science and invention—not to the enormous aggregation of capital.[16]

Support for the Bureau's inferences on innovation is provided by an analysis of data the Bureau staff failed to consider (presumably because it was not fashionable in economics to do so at the time, as it is now). From Jacob Schmookler's compilation of U.S. patents issued in various fields, Figure 1 shows the number of petroleum refining patents issued during five-year periods between 1850 and 1929, along with the amount

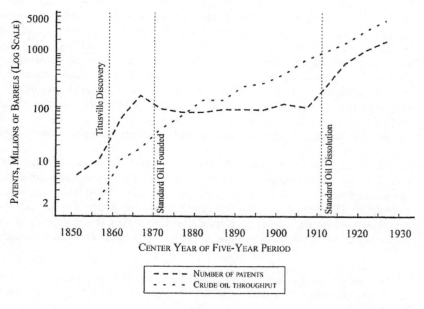

Figure 1.

Trends in petroleum refining patents and crude oil throughput.

---

15. *Id.* at 650-55.
16. *Id.* at 625-26.

of crude oil produced in the United States during the same periods.[17] The plot is in logarithmic form, so a straight line implies a constant annual growth rate. The growth of patenting is most rapid before Standard Oil was incorporated and began acquiring competitors in 1870. By 1880, Standard had acquired at least 80 percent of U.S. refining capacity. During its period of dominance, patenting shows no growth and is at lower absolute rates than in 1865-69. After the dissolution of the New Jersey Standard Company in 1912, there is new growth and a substantial increase in the level of patenting.

More detailed scrutiny suggests that the core components of Standard Oil generated only a small share of the 443 refining patents identified in Schmookler's tabulation for the years from 1875 to 1899. A search was conducted in the U.S. Patent and Trademark Office's *Annual Index of Patents* covering those 25 years for any patent assignment to an entity with the name "Standard Oil" along with 50 subsidiaries named, for various time periods, in historian John Moody's *The Truth About the Trusts*.[18] Patents pertaining to barrel-making, can-sealing, and petroleum applications inventions were excluded to maintain consistency with the Schmookler definitions. With the benefit of the doubt resolved in cases of imperfect name matches in favor of counting patents as Standard-originated, from 48 to 54 patents, or at most 12 percent of the comparable Schmookler count, had origins in Standard companies. It is possible that some inventions made by Standard employees were not assigned to the parent, and indeed, several cases were found in which employees assigned some patents to Standard units and retained individual rights to others. However, in 1871 U.S. law was revised to allow companies to require assignment of employee-made inventions, so Standard clearly had the right to require assignment, and 16 Standard units were found to have received assignments during the sample period.[19] It seems clear that Standard's operating entities made relatively few technological contributions other than those associated with Hermann Frasch, who single-handedly accounted for 21 of the assigned refining process inventions.

There is qualitative support for inferring that Standard Oil was not an outstanding technological innovator during its period of dominance. While the monopolization case was proceeding, the petroleum refining industry was subjected to two technological revolutions. The demand for kerosene illuminating oil—its principal early product— was threatened by the advent of electric illumination, but the emergence of the automobile created demand for gasoline, which until then had been a nearly worthless

17. For Patent Office classes 325 through 332, see 2 JACOB SCHMOOKLER, STATISTICS OF PATENTS CLASSIFIED BY INDUSTRY, UNITED STATES, 1837-1957 (undated, mimeographed, University of Minnesota).

18. JOHN MOODY, THE TRUTH ABOUT THE TRUSTS 120-24 (1904). The search utilized *Index of Patents* volumes located in the Patent Office's public search room, which were found to be in seriously deteriorated condition, and better maintained volumes (missing five years) in the Boston Public Library.

19. *See* CHRISTOPHER MAY & SUSAN K. SELL, INTELLECTUAL PROPERTY RIGHTS: A CRITICAL HISTORY 123 (2006). The count of Standard subsidiary assignees here includes several inventions on nonrefining inventions, of which numerous cases were found. In 1778 William Rockefeller, John D. Rockefeller's brother and business associate, took personal assignment on a nonrefining invention.

by-product of the refining process. In 1907, 8.0 percent of American homes were wired for electricity; by 1912, the figure had doubled and continued rising to 34.7 percent in 1920. In 1907, 43,000 passenger automobiles were produced; in 1912, 356,000; and after the first million-car year in 1916, factory sales reached 1.9 million in 1920. Using traditional methods, petroleum refiners were hard-pressed to extract enough gasoline to meet the burgeoning demand. A new process for obtaining a much higher fraction of gasoline from a barrel of crude oil—thermal cracking—was invented around 1909 by William Burton, co-inventor earlier of the Frasch process and in 1909 head of production at Standard Oil Company of Indiana. Indiana Standard applied to Standard headquarters in New York for authorization to spend $1 million developing and installing thermal crackers. The request was turned down; the invention was considered too dangerous.[20] Only when Standard of Indiana became independent in 1912 could the project go forward. The Burton process was widely licensed. Between 1913 and 1920, when competing cracking processes began to emerge, 91 million (42-gallon) barrels of gasoline had been refined using the Burton process.[21]

3. The electric lamp industry

If the kerosene lamp repelled the forces of darkness, electric illumination vanquished them. Thomas Edison, every American school child knows, is the one who struck the decisive blow. But the full story is more complex. By the 1870s, the scientific knowledge base required for an incandescent lamp had evolved to a state under which, given the powerful demand for low-cost illumination, the "invention" of electric lamps had become virtually inevitable.[22] Thus, carbon filament lamps were conceived almost simultaneously between 1879 and 1881 by a number of individuals, including Edison, Great Britain's Joseph Swan (who had experimented with filament lamps as early as 1848), and others. Edison had two advantages: he more than any other perfected an entire system for electric lighting, and he sought patents aggressively. Erroneously believing that patenting was precluded by prior art, Swan lagged Edison in seeking patents. Nevertheless, many companies entered the new business, and a tangle of potentially interfering patents materialized.

The strategies of Edison and the General Electric Company (GE), the successor to the various Edison companies formed in 1891, included vigorous acquisition of other inventors' key patents, restrictive cross-licensing of patents when outright acquisition was not possible, merger with competing companies producing electric lamps and ancillary equipment, and leveraging their powerful patent position to organize both

---

20. *See* DANIEL YERGEN, THE PRIZE 111-12 (1991); GEORGE S. GIBB & EVELYN H. KNOWLTON, HISTORY OF STANDARD OIL COMPANY: THE RESURGENT YEARS: 1911-1927, at 116-17 (1956). Gibb and Knowlton observe more generally that "[l]ittle creative research of an important nature . . . was undertaken" by New Jersey Standard. *Id.* at 123.

21. JOHN L. ENOS, PETROLEUM PROGRESS AND PROFITS: A HISTORY OF PROCESS INNOVATIONS app. tbl.1a (1962).

22. *See* William F. Ogburn & D.S. Thomas, *Are Inventions Inevitable?*, 37 POL. SCI. Q. 83-98 (1922); F.M. SCHERER, *Economics of Innovation and Technological Change, in* 11 ENCYCLOPEDIA OF THE SOCIAL AND BEHAVIORAL SCIENCES 7531-33 (2001).

national and international cartels.[23] By 1896, GE and its cross-licensee Westinghouse dominated the industry with a combined 75 percent market share, surrounded by a fringe of licensed and (typically short-lived) smaller rivals. In 1896 GE took the lead in organizing the Incandescent Lamp Manufacturers trade association, which fixed prices, allocated customers, and assigned each member a maximum percentage quota oriented around GE's sales. Cross-licenses with European rivals limited the participating companies to their agreed-upon national spheres of influence. As the basic Edison and complementary patents expired, GE sustained its dominant position and its ability to orchestrate the cartel through further acquisitions of key patents and rival companies. GE was slow to embrace superior metal lamp filament designs and other improvements,[24] but when the expiration of carbon filament lamp improvement patents weakened its position and after European companies had blazed the trail by introducing lamps with metal (e.g., tungsten and tantalum) filaments, GE caught up by developing between 1904 and 1907 superior lamps with ductile tungsten filaments, to which the advantages of argon gas filling were later added.[25]

The first government attack on the lamp cartel was initiated in March 1911, two months after the Supreme Court's *Standard Oil* decision. A consent decree entered on October 12, 1911, enjoined many of the cartel's practices. However, following precedents confirmed in the *Bement* case,[26] the consent decree did not restrict GE's ability to acquire competing patents or its ability to specify in patent licenses the prices at which the licensees sold their bulbs, assign them market share quotas, and limit the kinds or sizes of lamps they could supply. It did, however, prevent GE from stipulating the prices its own and licensees' downstream distributors could charge. GE and Westinghouse circumvented this restriction by designating their retailers as agents, maintaining de jure property rights in the patented lamps carried in retailers' inventories. With restrictive license terms and the agency system substituting for the earlier cartel arrangements, the electric lamp cartel was minimally discommoded. GE's share of U.S. lamp production in 1923 was estimated to be 61 percent; Westinghouse's share 16 percent; that of other licensees 9 percent, and other vendors (mostly specialized) 14 percent.[27]

The agency system was challenged under a new antitrust suit in 1924, but it was sustained as legitimate by a district court in 1925 and by the Supreme Court in 1926.[28] Among other things, the Supreme Court reiterated its *Bement* conclusion that fixing the prices at which direct licensees (e.g., Westinghouse) sold their products was a condition "normally and reasonably adapted to secure pecuniary reward for the patentee's monopoly"—downplaying the fact that GE's patents were often acquired from would-be

---

23.   The most comprehensive source on this history is ARTHUR A. BRIGHT JR., THE ELECTRIC LIGHT INDUSTRY (1949). Edison withdrew from the active management of his electric light companies in 1884.

24.   *See* Robert P. Merges & Richard R. Nelson, *On the Complex Economics of Patent Scope*, 90 COLUM. L. REV. 839, 885-87 (1990) (citing inter alia BRIGHT, *supra* note 23).

25.   *See* JAMES M. UTTERBACK, MASTERING THE DYNAMICS OF INNOVATION 66-70 (1994).

26.   E. Bement & Son v. Nat'l Harrow Co., 186 U.S. 70 (1902).

27.   BRIGHT, *supra* note 23, at 242.

28.   United States v. Gen. Elec. Co., 272 U.S. 476 (1926).

rivals in what was transparently an attempt to monopolize the field and that they were conditioned on a rich network of restrictive cross-licenses.

Public attitudes toward patent-based cartels changed dramatically during the Great Depression of the 1930s. The failure of the cartel-friendly National Recovery Administration (NRA) to restore prosperity was one reason. Investigations by the Temporary National Economic Committee (TNEC) also altered policy makers' perceptions, among other things by revealing in detail the stranglehold the Hartford Empire Company and its bottle making licensees had secured over the glass container industry. At an American Economic Association symposium reviewing the TNEC's findings, later Nobel laureate George Stigler found Hartford Empire "an eloquent example of an evil demanding correction" and concluded flatly that "[t]he case for limitation of restrictive licensing is surely irrefutable."[29] The TNEC findings spurred the Department of Justice (DOJ) to launch a broad investigation of patent system abuses and to initiate numerous complaints challenging patent practices. The electric lamp cartels, national and international, were one target. Westinghouse consented in 1942 to end its cartel participation and license its patents royalty-free, but for GE and some licensing partners who chose to fight the battle in court, prosecution was delayed until the end of World War II to avoid distracting executives' attention from the war effort.

In 1948, the U.S. District Court for the Northern District of Ohio found that GE and its licensees had in fact violated Sections 1 and 2 of the Sherman Act. Weighing what had been accomplished to provide U.S. consumers with low-cost illumination against the restraints maintained, Judge Phillip Forman concluded:

> The record of General Electric's industrial achievement has been impressive. Its predecessors pioneered the lamp industry and it organized through the years an establishment that stands as a model of industrial efficiency . . . . By means of extensive research . . . mechanical and technological advances were accomplished . . . which made possible a progressive price reduction policy . . . . It can take just pride in the more graphic statistic that the price of a 60 watt bulb was 45 cents in 1922 and 10 cents in 1942 . . . .
>
> On the other hand there can be no doubt that it paced its industrial achievements with efforts to insulate itself from competition. It developed a tremendous patent framework and sought to stretch the monopoly acquired by patents far beyond the intendment of those grants. It constructed a great network of agreements and licenses, national and international in scope, which had the effect of locking the door of the United States to any challenge to its supremacy in the incandescent electric lamp industry arising from business enterprise indigenous to this country or put forth by foreign manufacturers. Its domestic licenses gave fiat to a few licensees whose growth was carefully limited to fixed percentages of its own production and expansion so that over the years its share of the business was not materially diminished and its dominant proportion was never exposed to any hazard in that direction.[30]

The remedial order was deferred to a subsequent stage, concluded in 1953. At the time, GE's share of domestic incandescent lamp production was estimated to be 60

---

29. George J. Stigler, *The Extent and Bases of Monopoly*, 32 AM. ECON. REV. 14 (June Supp. 1942).
30. United States v. Gen. Elec. Co., 82 F. Supp. 753, 905 (D.N.J. 1949).

percent. The government's petition that half of GE's principal lamp production capacity be spun off into a separate entity was denied. However, the restrictive agreements between GE and its domestic and foreign licensees were enjoined. GE had argued, citing a Supreme Court pronouncement in the *Hartford-Empire* case,[31] that it should receive appropriate compensation for any patent licenses it was required to issue. However, finding GE and its licensees to be "mounted upon an arsenal of a huge body of patents that can easily overwhelm and defeat competition by small firms," Forman asserted what the Supreme Court had deemed in another compulsory licensing case to be "sound judicial discretion" and ordered that the lamp patents be dedicated to the public without compensation:

> Royalty free licensing and dedication are but an extension of the same principle, not to be directed indiscriminately, of course, but well within the therapeutic measures to be administered under circumstances such as were made to appear in this case.[32]

Thus, a patent monopoly position engendered when Thomas Edison received his basic carbon filament lamp patent in 1880 ended by judicial decree 73 years later. A congressional survey found that as of January 1956 nine compulsory licenses had been issued by GE and eight by Westinghouse.[33] Price competition from both domestic and foreign sources has undoubtedly intensified since then. In 1985 imports rose to 10.9 percent of domestic firms' output value. The domestic industry structure, however, was not radically transformed; it continues to be a relatively tight oligopoly, with a four-firm concentration ratio of 93 percent in 1954 and 87 percent in 1992.[34]

4. AT&T

The early history of American Telephone and Telegraph Company (AT&T) is remarkably similar to that of GE. Alexander Graham Bell filed his first telephone patent application on February 14, 1876. Patent no. 174,465 was approved three weeks later. Only a few hours after Bell's initial application was filed, Elisha Gray of Chicago filed a patent application for his own version of the telephone. Bell's first and subsequent patents were assigned to a series of companies that eventually became AT&T; Gray's to the powerful Western Union Company (which in August 1877 turned down an opportunity to purchase Bell's initial patent). Each company began installing or licensing newly created local firms to install telephone networks. Given the conflicting claims resulting from third-party inventions, various infringement suits were initiated. They were eventually resolved in favor of the Bell derivative companies in a 4-3 decision of the U.S. Supreme Court.[35] In the meantime, Western Union had also

---

31. Hartford-Empire Co. v. United States, 323 U.S. 386, 414 (1945).
32. United States v. Gen. Elec. Co., 115 F. Supp. 835, 844 (D.N.J 1953).
33. STAFF OF SUBCOMM. ON PATENTS, TRADEMARKS, AND COPYRIGHTS OF THE S. COMM. ON THE JUDICIARY, 86th Cong., REPORT ON COMPULSORY LICENSING UNDER ANTITRUST JUDGMENTS 20 (1960).
34. From relevant U.S. Bureau of the Census publications and Web filings under the general title, Concentration Ratios in Manufacturing. Historical data are found at www.census.gov/eped/www/concentration92-47.xls.
35. Dolbear v. Am. Bell Tel. Co., 126 U.S. 1 (1888).

purchased relevant patents from Amos E. Dolbear and Thomas A. Edison. These additional inventions were sufficiently superior to those of Bell that, despite Bell's purchase of an improved transmitter patent, Western Union "methodically beat [Bell] each time the two systems were in direct competition."[36]

Each company found itself threatened by the other's patent claims and telephone system investments. In November 1879 a settlement was reached. Under it, Western Union agreed not to contest the validity of Bell's patents, to cede exclusive rights for the construction and operation of telephone networks to the Bell companies, and to grant Bell rights in 42 existing and any subsequent telephone patents owned by Western Union. The quid pro quo was an agreement by Bell not to compete in the field of telegraphy and to pay between 1879 and 1896 20 percent of Bell's license revenues from its telephone operating company franchisees. In addition, Bell agreed to purchase Western Union's already existing telephone operations.[37]

To consolidate its patent position, the Bell derivative (AT&T predecessor) companies acquired a 40 percent interest in the Western Electric Company, which had been organized in 1856 to supply telegraph equipment to Western Union and which, when Western Union entered telephony, had made numerous additional telephony inventions. By 1883, AT&T had acquired majority control of Western Electric. Among other things, these actions prevented Western Electric from supplying telephone apparatus to other companies that might compete with the Bell affiliates.

Despite Bell's consolidated patent position, many other companies did try to enter the newly emerging telephone service and equipment supply industries. Bell's largely successful strategy in combating them was to deny them Western Electric as an equipment supplier and to sue them for infringement when other equipment sources were tapped. Between 1877 and 1893, when the original Bell patent expired, roughly 600 infringement suits were brought. Most of the respondents promptly went out of business when challenged; only a few suits were pursued to the final Supreme Court decision of 1888.[38] With the expiration of another key Bell patent in 1894, however, Bell's ability to exclude competition merely on the basis of its extensive continuing patent portfolio was severely weakened. Again, new companies began providing telephone service, especially in smaller towns Bell had not yet entered but also some directly competing in the larger metropolitan areas. By 1902, there were 1.32 million Bell telephones in use and 1.05 million independent units.

AT&T (incorporated in 1885 and reorganized to control all Bell affiliates in 1900) pursued several strategies to restrain the growth of independent competition. It acquired from outside inventors additional patents, including Lee de Forest's basic triode amplifier tube patent. It continued to bring infringement suits, not all of them successful. Efforts to strengthen this barrier further by purchasing two particularly important equipment manufacturers who supplied the independent telephone companies

---

36.   JOSEPH C. GOULDEN, MONOPOLY 35 (1970).

37.   1 FEDERAL COMMC'NS COMM'N STAFF REPORT ON TELEPHONE INVESTIGATION 183-85, 318, 356 (1939) [hereinafter FCC STAFF REPORT]. The early sections of this account rely heavily upon the FCC report.

38.   *Id.* at 186.

were defeated by federal and state antimerger actions in 1906 and 1907.[39]   Having steadily increased the "long lines" connections among individual metropolitan telephone systems, AT&T denied interconnection to competing local operating companies and hence deprived them of network advantages.[40]   With its superior access to financial capital and its network advantage of long lines interconnectivity, the Bell System engaged in an aggressive program of buying up competitive telephone companies.   By 1912, Bell control of telephone sets in service had risen to 5.09 million, compared to 3.64 million associated with independent companies.[41]

A T&T's continuing efforts to acquire rivals and its refusal to interconnect those who remained independent, however, provoked antitrust intervention beginning in 1913. This led in late 1913 to the so-called Kingsbury commitment,[42] named after a vice president of AT&T.   Under it AT&T agreed not to acquire control over any additional competing telephone service companies, to dispose of its controlling stock interest in Western Union (acquired in 1909), and to interconnect its intercity and local networks with competing companies if they provided standardized connecting lines.   The undertaking was modified in 1918 to permit Bell to acquire competing companies if the Bell System in turn spun off an equal number of telephone stations to independent companies.   Some independent companies apparently protested that the Kingsbury commitment prevented them from selling out on advantageous terms to AT&T, and in 1921, after the passage of permissive legislation, the DOJ voided the commitment.   As a result of these changes, the number of independent telephone sets peaked at 4.8 million in 1922 while Bell's network of sets rose to 9.5 million in 1922 and 13.7 million in 1927.

Even before the Kingsbury commitment was negotiated, some of Bell's restrictive policies were relaxed beginning with the return of Theodore Vail to the leadership of AT&T in 1907.   Vail believed that telephone service should be a universal monopoly regulated by governmental authority at either the state or federal level.   He was also concerned by escalating threats of antitrust intervention.   Some (largely ineffective) regulation was exercised by the Interstate Commerce Commission beginning in 1910, replaced in 1934 by the creation of the Federal Communications Commission (FCC). Also, recognizing that Bell's ability to block independent competition through patent suits was weakening, Vail authorized Western Electric to begin selling equipment to the independent operators.   The loss of leverage motivating independent companies to sell out to Bell in order to gain interconnection with Bell's long lines was apparently compensated by arbitrary toll revenue "divisions" that favored Bell, given the independents' need to connect with Bell in order to supply their patrons with comprehensive nationwide service.[43]

---

39.   *Id.* at 204.
40.   On network externalities, see Michael L. Katz & Carl Shapiro, *Systems Competition and Network Effects*, 8 J. ECON. PERSP. 93-115 (1994).
41.   FCC STAFF REPORT, *supra* note 37, at 208.
42.   *Id.* Prior to 1913, 16 states had passed laws requiring interconnection, but some were undermined through technical incompatibilities.
43.   *Id.* at 213.

The emergence of radio technology posed a new threat to AT&T's increasingly dominant position. With its control of the de Forest triode patent and many improvement inventions, AT&T held a key blocking position. But other companies had equally important patents on related aspects of radio technology. To ensure that advances in the military use of radio did not bog down through a welter of infringement suits, the U.S. Navy required in 1917 (as the United States entered World War I) that the principal patent holders cross-license their patents into a patent pool. After the war, the leading radio patent holders—AT&T, GE, RCA (created as a patent-pooling entity in 1919), and Westinghouse—entered into cross-licensing agreements, with each participant receiving exclusive rights to develop its strategic interests—e.g., for AT&T, to use the patents for wire telephone and telegraph technology and public network radiotelephones. However, the rapid rise of radio broadcasting was not anticipated in the agreements. AT&T began setting up broadcasting stations, initially with WEAF in New York during 1922, and demanding that other radio broadcasters take licenses from AT&T calling for royalty payments and restrictions on the commercial sale of radio time. They initiated political countermeasures, leading Secretary of Commerce Herbert Hoover to declare in 1924:

> I can state emphatically that it would be most unfortunate for the people of this country to whom broadcasting has become an important incident of life if its control should come into the hands of any single corporation, individual or combination.[44]

This controversy led to arbitration over the terms of the original patent pool and eventually, in 1926, to a cross-licensing agreement modification under which AT&T sold its broadcasting operations to RCA and agreed to stay out of broadcasting in return for exclusive "pickup" rights to transmit programs between radio stations over its land telephone lines. The agreement provided that if AT&T failed to furnish the desired services, RCA could do so. AT&T retained exclusive rights to all other applications of wire telephony, to commercial two-way radiotelephony operations within the United States, and to the provision of equipment used in the United States for transoceanic radiotelephone calls.[45] This agreement drew an antitrust challenge, eventually settled in 1932. The revised agreement did little to restrict AT&T's ability to control its chosen fields.[46]

With a secure monopoly in telecommunications service and the supply of equipment to its operating companies, AT&T was, according to the FCC's 1939 staff report, slow in introducing such technological innovations as automatic dialing, monolithic handsets, anti-sidetone circuitry, and office switchboards with enhanced features.[47] Following World War II,[48] AT&T continued to delay the implementation of certain technological

---

44. W.R. MACLAURIN, INVENTION AND INNOVATION IN THE RADIO INDUSTRY 114 (1949).
45. *See* FCC STAFF REPORT, *supra* note 37, at 334-36; GERALD W. BROCK, THE SECOND INFORMATION REVOLUTION 36-38 (2003).
46. *See* FCC STAFF REPORT, *supra* note 37, at 340.
47. *Id.* at 323-98, 404-05.
48. For an analysis of ten postwar innovations showing rapid introduction in some monopoly cases (e.g., touch-tone dialing) but on average faster introduction under more recent competitive conditions, see

innovations despite the work of its Bell Telephone Laboratories, called by *Fortune* in November 1958 "the world's greatest industrial laboratory," responsible among other things for the invention of the transistor,[49] the discovery of cosmic microwave background radiation presumably resulting from "the Big Bang," a leading role in the invention of the laser, and shared development of optical fiber transmission cables. Delayed implementation occurred because Western Electric designs were favored over alternative equipment available on the outside market and through stringent interpretation of its tariff rules barring the attachment of "foreign devices" to Bell's lines and telephones. Examples included Bell's discontinuation of service to customers using answering machines and recording devices not designed by Western Electric; actions to discourage customers from using one-piece telephones, facsimile machines, designer telephones, and speakerphones available on the market; the insistence that large-volume customers use Bell-design office switchboards rather than allegedly superior models available from other sources; and actions taken to prevent the use of Hush-a-Phone (a device attaching to handset speakers to prevent bystanders from overhearing conversations) and the Carterphone, which permitted users to "patch" telephone calls back and forth into over-the-air radio communication devices, including ham radios. The Hush-a-Phone and Carterphone disputes led to regulatory proceedings before the FCC and litigation in the federal courts, precipitating escalating requirements that AT&T lessen its barriers to foreign attachments.[50]

Another exception to Bell's slow innovation pace is revealing. By the end of World War II, radio, radar, and radio tube technology had advanced to the point where transmitting large quantities of information using microwave radio had become feasible. At the same time, the rapid emergence of the television industry created a demand for the ability to carry broadband television signals for long distances between various parts of the country. To facilitate microwave technology, the FCC allocated blocks of the microwave radio spectrum for use by relay systems. By 1947, several companies, including Philco, Raytheon, Western Union, GE and IBM jointly, and DuMont had applied for microwave spectrum allocations and had either begun or were about to begin construction of experimental microwave relay networks.[51] These ventures were a serious threat to the Bell System's long-established monopoly position in the intercity transmission of all but telegraph signals. Bell responded by developing at record speed its TD-2 radio relay system, initiating service with a New York-Chicago link in

Howard A. Shelanski, *Competition and Deployment of New Technology in U.S. Telecommunications*, 2000 U. CHI. LEGAL F. 85, 98-117 (2000).

49. For an obituary observing that a lack of competitive urgency slowed AT&T's use of Bell Laboratories inventions, see *AT&T Inventions Fueled Tech Boom, And Its Own Fall*, WALL ST. J., Feb. 2, 2005, at 1. Remarkably, Bell Laboratories lagged Northern Telecom of Canada in the development of digital central office switches because Bell failed to extrapolate, consistent with Moore's Law, the future decline of integrated circuit prices. *See* F.M. SCHERER, INTERNATIONAL HIGH-TECHNOLOGY COMPETITION 87-88 (1992).

50. Hush-a-Phone Corp. v. United States, 238 F.2d 266 (D.C. Cir. 1956); Hush-a-Phone Corp., 22 F.C.C. 113 (1957); Carter v. AT&T Co., 250 F. Supp. 188 (N.D. Tex.), *aff'd*, 365 F.2d 486 (5th Cir. 1966); Use of Carterphone Device in Message Toll Tel. Serv., 13 F.C.C.2d 420 (1968).

51. *See* Donald C. Beelar, *Cables in the Sky and the Struggle for Their Control*, 21 FED. COMM. BAR J. 27-37 (1967).

September 1950.[52] It simultaneously retarded or blocked rival developments by staking claims to the most desirable relay locations, refusing to interconnect its microwave and telephone facilities with non-Bell microwave systems, and persuading the FCC to restrict the use of key spectrum blocks to common carriers. Through the "crash" TD-2 program, AT&T successfully defended most of its monopoly position in intercity message transmission—at least until later regulatory developments altered the environment in the 1960s.[53]

Eventually, however, AT&T's efforts to maintain its service and equipment near-monopoly positions induced aggressive antitrust intervention. A complaint was filed in 1949 seeking divestiture of Western Electric from AT&T, fragmentation of Western Electric into three parts, and the end of other restrictive arrangements. Adjudication was delayed by the Korean War. In 1953, Secretary of Defense Charles E. Wilson sent to Attorney General Herbert Brownell a letter observing that the proposed divestiture of Western Electric "seriously threatens the continuation of important work which the Bell System is now carrying forward in the interests of national defense." It urged that "a mere postponement . . . does not adequately protect the vital interests involved" and asked that the DOJ review "how this potential hazard to national security can be removed or alleviated."[54] This paved the way for a consent settlement in 1956 requiring compulsory licensing of roughly 9,000 AT&T patents and limitations on third-party commercial product sales by Western Electric.[55] A congressional investigation revealed later that the letter was drafted by Bell Laboratories president Mervin J. Kelly.[56] The Western Electric case was cited, along with more recent settlements involving the automobile industry and various mergers, in congressional hearings that led to the so-called Tunney Act, which requires publication of the rationale for antitrust consent decrees and judicial oversight of their provisions.[57]

How AT&T responded to post-1956 FCC mandates allowing companies such as MCI and Datran to commence intercity service competitive with AT&T and requiring it to interconnect "foreign devices" set the stage for a new monopolization complaint in November 1974. In addition to showing that AT&T and Western Electric held monopoly positions, the government alleged a laundry list of restrictive practices, including failure to interconnect competing carriers with its network on reasonable terms, discriminatory price reductions confined to the markets in which competition had emerged, and much else, which, the government alleged provided proof of intent to monopolize. The government sought divestiture of local Bell operating companies and

---

52. F.M. Scherer, *The Development of the TD-X and TD-2 Microwave Radio Relay Systems in Bell Telephone Laboratories*, cleared case study, *in* HARVARD BUSINESS SCHOOL WEAPONS ACQUISITION RESEARCH PROJECT (1960).

53. Specifically, the FCC's *Above 890* decision in 1959 followed by the FCC's approval of MCI's radio relay system application in 1969.

54. *Consent Decree Program of the Department of Justice, Part II: Hearing Before the Subcommittee on Antitrust of the H. Comm. on the Judiciary*, 85th Cong. 2029-31 (1958) [hereinafter *Consent Decree Program*].

55. United States v. W. Elec. Co., 1956 Trade Cas. (CCH) ¶ 68,246 (D.N.J. 1956).

56. *Consent Decree Program*, *supra* note 54, at 2015-39.

57. *Antitrust Procedures and Penalties Act: Hearing Before the Subcommittee on Antitrust and Monopoly of the S. Committee on the Judiciary*, 93d Cong. (1973); Pub. L. No. 93-528 (Dec. 1974).

Western Electric from AT&T and (more tentatively) fragmentation of Western Electric. A clumsily punctuated paragraph in the government's brief also implied that Bell Telephone Laboratories would be separated from the Western Electric manufacturing operations[58]—a proposal which, if in fact intended, showed serious misunderstanding of how research and development are best conducted. AT&T replied inter alia that its monopolistic positions and the vertical integration of its operations resulted from conscious regulatory policies and that the restrictive practices of which it was accused were approved, either actively or passively, by the FCC. They reflected among other things regulators' desire to preserve the integrity of the U.S. telecommunications network from technological failures and from "cream-skimming" behavior by new rivals exploiting an accepted uniform-price policy by entering only high-volume, low-cost segments. Equally importantly, there was what the AT&T brief called its "economic and technological defense":

> [T]he integrated structure of the Bell System which the Government seeks to destroy in this case, and the interactions and common purpose which that structure makes possible, have enabled the Bell System to provide the public with the finest telecommunications system in the world at rates that compare very favorably with those available in any other country.... The Bell System's price and quality performance has only been matched by its record of introducing innovative equipment better to fulfill its service mission.[59]

After the government's case-in-chief was completed, AT&T moved for summary judgment. Placing little weight on the economic and technological defense, District Judge Harold Greene concluded that AT&T possessed monopoly power "notwithstanding regulation," adding his supposition that the FCC "may realistically be incapable of effectively regulating a company of AT&T's size, complexity, and power."[60] He ruled further, subject to possible rebuttal in the case's defense phase, that the evidence gave reason to believe that the Bell System had violated the antitrust laws over a lengthy period of time, citing in particular its conduct with respect to the connection of customer-owned equipment, intercity service competitors, and the procurement of equipment.

A series of surprises followed. Settlement negotiations already underway at the time of Greene's decision were accelerated, and on January 8, 1982, AT&T and the government announced that they had reached a consent agreement. Twenty-two Bell companies providing preponderantly local telephone service were to be separated from AT&T and reorganized into an unspecified number (eventually, seven) of regional clusters (RBOCs, for Regional Bell Operating Companies). AT&T would retain the interstate service (long lines) part of its activities as well as Western Electric and Bell Telephone Laboratories. The parts retained by AT&T, the settlement's rationale implied, were activities that would be exposed to actual and potential competition, whereas the divested regional operating companies were considered to be natural

---

58.   Plaintiff's First Statement of Contentions and Proof, United States v. AT&T, Civil Action No. 74-1698, at 528 (D.D.C. Nov. 1978).

59.   Defendants' First Statement of Contentions and Proof, United States v. AT&T, Civil Action No. 74-1698, at 44-45, 436-37 (D.D.C. Jan. 1979).

60.   United States. v. AT&T, 524 F. Supp. 1336, 1381, 1359 (D.D.C. 1981).

monopolies that would continue to be regulated by the FCC and state authorities.[61] As in 1955, AT&T secured support from other government agencies against divestiture, but even President Ronald Reagan's cabinet was unwilling to prevent Assistant Attorney General William Baxter from going forward.[62] Restraints from the 1956 consent decree barring Western Electric from commercial sales to non-Bell customers were relaxed, permitting Western Electric to enter the computer industry (which it later did, unsuccessfully) and merchant semiconductor sales. The divested operating companies were required to provide local connection access to AT&T and its rivals on essentially equal but unspecified terms.

Why AT&T accepted this settlement rather than continuing to contest the monopolization charges, insisting as it had for decades that its integration offered major efficiencies, remains somewhat of a mystery. Its management undoubtedly feared that a litigated judgment against it, which Greene's preliminary decision foreshadowed, would lead to crippling treble damages suits. It almost surely overestimated the chances that Western Electric with Bell Laboratories could achieve major success in computers. And it may have been blinded by the tight-money policy pursued by the Federal Reserve Board at the time. With high-grade bond interest rates of 14 percent, the cost of new capital to AT&T was higher than the rates of return on capital allowed by local regulatory authorities for Bell operating companies, which were under pressure to continue investing vigorously. Thus, every $1 million invested by Bell cost more in interest than it yielded in additional regulated returns, making the Bell operating companies a "dog" in the eyes of stock market investors.[63] This anomaly faded by the late 1980s, but by then, the divestiture was history.

The divestiture itself proved to be more complex than originally contemplated.[64] It was accompanied and followed by tumultuous technological and economic changes: the rapid growth of cellular telephony, which created competition to local Bell operating companies; an explosion of optical fiber cable installations by Bell companies, long-distance telephone rivals, and cable television providers; the emergence and growth of the Internet; and, in the first years of the twenty-first century, the appearance of new competition to traditional long-distance voice telephony from voice-over-Internet-protocol service offered by cable television firms. Rules governing the pricing of access to local telephone company networks were revised repeatedly. Three of the seven divested regional Bell operating companies were acquired by the others, leaving only four. In 1996, AT&T chose to abandon the crown jewel it had defended from antitrust for four decades: it spun off its Western Electric manufacturing subsidiary, renamed Lucent Technologies, along with Bell Telephone Laboratories, because their affiliation with Bell was a disadvantage in selling to non-Bell telecommunication companies. By that time, deprived of annual taxes levied on the Bell operating companies, Bell Laboratories retained only a shadow of its former glory. In 2006, Lucent was acquired by Alcatel, the leading French telecommunications supplier. And in 2005, the original

---

61.   *See* GERALD W. BROCK, TELECOMMUNICATION POLICY FOR THE INFORMATION AGE 157-67 (1994).
62.   *Id.* at 157-59.
63.   For a proof, see F.M. SCHERER, INDUSTRIAL MARKET STRUCTURE AND ECONOMIC PERFORMANCE 526 (1st ed. 1970).
64.   *See* BROCK, *supra* note 61, at 167-72.

AT&T was acquired by SBC, the merged successor from one of its original regional operating companies. The combined company was renamed AT&T.

A crucial question is whether the Bell system divestitures accelerated or retarded the technological changes that were occurring. Because the changes were rapid and revolutionary, it would be hard to infer substantial support for the proposition that they retarded progress. Reorganization surely made the divested Bell operating companies more amenable to purchasing from vendors other than Western Electric, and the resulting competition probably accelerated innovation in at least optical fiber cables and digital central office switches.[65] However, most of the communications technology advances following 1982 were facilitated more by FCC actions opening up the telephone network to foreign devices such as computer modems and facsimile machines and allowing providers such as MCI, Sprint, and Datran to build and interconnect their own intercity cable networks than by the divestiture per se. An analysis by the author of labor productivity growth in the telephone communications industry revealed an average growth rate of 6.08 percent per year between 1952 and 1982, before the divestiture, and 5.59 percent between 1985 and 2000.[66] The series is quite noisy, and the mean differences are not statistically significant. Because productivity growth tends to be underestimated by the Bureau of Labor Statistics when there is a high rate of product innovation, as there was in the 1990s, the most plausible inference is that divestiture did no perceptible harm.

5. Cellophane

Tough precedents articulated by the federal courts in the *Alcoa* (1945), *American Tobacco* (1946), *A&P* (1946-49), motion picture exhibition chain (1944-48), and *United Shoe Machinery* (1953-54) cases suggested that charges of illegal monopolization could be more readily sustained than they were during the 1920s and 1930s. With the possible exception of *United Shoe Machinery*, however, technological innovation was not a prominent consideration in those cases.[67]

The so-called *Cellophane* case was therefore a post-World War II test of how the federal antitrust authorities and courts would deal with a technologically progressive monopolist. One might view cellophane now as ancient technology, but when it was

---

65. For case studies, see SCHERER, *supra* note 49, 86-97.

66. The raw data are found at www.ftp://ftp.bls.gov/pub/special.requests/opt/dipts/oaeh3drt.txt and /oaehhirt.txt. The only year in the series with negative productivity growth, –0.2%, was 1984, the year of maximum reorganizational turmoil. The analysis was presented at a University of Colorado Law School seminar in October 2003.

67. Judge Charles E. Wyzanski's decision in 1953 rejected divestiture of United's single main machine manufacturing plant into three components, but cautioned that the issue might be revisited (as it was in 1968) if more competition in shoe machinery supply did not emerge. United States v. United Shoe Mach. Corp., 110 F. Supp. 295 (D. Mass. 1953). An interview with a USM executive by the author in 1958 revealed that, with future divestiture threats hanging over its head, USM was redirecting its research toward diversification opportunities. USM's shoe machinery position declined in subsequent years and the company itself disappeared, initially by merger and then by closure of the Beverly, Massachusetts, plant. The best shoe machinery is now imported preponderantly from Italy. A careful case study would be desirable.

introduced to the United States by DuPont in the mid-1920s, it was considered high technology, as suggested by the lyrics of a 1934 Cole Porter song "You're the Top":

> You're the top, you're Mahatma Gandhi,
> You're the top, you're Napoleon brandy.
> . . .
> You're cellophane! [68]

Cellophane was invented in France. In 1923, the E. I. du Pont de Nemours Company (DuPont) entered into a joint venture with the French cellophane producer, La Cellophane, receiving through it exclusive North American patent rights and, more importantly, extensive trade secrets required for successful production. Both companies had roots in rayon production, using similar chemical antecedents. DuPont later gained full ownership of the U.S. operation. Beginning in the late 1920s, it developed and patented coating processes through which cellophane could be made moisture-proof and also production process improvements that reduced costs, improved product quality, and made the product easier to use by packagers. In 1930 Sylvania, a Belgium-based company (unrelated to the light bulb producer of identical name), began producing and selling cellophane in the United States. A patent infringement suit by DuPont led to a settlement under which DuPont licensed Sylvania to its patents at a 2 percent royalty rate which, however, increased to at least 30 percent if Sylvania's output exceeded quotas stipulated by DuPont. It was alleged that DuPont, la Cellophane, and other cellophane producers reached spheres of influence agreements under which non-U.S. firms were prevented from selling in the U.S. market, but DuPont executives denied under oath that they had actually participated in those agreements. DuPont did lobby for and obtained in 1929 U.S. import tariffs of 60 percent (later, 45 percent) that kept virtually all cellophane imports out of the United States. During the 1930s and 1940s, therefore, DuPont, with a share of approximately 75 percent, and Sylvania, with 25 percent, were the only significant suppliers of cellophane in the United States. Except for the early infringement suit against Sylvania and one other minor incident, there was no evidence of DuPont actions like those of GE or Standard Oil seeking to prevent entry through extensive patent litigation, predatory pricing, or acquisition of competitors.

In 1947 the DOJ charged DuPont with monopolization. A decision in 1953 by Judge Paul Leahy of the U.S. District Court for Delaware began with a review of economic theories and then laid down extensive findings of fact and law. [69] The court's emphasis was on the question of whether the relevant market was cellophane, dominated by DuPont, or flexible packaging materials, in which DuPont's share was less than 20 percent—too small for a monopolization finding. However, Leahy also ruled that the evidence did not support a finding that DuPont had exhibited more intent to monopolize and exclude competitors than what one would reasonably expect of a company striving for success in its commercial efforts. Rather, Leahy concluded:

> [DuPont's] "monopoly" was "thrust upon" it within the true meaning of the [precedential] decisions . . . and the facts as to how du Pont achieved its position . . . . [D]u Pont's

---

68. From the 1934 musical *Anything Goes.*
69. United States v. E.I. du Pont de Nemours & Co., 118 F. Supp. 41 (D. Del. 1953).

position is the result of research, business skill and competitive activity. Much of du Pont's evidence was designed to show research, price and sales policies of that Company are responsible for its success and these policies were conceived and carried forward in a coordinated fashion with skill, gaining for du Pont substantial recognition in the packaging industry . . . . The record reflects not the dead hand of monopoly but rapidly declining prices, expanding production, intense competition stimulated by creative research, the development of new products and uses and other benefits of a free economy.[70]

On the question of market definition, which was the only part of the district court's decision appealed to and broadly sustained by the Supreme Court,[71] Leahy observed that cellophane competed with a broad range of flexible packaging materials, including lower cost materials such as waxed paper and bleached glassine as well as higher cost polyethylene, pliofilm, and Saran wrap. DuPont, he said, competed vigorously, among other things reducing its costs and its average price per pound from $1.06 in 1929 to 38 cents in 1940, to have its cellophane substituted for alternative packaging materials. He continued:

> Du Pont has no power to set cellophane prices arbitrarily. If prices for cellophane increase in relation to prices of other flexible packaging materials it will lose business to manufacturers of such materials in varying amounts for each of du Pont cellophane's major end uses. Relative increases would make competition more difficult to obtain new business.[72]

Leahy's view of the constraints facing DuPont in its cellophane pricing decisions is characterized by some economists as "the *Cellophane* fallacy."[73] The essence of the fallacy is that firms with some degree of product differentiation, and hence some discretion as to what price to charge, will maximize their profits by raising their prices near to, but not all the way up to, the level at which they lose substantial sales as a result of cross-elasticity of demand imparted by the competition from substitute products. In other words, they raise their prices into a range of substantially elastic demand. This concept is illustrated, crudely but with an attempt to track the cellophane facts of the late 1940s, in Figure 2. DuPont's demand function, given the prices of potential substitute products, is the wavy solid line, giving rise to a wildly fluctuating and discontinuous marginal revenue (MR) function.[74] The intuition is as follows. At a price of 5 cents per 1,000 square inches, cellophane is (a bit unrealistically) so high priced relative to substitutes that no sales occur. As the price is reduced, cellophane gains sales volume from high-priced substitutes such as pliofilm and Saran wrap. As the price is reduced further into a range slightly above 2 cents, it captures most of the volume those substitutes otherwise would have enjoyed. But around point B it has largely exhausted

---

70.   *Id.* at 217, 233.
71.   United States v. E.I. du Pont de Nemours & Co., 351 U.S. 377 (1956).
72.   *Du Pont*, 118 F. Supp. 179.
73.   The term came to me by oral tradition; its origin is unknown, at least to this author. A predecessor without the word "fallacy" was Donald F. Turner, *Antitrust Policy and the Cellophane Case*, 70 HARV. L. REV. 281, 288, 297, 308-10 (1956).
74.   The curves were plotted using two spliced algebraic equations, simplifying the otherwise difficult task of ensuring that the marginal revenue function was drawn correctly.

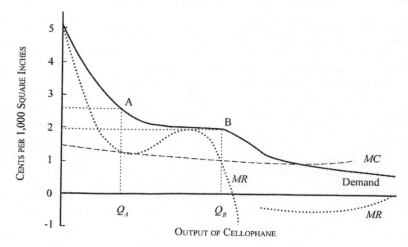

Figure 2.

Illustration of the Cellophane *fallacy.*

the opportunities for capturing such high-quality applications, so demand becomes more inelastic. If, however, it can bring its price into the one-cent range, it can capture a large volume of applications from low-quality substitutes such as glassine and waxed paper, so demand turns price-elastic again.

Given this curvilinear demand function, which, I believe, typifies many differentiated product situations,[75] multiple profit-maximizing equilibria exist. One, where the first intersection of marginal cost (MC) with marginal revenue occurs, leads to an equilibrium at point A, with a price of roughly 2.6 cents and quantity Q_A. A second equilibrium occurs at point B, with a price of approximately 1.95 cents and quantity Q_B. Of the two, profits—the summed surplus of revenue above marginal cost—are higher at equilibrium B, so this is what one would expect DuPont to choose. If it raised its price just a fraction of a penny, it would experience massive volume losses to superior substitutes, as Leahy implied—hence the *Cellophane* fallacy.

How much monopoly power a producer possesses under these conditions depends upon the varying curvature of the demand functions and the relation of the demand function to the marginal cost function. As Figure 2 is drawn, marginal costs are too high for cellophane profitably to capture volume from waxed paper and glassine. But at equilibrium B, the price is roughly twice marginal cost and substantial profits (ignoring fixed costs) are realized. The implication is that the producer facing the conditions of Figure 2 does have appreciable monopoly power, despite substantial substitution possibilities. In a critique of Leahy's decision, economists George Stocking and Willard Mueller argue that close attention should have been paid to DuPont's 24.2 percent

---

75. *See also* F.M. SCHERER & DAVID ROSS, INDUSTRIAL MARKET STRUCTURE AND ECONOMIC PERFORMANCE 181-83 (3d ed. 1990).

average after-tax profit return on investment in its cellophane operations.[76] Leahy acknowledged DuPont's profitability but accorded it little weight.[77]

Figure 1 presents a snapshot in time. In a more dynamic context, Leahy could nevertheless have been correct on the importance of substitution. DuPont did implement technological improvements and reduce cellophane costs substantially over time. If marginal costs had been two cents or more per 1,000 square inches, e.g., in an earlier phase of the cellophane marketing history, there would be only one equilibrium, northwest of point A at a price of roughly 3.4 cents, allowing most higher priced substitutes to retain their volume. By reducing costs and hence profit-maximizing prices over time, DuPont captured demand from substitute products. But around the 3.4 cent alternate equilibrium, it enjoys substantial discretion over what price to charge—the essence of monopoly power—and, again ignoring fixed costs, retains appreciable profits. Cost and price reductions by substitute products could also shift the cellophane demand curve and alter quantities. An analysis more subtle than Leahy's—one, to be sure, that would overwhelm the econometric competence of DuPont's and the government's economists at the time—would be needed to resolve the matter correctly.

Over the long run, rival packaging materials' prices could also change, shifting cellophane's demand curve to the left, if technological progress were more rapid in alternative materials than in cellophane. That something like this must have happened is suggested by census data showing an absolute decline in cellophane sales between 1954 and 1977. Also, in 1954, cellophane sales exceeded the sales of unsupported vinyl and polyethylene film by 14 percent; by 1977, sales of a wider array of plastic film and sheeting exceeded those of cellophane by 14 times.[78]

6. Xerox

Scholars and others who spend their lives working with text appreciate xerography as one of the greatest inventions of the twentieth century. The basic concepts were conceived through independent experiments by physicist Chester Carlson between 1934 and 1938. Several basic patents resulted. Realizing that developing a practical xerographic copying machine was beyond his means, and finding none of the roughly 20 companies he approached willing to pursue his invention, Carlson transferred his patents to the Battelle Memorial Institute, a not-for-profit research and development powerhouse, in exchange for a 40 percent share of profits. Battelle made and patented important improvements on Carlson's concepts, including the use of the photo-conducting element selenium as the image transfer basis. But commercial development required more resources than Battelle could allocate. The Haloid Corporation, with sales of roughly $6 million at the time, was the only business entity willing to take up

---

76.   George W. Stocking & Willard F. Mueller, *The Cellophane Case and the New Competition*, 45 AM. ECON. REV. 29-63 (1955) (see especially Table 3).

77.   *Du Pont*, 118 F. Supp. at 179; *see also* United States v. Aluminum Co. of Am., 148 F.2d 416, 426-27 (2d Cir. 1945) (Judge Learned Hand's caveat on the use of profit evidence).

78.   U.S. BUREAU OF THE CENSUS, CENSUS OF MANUFACTURES, INDUSTRY STATISTICS (1954, 1977). In 1954, such materials were classified in S.I.C. 2823, "organic chemicals." By 1977, they had been moved to S.I.C. 3079, "miscellaneous plastics products."

the challenge. In 1946 Battelle assigned Haloid a nonexclusive license to the xerography patents, amended in 1956 to confer upon Haloid exclusive rights to all existing and improvement xerography patents in exchange for $3.5 million cash and an eventual 1.1 million shares of Haloid stock. Haloid (later renamed the Xerox Corporation) pursued the development and in 1959 introduced to the world the first console plain-paper xerographic copier, the 914. It and subsequent models were enormously successful. Erwin Blackstone has estimated that the approximately $20 million Haloid invested in xerography research and development between 1946 and 1960 yielded an after-tax return of at least 25 percent.[79]

The Xerox Corporation continued to patent improvements on its copying machines, amassing a portfolio of nearly 1,000 patents by the mid-1970s. After winning a priority dispute, it licensed its patents on coated paper xerographic copying to numerous other firms but defended its exclusive position in lower incremental cost plain paper copying, inter alia, through infringement suits. With a monopoly on plain paper copying and 86 percent of total U.S. office copier sales and lease revenue in 1971, Xerox increased its profits through a sophisticated price discrimination strategy.[80] One way of extracting more revenue from high-use customers was to tie the sales of toner (priced at such levels that it was called "black gold" by Xerox insiders) to the use of Xerox copiers. A formal contractual tie was avoided because it would lead to patent misuse and Clayton Act problems, but Xerox sales representatives vigorously urged the use of Xerox toner rather than rival offerings said to be inferior. More importantly, Xerox set prohibitively high sale prices for its machines, inducing virtually all customers to lease rather than purchase. It offered more economical lease terms to high-volume users than to low-volume customers. Because available substitutes were quite inferior to xerography when only a few copies of an original were to be made, but Xerox machines faced tough competition from multilith and mimeograph machines for high-volume jobs, Xerox machines included a meter that charged much higher per-copy rates on small jobs than on large. Service was bundled with the lease of a Xerox machine, making it difficult for independent service vendors to compete. Plain-paper copier provision outside the United States was allocated to partly owned Rank Xerox of the United Kingdom and Fuji Xerox of Japan.

In 1973 the Federal Trade Commission (FTC), revitalized under new leadership after reports criticizing its performance were published by the American Bar Association and Nader's Raiders, issued a complaint alleging that Xerox had monopolized the copying machine market and a plain-paper copier submarket, thereby violating Section 5 of the Federal Trade Commission Act. The complaint emphasized Xerox's monopoly position, its continuing accumulation of patent barriers to entry, at first through acquisition from Battelle and then through internal development, its lease-only policies, the bundling of service with leases, its extensive pattern of price discrimination, and various other practices. Legally, the patent accumulation charge was a weak reed because it was unlikely that Battelle could have commercialized xerography, and if not Haloid, then

---

79. Erwin A. Blackstone, The Copying Machine Industry: A Case Study 238-39 (1968) (unpublished Ph.D. dissertation, University of Michigan).
80. The most comprehensive analysis is Blackstone. *Id.*

who else? Also, the mere accumulation of patents, however many, through internal research and development had been countenanced under an earlier Supreme Court dictum.[81] Certainly, the Xerox facts presented much less in the way of exclusionary practices than the other monopolization cases reviewed here. But by 1973, Xerox had enjoyed monopoly sales for 14 years, and by the time a litigation was concluded, it would have possessed a monopoly position for at least the statutory 17 years. This, one might extrapolate from the failures of antitrust in the electric lamp and telephone industries, ought arguably to be a time for therapeutic intervention.

Xerox chose to negotiate. In mid-1975, a consent agreement was reached and, after Tunney Act procedures, approved by the FTC.[82] The most important provision of the consent decree stipulated that Xerox would grant nonexclusive compulsory licenses to its existing patents, domestic and foreign, and any applied for during the three years following the decree. The first three patents chosen by the applicant for license were to be royalty-free; each additional patent bore a 0.5 percent royalty rate up to a maximum royalty rate of 1.5 percent. Other provisions called for know-how transfer, a ban on multimodel lease price discounts, the publication of toner quality specifications, and a mechanism for resolving disputes over whether a rival toner was unsuitable for use.

One naturally inquires, why did Xerox settle rather than litigating what would be a difficult case for the FTC to win? The answer has been provided by David Kearns, at the time group vice president of Xerox and later its CEO:

> We agreed to forfeit much of our patent protection through licensing arrangements, because McColough [the Xerox chairman] believed that the erosion of our hold on the market would not be that significant. After all, there was our unrivaled sales force to contend with and the two decades of experience building our brand in the marketplace. The patents were simply less important than when Xerox was small and fragile . . . . We already realized that if we didn't license people new competition would come into the business and infringe our patents anyway. We would sue and they would countersue, claiming antitrust. And the litigation would go on and on. We couldn't conduct a business like that. So once we decided we needed to license people there was no reason not to settle with the FTC.[83]

Subsequent events revealed that both Xerox and the FTC staff had misperceived the competitive situation. Both believed that the principal likely rivals to Xerox would be IBM and Eastman Kodak, both of which had commenced their entry into plain-paper copying. As Kearns recalls:

> [W]e were totally blinded by IBM and Kodak. The two of them could throw an awful light into someone's eyes . . . . It's wrong, however, to think that we were oblivious to the Japanese. My very first summer at Xerox, I remember going to meetings where the

---

81.   Automatic Radio Mfg. Co. v. Hazeltine Research, 339 U.S. 827, 834 (1950).
82.   As director of the FTC's Bureau of Economics, the author cosigned the recommendation that the FTC accept a consent settlement.
83.   DAVID T. KEARNS & DAVID A. NADLER, PROPHETS IN THE DARK: HOW XEROX REINVENTED ITSELF AND BEAT BACK THE JAPANESE 64-65 (1991). On the importance of innovators' nonpatent advantages, see Richard C. Levin, Alvin K. Klevorick, Richard R. Nelson & Sidney G. Winter, *Appropriating the Returns from Industrial Research and Development*, BROOKINGS PAPERS ON ECONOMIC ACTIVITY NO. 3 783-820 (1987).

Japanese came up for discussion. People would say, "The Japanese are coming. The Japanese are coming." So it wasn't a matter of Xerox not knowing about Japan. In fact, we predicted the Japanese would arrive sooner than they did. But what no one at Xerox seemed to have any good grasp of was the level of quality and the low cost of manufacturing that the Japanese were destined to achieve.[84]

Within a few years after the consent decree, Japanese firms such as Canon, Toshiba, Sharp, Panasonic, Konica, and Minolta had achieved significant inroads into the U.S. market with copying machines that were more reliable and lower priced than those of Xerox. Xerox was forced by this new competition into a strenuous program of "reinventing" itself. By 1977, at a major Xerox sales conference, Xerox CEO Peter McColough delivered

> a blunt appraisal of the marketplace and Xerox's position in it. In no uncertain terms he made it clear that Xerox was being "out-marketed, out-engineered, outwitted in major segments of our market. He underscored the fact that Xerox would never have it the way it did when it was protected by its patents, when it could take its sweet time developing and introducing products and when it made no difference how much it cost to make something because the company could charge almost whatever it wanted . . . . Peter stressed . . . "We are now faced with the urgent need for change within this company!"[85]

In hindsight, it seems clear that by facilitating the availability of well-designed foreign and domestic copiers and stimulating Xerox's efforts to enhance its competitiveness, the Xerox settlement provided major benefits to the copier-using American public.[86]

7. IBM

Building upon concepts developed for military purposes during World War II, Univac I, the first commercial general purpose digital electronic computer, was introduced by Remington-Rand in 1951.[87] An attempt by its designers to obtain basic patent protection failed. International Business Machines (IBM), which with its tabulating card machines dominated the automatic data processing field, saw its position threatened.[88] It developed a series of electronic computers, the first of which, the IBM 702, was introduced in 1953. After retraining and refocusing its large tabulating card sales force, IBM was much more successful than Remington and other rivals in persuading business organizations to embrace the mysteries of digital computing. By 1955, IBM's share of rapidly increasing general purpose digital computer installations had risen to 75 percent, and from then until the 1980s, it retained a dominant position.

---

84.   KEARNS & NADLER, *supra* note 83, at 75.

85.   *Id.* at 100; *see also id.* at 68, 123.

86.   See also Timothy F. Bresnahan, *Post-Entry Competition in the Plain Paper Copier Market*, 75 AM. ECON. REV. 15-19 (1985), and the longer unpublished study on which it is based.

87:   Excellent early histories are JOEL SHURKIN, ENGINES OF THE MIND (1984), and KENNETH FLAMM, CREATING THE COMPUTER (1988). This section is adapted from F.M. SCHERER, INDUSTRY STRUCTURE, STRATEGY, AND PUBLIC POLICY ch. 7 (1996).

88.   IBM's tabulating card monopoly was the subject of a consent decree that among other things required compulsory licensing of IBM's computer patents. United States v. IBM Corp., 1956 Trade Cas. (CCH) ¶ 68,245 (S.D.N.Y. 1956).

As computer users built their data processing operations around IBM software and data formats, they became "locked in" to new and backward-compatible IBM computer versions. Other firms tried to break the lock by designing computers that emulated the IBM architecture, but without great success. Repair service, needed often in the early days of computing, came bundled with lease or purchase contracts, as with Xerox, making it difficult for outside service firms to flourish. From early on, required to do so under a 1956 consent decree, IBM offered either to lease or sell its computers.[89] Most customers were averse to obsolescence risks and therefore preferred leases. This aggravated a classic dominant firm problem for IBM.[90] Bringing out a more powerful machine led customers to cancel their leases, cannibalizing IBM's existing revenues, to install the newer machine. IBM therefore tended to pursue a "fast second" strategy, delaying the introduction of new machines until inroads from rival machines became a serious threat.[91]

As fringe rivals redoubled their innovative efforts with transistorized models during the early 1960s, IBM was induced to escalate the fast second strategy on its ambitious System 360 development. To avert customers' defection to more advanced rival machines, it not only accelerated the development but announced the complete 360 line before development had proceeded far enough to ensure that quality goals and delivery dates could be met. Particularly serious slippage occurred on its time-sharing machines and the high-end System 360/90 targeted at Control Data Corporation's superior scientific data processing computer and expected from the outset to incur substantial out-of-pocket losses. A successful Sherman Act suit by Control Data Corporation followed. By embodying standardized plug-in interfaces, System 360 also created another problem. Part of IBM's strategy was to price entry-level computers low but sustain high margins on peripherals such as add-on memory, tape drives, and disk drives. Because inexperienced customers almost always underestimated their need for peripherals, the sale of a computer at a low price informally "tied" customers to the purchase of high-margin peripherals. With System 360's standardized interfaces, plug-compatible peripheral manufacturers proliferated. To combat them, IBM pursued an array of strategies, including the sale of "fighting machines" at arguably predatory prices; lease plans with discounts tailored to lock customers in until rival peripherals were unprofitable; moving control functions into the central processing unit, where they could be altered to render rival peripherals inoperative; delaying the release of interface information to the disadvantage of competitive peripheral developers; and changing the traditional sales price versus lease price ratio to undermine the profitability of firms that leased rival peripherals to IBM computer users. More private antitrust suits followed, most of which IBM eventually won, in part because contemporary decision-making

---

89.   Xerox's leasing and pricing strategies were said to have been modeled on those of IBM.

90.   *See* GERALD O. BROCK, THE U.S. COMPUTER INDUSTRY ch. 7 (1975).

91.   On the original and more general theory, see W.L. Baldwin & G.L. Childs, *The Fast Second and Rivalry in Research and Development*, 36 S. ECON. J. 18-24 (1969). A crucial "fast second" error by IBM occurred after its antitrust contest with the government was concluded. To avoid cannibalizing mainframe computer sales, it delayed using Intel's new 32-bit 80386 microprocessor in its personal computers until 1987, seven months after Compaq did so. It rapidly lost leadership in personal computers.

memoranda had been screened by internal counsel to ensure that they contained no smoking gun language.

On January 17, 1969, the last day of the Johnson administration, the DOJ filed a broad Sherman Act complaint against IBM, alleging monopolization and citing most of the practices outlined above.[92] After extensive discovery, the trial in the U.S. District Court for the Southern District of New York began in 1975 and continued into 1981.[93] IBM fiercely contested the government's allegations—on defining the market as "general-purpose digital computers," on how much pricing discretion it enjoyed, on the relevance of IBM's high accounting profits as an indicator of monopoly, on whether IBM's pricing was predatory and on alternative tests for predation,[94] on IBM's fast second innovation strategy, renamed "leapfrogging," on whether there was such a thing as software lock-in, on customers' preferences for leases and bundled service, and on many other facets of IBM's practices.[95] The presiding judge was unwilling or unable to bring the parties to focus issues and expedite the trial. The government's team was led by senior DOJ attorneys with much trial experience but a limited understanding of economics and high-technology issues, who ceded much of the trial's strategic direction to staff economists.

As the trial neared completion, the Reagan administration took office. A new Assistant Attorney General, William Baxter, began a thorough review of the case's merits (along with the parallel AT&T case). On January 8, 1982, he announced simultaneously the consent settlement reached in AT&T along with his decision to abandon the IBM case—13 years after its initiation. In Baxter's asserted view, "continuing the case would be an expensive and ultimately futile endeavor,"[96] in part because events since the case commenced had significantly transformed computer industry structure. In particular, IBM had reacted too slowly to retain leadership in top-end scientific computer placements, it had been thoroughly defeated at the lower end by minicomputer makers such as Digital Equipment, Data General, Tandem, and Prime; and the personal computer (PC) revolution was underway.

An appropriate epitaph is found in the memoirs of IBM's chairman, Thomas J. Watson Jr.:

> Looking back, I see a lot of sad irony in the whole affair. I think a lot of people would
> agree that at the outset the Justice Department's complaint had merit. IBM was clearly in
> a commanding position in the market, and some of our tactics had been harsh. We

---

92. The case had been vetted by President Lyndon Baines Johnson's Council of Economic Advisers and was vetted again by Richard Nixon's council. The PCM practices were added in a later amendment.
93. The author was the initial economist witness of several appearing for the government.
94. *See* Phillip Areeda & Donald F. Turner, *Predatory Pricing and Related Practices under Section 2 of the Sherman Act*, 88 HARV. L. REV. 697 (1975), which was apparently written as a result of consulting for IBM and which precipitated a string of articles presenting alternative theories.
95. For the best summary of IBM's economic case, see FRANKLIN M. FISHER, JOHN J. MCGOWAN & JOEN E. GREENWOOD, FOLDED, SPINDLED, AND MUTILATED: ECONOMIC ANALYSIS AND U.S. V. IBM (1983). The best statement of the government's case is RICHARD T. DELAMARTER, BIG BLUE: IBM'S USE AND ABUSE OF POWER (1986).
96. Memorandum of William F. Baxter to William French Smith, U.S. Attorney General, Jan. 6, 1982, *reproduced in* Lawrence A. Sullivan, *Monopolization: Corporate Strategy, The IBM Cases, and the Transformation of the Law*, 60 TEX. L. REV. 587, 639 (1982) (Appendix A).

eliminated many of these practices ourselves, and our overall record during the case was pretty clean . . . [T]he case stretched on unresolved for so long that before it was over history showed my argument . . . to have been right. IBM kept growing, but the computer industry grew even more, and the natural forces of technological change etched away whatever monopoly power we may have had.[97]

Despite dissuasion by the U.S. government, the European Commission persisted in a parallel antitrust complaint against IBM. In August 1984 a settlement was negotiated under which IBM agreed to "unbundle" all add-on memory but the minimum amount needed for machine operation and to provide in advance the interface information needed for peripheral manufacturers to attach their products to IBM computers.[98]

8. Microsoft

IBM was slow in recognizing the possibilities of PCs, lagging even more than one might expect under a fast second theory.[99] In its crash catch-up development program to introduce the first IBM personal computer on August 12, 1981, IBM departed from its usual practice of developing its own operating system and instead chose one it believed (somewhat erroneously) to be already available. It licensed MS/DOS from a fledgling Seattle software house, Microsoft, which obtained it from another firm, Seattle Computer Products. Microsoft secured from SCP nonexclusive rights for $50,000 and later exclusive rights for $925,000. IBM's imprimatur convinced business enterprises that PCs were more than a children's plaything, and sales soared. Since IBM's contract with Microsoft was nonexclusive, a PC "clone" industry emerged using the MS/DOS operating system. The large number of PCs, from IBM and clones, residing on desktops induced applications software houses to assign first priority to writing applications programs—thousands of them—running on the MS/DOS platform. Superior availability of applications software in turn stimulated consumers to prefer desktop computers running MS/DOS, giving Microsoft a leading position in the provision of operating systems.

Personal computer pioneer Apple sought to escape this snowball effect by introducing in January 1984 its Macintosh computer, the first economically priced desktop computer to offer a graphical user interface (GUI) (conceived but not successfully commercialized by the Xerox Corporation's Palo Alto Research Center). Commissioned by Apple in 1982 to write applications programs for the Macintosh, Microsoft learned the Macintosh operating system's structure and devised its own GUI operating system, Windows, preannounced in November 1983 but not available to consumers until two years later. A suit by Apple alleging that Windows infringed the Macintosh copyright's "look and feel" was unsuccessful. So also were the early underpowered versions of Windows, but Windows 3.0, rolled out in May 1990, became

---

97. THOMAS J. WATSON JR. (WITH PETER PETRE), FATHER, SON & CO.: MY LIFE AT IBM 415 (1990). See also my review of the DeLamarter book in 32 ANTITRUST BULL. 829, 840 (1987).
98. On the consequences, see F.M. Scherer, *Microsoft and IBM in Europe*, 84 Antitrust & Trade Reg. Rep. (BNA) 65-66 (2003).
99. For a complementary sociological explanation, see CLAYTON M. CHRISTENSEN, THE INNOVATOR'S DILEMMA: WHEN NEW TECHNOLOGIES CAUSE GREAT FIRMS TO FAIL (1997).

a spectacular market success. One reason for the success of Windows 3.0 was that it resided on an MS/DOS platform and could therefore run applications programs written for either MS/DOS or Windows. Software houses offering the leading PC application programs at the time were focusing their GUI efforts on IBM's OS/2 operating system, which both IBM and Microsoft predicted would be the PC operating system of the future. But Microsoft was ready with its Excel spreadsheet and Word word processing programs optimized for Windows 3.0, and it soon captured a dominant position in office applications programs to complement its 85 to 90 percent share of desktop computer operating systems placements. By choosing not to "port" Excel and Word to operating systems other than Windows and Macintosh, Microsoft enhanced what came to be called an "applications barrier to entry" congealing the preferences of users trained on and loyal to Excel and Word.

Microsoft's dominance was investigated in the early 1990s by the FTC, which reached no decision to act, and then by the DOJ, which filed a complaint in July 1994. The complaint addressed an array of Microsoft practices, including premature product preannouncement to combat rival products and unfair advantages allegedly possessed by Microsoft applications program writers through earlier and more complete knowledge of operating system interface parameters. But the negotiated consent decree filed on the same day as the complaint remedied mainly Microsoft's practice of charging computer assemblers a royalty for every PC they sold, whether it contained a Microsoft operating system or one offered by competitors. To install a rival's Windows clone, therefore, the PC producer paid twice, which was unattractive, solidifying Microsoft's dominance. The consent decree banned this practice. Reviewing the proposed decree under the Tunney Act, district Judge Stanley Sporkin rejected it, stating that it was insufficient to correct other named abuses.[100] Microsoft appealed. The appellate court found that Sporkin had exceeded his authority and remanded the case to a new judge with instructions to enter the decree.[101]

The mid-1990s brought a new threat to Microsoft's dominance. The Internet evolved from a Department of Defense computer-linking system in the 1970s through the National Science Foundation's NSFnet to an open system in 1995. The extensive installation of optical fiber cables made it possible to transmit computer data inexpensively, and the relaxation of AT&T's "foreign attachments" restrictions permitted easy coupling of computers with telephone-cable networks. In November 1994 Netscape introduced a full-scale test version of its Navigator browser, which made it possible for computer users to access materials stored on servers throughout the world. It achieved extraordinarily rapid growth in 1995. Microsoft officials saw in Navigator a threat to the dominant position of Windows. Software writers might write applications programs not to Windows but target them to Internet servers, optimized for applications program interfaces (APIs) exposed by a "middleware" browser such as Navigator, and allowing computer users to combine a browser with a stripped-down operating system to bypass Windows. Meeting with Netscape officials in June 1995, Microsoft officials allegedly offered Netscape 20 percent equity financing in exchange for Netscape's

---

100. United States v. Microsoft Corp., 159 F.R.D. 318 (D.D.C. 1995).
101. United States v. Microsoft Corp., 56 F.3d 1448 (D.C. Cir. 1995).

limiting its browsers to older Windows operating systems and leaving the nascent market for significantly improved Windows 95 to Microsoft. Netscape refused. Microsoft thereupon denied Netscape Windows 95 API information until two months after Windows 95 was on the market, putting Navigator software writers at a disadvantage. In December 1994 Microsoft had licensed an alternative browser, Spyglass, from a small firm. It revised the Spyglass instructions to create Internet Explorer, which in late 1995 it began including on a separate diskette free with every copy of Windows 95, forcing Netscape to follow suit and offer Navigator free to all customers. Microsoft also brought pressure to bear upon computer assemblers, threatening them with Windows license cancellation, forfeiture of discounts, or other retaliatory measures if they favored Navigator over Internet Explorer.

At about the same time Sun Microsystems devised a new programming language, Java, for Internet applications. Sun's announced intention was to make Java a universal language with a compiler that would run applications written for it on any computer operating system, with or without Microsoft operating systems. Microsoft officials saw Java as another threat that would divert applications program writers from writing first for Windows. In March 1996 Microsoft contracted with Sun to include unmodified Java compilers with Windows. But to prevent Java from becoming a universally available standard, it changed the Windows Java installations so that applications written for them would not run on the standard Java system.

In the fall of 1997 Microsoft took another decisive step. It announced that Windows 98, to be marketed beginning in mid-1998, would have its Internet Explorer browser physically bundled with the operating system, so new PC buyers could not avoid installing Explorer with Windows 98. When this happened in 1998, it accelerated the increase in Explorer's usage share relative to Navigator. The announcement prompted the DOJ to sue, alleging that physical bundling of Internet Explorer violated the 1995 consent decree. District Judge Thomas Penfield Jackson issued a preliminary injunction requiring that Microsoft provide a version of Windows 98 from which Explorer was unbundled. But Microsoft had bargained hard to have language in the 1995 consent decree stating that Microsoft was not prohibited from "developing integrated products," deleting from a government draft four trailing words, "which offer technological advantages."[102] This permissive language was stressed in the appellate court's reversal.[103] The court reserved judgment on whether the bundling independently violated the Sherman Act.

Stung by this defeat, the DOJ filed a more sweeping complaint accusing Microsoft of violating Sherman Act Sections 1 and 2, citing the practices articulated in the previous three paragraphs and others. Jackson scheduled a fast track trial, among other things limiting each party to 12 trial witnesses plus two rebuttal witnesses. The trial began in October 1998 and lasted 76 days. The government took the unusual step of having as its lead counsel a prominent private sector antitrust attorney, David Boies, who had been second-in-command on IBM's defense team in the 1970s litigation. Another curious

---

102. For a fascinating chronicle of the later *Microsoft* case's procedural history, see John Heilemann, *The Truth, The Whole Truth, and Nothing but the Truth*, WIRED, Nov. 2000, at 275.

103. United States v. Microsoft Corp., 147 F.3d 935 (D.C. Cir. 1998).

feature of the government's otherwise vigorous prosecution was the failure to present testimony on Microsoft's profits, which, a private study had shown, translated to an extraordinary 88 percent return on invested capital for 1998 when one did the accounting properly.[104] The government's case was strengthened by a plethora of e-mail messages among Microsoft executives explaining how and why the company was taking strategic actions against various rivals and uncooperative business partners—discovered, apparently, because the company's leaders had chosen not to implement the thoroughgoing antitrust compliance programs maintained by most U.S. companies with a dominant market position.

On November 5, 1999, Jackson issued lengthy findings of fact indicating that Microsoft's market position and its practices constituted probable Sherman Act violations.[105] He found inter alia that the bundling of Internet Explorer with Windows 98 had improved the quality of Web browsing software, reducing its cost, and increasing its availability, "thereby benefiting consumers."[106] However, to the detriment of consumers, Jackson added, the bundling forced computer assemblers to ignore consumer demand for a browserless version of Windows, increased confusion, degraded system performance, and restricted memory.[107] He concluded with an admonition:

> Most harmful of all is the message that Microsoft's actions have conveyed to every enterprise with the potential to innovate in the computer industry. Through its conduct toward Netscape, IBM, Compaq, Intel, and others, Microsoft has demonstrated that it will use its prodigious market power and immense profits to harm any firm that insists on pursuing initiatives that could intensify competition against one of Microsoft's core products. Microsoft's past success in hurting such companies and stifling innovation deters investment in technologies and businesses that exhibit the potential to threaten Microsoft. The ultimate result is that some innovations that would truly benefit consumers never occur for the sole reason that they do not coincide with Microsoft's self-interest.[108]

Jackson thereupon engaged appellate judge Richard Posner to mediate between the government and Microsoft with the objective of finding mutually acceptable remedies. Four months of mediation yielded no positive result. On April 3, 2000, Jackson issued conclusions of law, finding that Microsoft had violated Sherman Act Section 1 through its tying of Internet Explorer to Windows 98 and Sherman Act Section 2 through monopolization and attempted monopolization. He asked the plaintiffs to file a brief on remedies and consolidated actions brought by 19 state attorneys general with the federal government case. The plaintiffs then proposed that Microsoft be divided into two separate companies, one with responsibility for applications and one for operating systems. They requested diverse prohibitions against bundling middleware products within the Windows operating system unless an otherwise identical unbundled version

---

104. Remedies Brief of Amici Curiae Robert E. Litan et al. app. at 2, United States v. Microsoft Corp., 84 F. Supp. 2d 9 (D.D.C. 1999). The probable reason was that the government's lead economic expert, Franklin Fisher, had testified in *United States v. IBM* that profitability data were meaningless.

105. United States v. Microsoft Corp., 84 F. Supp. 2d 9 (D.D.C. 1999).

106. *Id.* ¶ 408.

107. *Id.* ¶ 410, at 111.

108. *Id.* ¶ 412, at 112.

was offered, against contractual ties, and against exclusive dealing arrangements. In addition, Microsoft would be required to provide information to third-party software developers needed to ensure that their software interoperates effectively with the Windows operating system. On June 7, 2000, the court ordered that the plaintiffs' proposed remedies be implemented without significant changes.[109]

Needless to say, Microsoft appealed. And from that point on, the tide turned against the plaintiffs. The Supreme Court denied certiorari and remanded the appeal to the District of Columbia Court of Appeals for en banc hearing. The Clinton administration left office, and a new team was appointed by President George W. Bush. The Bush team chose to have the appeal argued by a Solicitor General staff with no prior connection to the case and minimal understanding of its facts and economic principles.[110] In its decision, the court of appeals sustained the lower court's finding that Microsoft had monopolized the PC operating system market through its dominant position and its conduct.[111] It vacated, however, Jackson's conclusion that Microsoft had attempted to monopolize a browser market, ruling that the market had been insufficiently defined. It remanded for further analysis on a rule of reason basis Jackson's decision that Microsoft's bundling of Internet Explorer with Windows was a per se violation of Section 2 of the Sherman Act, observing that

> Microsoft does not dispute that many consumers demand alternative browsers. But on industry custom Microsoft contends that no other firm requires non-removal because no other firm has invested the resources to integrate web browsers as deeply into its OS as Microsoft has .... Microsoft contends not only that its integration of IE into Windows is innovative and beneficial but also that it requires non-removal of IE .... Microsoft argues that IE and Windows are an integrated physical product and that the bundling of IE APIs with Windows makes the latter a better applications platform for third-party software. It is unclear how the benefits from IE API's could be achieved by quality standards for different browser manufacturers. We do not pass judgment on Microsoft's claims regarding the benefits from integration of its APIs. We merely note that these and other novel, purported efficiencies suggest that judicial "experience" provides little basis for believing that, "because of their pernicious effect on competition and lack of any redeeming virtue," a software firm's decisions to sell multiple functionalities as a package should be "conclusively presumed to be unreasonable and therefore illegal without elaborate inquiry as to the precise harm they have caused or the business excuse for their use."[112]

Because it chose not to sustain two of the three broad violation findings, which might arguably render the divestiture remedy excessive, and also because it believed Jackson had erred by not holding hearings on the efficacy of the proposed remedies, the court of appeals vacated the remedial order and remanded the matter to a lower court for reconsideration. And because, it said, Jackson had violated judicial canons by talking to representatives of the press before the proceedings had ended and made to them

---

109. United States v. Microsoft Corp., 97 F. Supp. 2d 59 (D.D.C. 2000).

110. *Upfront: Trustbusters: Did Microsoft Catch a Break?*, BUS. WK., Mar. 12, 2001, at 14. The author listened to the proceedings on public radio and reached the same conclusion.

111. United States v. Microsoft Corp., 253 F.3d 34 (D.D.C. 2001).

112. *Id.* at 88-90.

disparaging remarks about Microsoft's good faith, the appellate court disqualified Jackson from further participation in the case. A new district judge, Colleen Kollar-Kotelly, was appointed to preside over the remaining proceedings.

In renewed negotiations, Microsoft and the DOJ agreed upon a settlement without divestiture or mandatory unbundling provisions. The settlement was widely criticized in the press as mild and insufficient.[113] Ten state attorneys general dissented and elected to pursue their own remedy proceedings—ultimately, with little effect. The government chose not to follow through on the appellate court's invitation to retry the bundling issue on a rule of reason basis. After complex hearings, a final judgment with remedial order was issued by Kollar-Kotelly in November 2002, five years after the initial complaint against Microsoft's bundling announcement.[114] It mandated nondiscriminatory licensing of the Windows operating system at publicized terms, barred restrictive agreements limiting computer assemblers' freedom to feature middleware competitive with Microsoft's and retaliation by Microsoft against firms that installed rival software, and required disclosure of interface specifications and communications protocols used by Microsoft middleware software to interoperate with the Windows operating system, along with other procedural measures.

Disputes continued over the level of Microsoft's interoperability information access charges, which were reduced following a court proceeding in July 2003,[115] and in 2007, over the introduction of a revised operating system, Vista, which was alleged to slow the functioning of alternative search engines such as Google.[116]

Throughout the litigation extending from 1997, Microsoft argued that limitations on its ability physically to integrate (i.e., bundle) software features with its operating system would be an unjustifiable constraint on its ability—indeed, its right—to innovate. The claim must be received with a grain of salt because in Microsoft's history since the early 1980s licensing or cloning other firms' software innovations, to be sure with Microsoft's own improvements, vastly predominated over coming up with successful, really new software features. And equally clearly, strategic objectives—disadvantaging rival vendors—played a major or even decisive role in its bundling decisions.

Despite being put on notice in 1997 that it risked antitrust prosecution through strategic bundling, Microsoft in May 1999 physically integrated its Windows Media Player, which up to that time had been supplied as a separate product, into its Windows operating systems. This bundling action became one key focus of a major European

---

113. *See, e.g., It's Still a Safe World for Microsoft*, N.Y. TIMES, Nov. 9, 2001, at 27; *An Unsettling Settlement*, ECONOMIST, Nov. 10, 2001, at 57-58; *Settlement or Sellout?*, BUS. WK., Nov. 19, 2001, at 112-16; *Slapping Microsoft's Wrist* (editorial), BUS. WK., Nov. 19, 2001, at 152; and *Skepticism in Senate Panel Over Accord with Microsoft*, N.Y. TIMES, Dec. 13, 2001, at D1. See also the Reuters news dispatch of February 9, 2005, in which Kollar-Kotelly is quoted as saying that her job was not to ensure that new competition is stimulated, but only to make sure that Microsoft abides by the agreements reached.

114. New York v. Microsoft Corp., 224 F. Supp. 2d 76, 266 (D.D.C. 2002).

115. *Microsoft Eases Licensing Under Pressure from U.S.*, N.Y. TIMES, July 4, 2003, at C3. The new royalty rates were posted on Aug. 19, 2003. Prepayments were reduced from $100,000 to $50,000 and ad valorem royalties into the 1 to 5% range.

116. *See Microsoft Finds Legal Defender in Justice Dept.*, N.Y. TIMES, June 10, 2007, at 1.

Commission (EC) competition policy complaint and adverse decision.[117] The other focus entailed Microsoft's promotional claims that its server software interoperated more smoothly than rival server software with ubiquitous Microsoft desktop operating systems because of secret communications protocols and Microsoft's superior knowledge of APIs. In April 2004 the EC ordered Microsoft to market Windows versions with Windows Media Player unbundled and to undertake much more extensive disclosure of applications interface specifications and communications protocols than had been required by U.S. courts. Microsoft petitioned to stay implementation of the remedies until appeals had been exhausted, but its petition to the European Court of First Instance (CFI) was denied in December 2004.[118] In September 2007 the CFI formally upheld most aspects of the Commission's decision.[119]

In the 2004 proceedings before the CFI, Microsoft argued that it could not successfully implement the unbundling and information disclosure remedies sought. The Windows Media Player was too closely integrated with the operating system to be unbundled; the intercommunications code was too complex and changing too rapidly to be disclosed. Some truth may lurk in these arguments.[120] But to a witness at the October 2004 European court hearings in Luxembourg, 30 miles from Bastogne, it was dismaying to hear the word "can't" invoked so often by representatives of a nation that had demonstrated American "can do" in the 1944 Battle of the Bulge. Given this "can't do" attitude, additional fines and/or stringent structural reorganization were threatened by European Community authorities.[121]

Controversy persisted over implementation of the remedies ordered by the EC and the CFI. Two main points of contention were the alleged inadequacy of Microsoft's information disclosure, said by the EC's technical advisor to be "devoted to obsolete functionality" and "self-contradictory,"[122] and Microsoft's insistence that recipients pay for the use of its communications protocols—payments to which, the EC responded, Microsoft had no right. In 2006 the EC began levying noncompliance fines of 2 million euros per day, cumulating eventually to 1.18 billion euros, supplementing its originally imposed fine of 497 million euros.

A curiosity of the EC proceedings is that, just as it did not prespecify the fees Microsoft could charge for interoperability information, the EC failed in its media player remedy to set a percentage price differential between the unbundled version of Windows and the version with Windows Media Player bundled. At a zero differential, it was plain

---

117. Commission of the European Communities, Commission Decision, Case COMP/C-3/37.792 (Microsoft), Apr. 21, 2004.

118. Order of the President of the Court of First Instance, Case T-201-04R, 22 December 2004. The author appeared as a witness on behalf of Real Networks in the hearing and consulted previously for Sun Microsystems in its litigation against Microsoft.

119. Microsoft Corp. v. Comm'n, Case T-201/04 (Ct. First Instance Sept. 17, 2007).

120. It has been suggested, for example, that Microsoft's software-writing operations were so chaotic that no single person or group knew what was in the code at any moment in time.

121. In 2007, the EC's competition commissioner suggested that one might conclude that "behavioural remedies are ineffective and that a structural remedy is warranted." Reuters internet dispatch by David Lawsky, Apr. 23, 2007.

122. Reuters internet dispatch by David Lawsky, Mar. 10, 2006.

to all, the bundled version would almost always be preferred.[123] Testimony in 2006 revealed that only 0.005 percent (i.e., one in 20,000) of the Windows systems sold in the European Community during the first nine months of its availability comprised the unbundled version.[124] A possible explanation is that the EC was expressing its implicit fear of having to determine what a reasonable price (or in the case at hand, a reasonable price differential) was—something on which it had been overruled on appeal by the European Court of Justice in prior abuse of dominant position cases.[125] It is also possible that EC decision makers were haunted by the ghost of Friedrich von Hayek, believing that in the absence of effective competition, "it is not possible to construct a hypothetical "as if" price, as nobody knows this price."[126] In the end, however, they were forced to act, at least on interoperability information and patents, even if not on the unbundled system price differential.[127] After negotiations between EC competition policy chief Neelie Kroes and Microsoft CEO Steven Ballmer, Microsoft abandoned its original 5.95 percent royalty demand and settled for royalty rates of 0.4 percent.

9. Conclusion

Reviewing the history of seven great monopolization cases, one is forced to a mixed verdict on whether the antitrust authorities are able competently to deal with structural monopoly and related sustaining practices in high-technology industries. In a majority of the cases, it took far too long, and in some instances several attempts, to come to grips with the problems. By the time the courts were ready for judgment, technological and economic changes had radically altered the environment in which the remedies originally sought would apply. This holds true also for the unusually expeditious Microsoft litigation, which, at least in the United States, achieved little or nothing in the end. The most rapid solutions were achieved through negotiated consent decrees, which require a belief on the part of respondents that they will not be seriously disadvantaged. In *Xerox* and *AT&T* (1982), the corporate settlers were probably too optimistic—the decrees did open up avenues for substantially enhanced technological competition. In early cases the courts shunned balancing technological gains, measured in terms of actual performance or theoretical arguments for patent accumulation, against strategies that suppressed competition. In later cases the courts' balancing record is more mixed. In *Microsoft* Jackson struggled admirably to weigh the benefits of browser integration against competitive harm, but his efforts were insufficient to convince a skeptical court

---

123. *See* Steve Lohr & James Kanter, *Microsoft Facing Fines in Europe*, N.Y. TIMES, Dec. 23, 2005, at C16.
124. *Microsoft in European Court Says 2004 Ruling Is a Failure*, N.Y. TIMES, Apr. 26, 2006, at 1 and C-4.
125. *See* Eleanor M. Fox, *Monopolization and Dominance in the United States and the European Community*, 61 NOTRE DAME L. REV. 891, 990-92 (1986).
126. *See* Ingo Schmidt, *Different Approaches and Problems in Dealing with Control of Market Power*, 28 ANTITRUST BULL. 434 (Summer 1983). It is striking that in its *Discussion Paper on the Application of Article 82 of the Treaty to Exclusionary Abuses*, released December 2005, the Commission's Directorate-General of Competition made no mention of excessive prices as an indication of dominance or a problem to be remedied.
127. Press Release IP/07/1567, European Commission, Antitrust: Commission Ensures Compliance with 2004 Decision against Microsoft (Oct. 22, 2007).

of appeals fearful of impeding technological progress and reluctant to undertake the job on its own.

The courts' adjudication of complex technological tradeoff questions would be facilitated if the presiding judge were able to retain as a clerk an expert with the requisite specialized knowledge. Jackson attempted to do so in *Microsoft* but was blocked in 1998 when Microsoft objected to his choice. Securing unbiased expertise is undoubtedly difficult, but its solution must lie within the bounds of judicial ingenuity.

From the great cases reviewed here, it would appear that dominant firms have accumulated far more monopoly power than is necessary to motivate and sustain the most rapid and beneficial rate of technological progress. All seven of the seminal products that gave rise to monopolization actions were invented or initially developed by entities other than the eventual monopoly or by small firms that only later grew to dominance. In several cases, such as electric lamps, the telephone, and computers, early inventions were made simultaneously but independently by multiple sources of initiative. In many instances, once a single firm came to dominate a new technology, it was palpably resistant to innovation after its position was secured. And in several such cases, the fast second phenomenon was evident: dominant firms delayed feasible innovations until their dominance was threatened by an upstart. Quite generally, the underlying economic literature suggests, new competition and the threat of being left behind—Schumpeter's "creative destruction"—are the most powerful spurs to innovation for well-established enterprises.[128] By learning the lessons of history, the courts and the antitrust enforcement agencies would be better able not to repeat past mistakes.

This suggests a reorientation of policy. The benefit of the doubt in high-technology monopolization matters ought to be resolved in favor of keeping structural and behavioral barriers to innovative new entry as low as possible. Even for cases in which monopoly was the natural result of significant innovation rather than other exclusionary practices, it implies skepticism toward monopoly positions that have been sustained through the accumulation of internally developed patents for longer than the 20 years contemplated in current patent law.[129] The "for limited Times" language in Article I, Section 8, of the U.S. Constitution should be taken seriously in order to promote the progress of science and the useful arts. Since properly conservative courts are unlikely to change the law in this direction without congressional guidance, appropriate legislation should be enacted to ensure the vibrancy of U.S. industrial technology in a world of increasingly tough technological challenges from abroad.

---

128. For wide-ranging historical evidence, see BURTON KLEIN, DYNAMIC ECONOMICS (1977).

129. On the implications for R&D expenditures of compulsory patent licensing decrees, see F.M. SCHERER, THE ECONOMIC EFFECTS OF COMPULSORY PATENT LICENSING 66-78 (New York Univ. Graduate School of Business Administration Monograph 1977-2, 1977).

2

Rev Ind Organ (2011) 38:225–233
DOI 10.1007/s11151-011-9283-y

Standard Oil as a Technological Innovator

F. M. Scherer

Published online: 27 February 2011
© Springer Science+Business Media, LLC. 2011

Abstract   A century ago, in 1911, the U.S. Supreme Court issued its path-breaking decision in the monopolization case against the Standard Oil Companies. Standard pleaded inter alia that its near-monopoly position was the result of superior innovation, citing in particular the Frasch-Burton process for refining the high-sulfur oil found around Lima, Ohio. This paper examines the role of Hermann Frasch in inventing and developing the desulfurization process, showing that Standard failed to recognize his inventive genius when he was its employee and purchased his rights and services only after he had applied it in his own Canadian company.

Keywords   Monopolization · Innovation · Antitrust · Patents · Standard Oil

1 Introduction

The 1911 *Standard Oil* case, everyone knows, was all about price discrimination, "predatory" pricing, acquisitions under duress, and the like. But there was also a technological element. Defending against monopolization charges, Standard Oil claimed that it had innovated both technologically and in the scale economies-enhancing investments by which it aggressively expanded its business:

> They have been unremitting in their efforts to improve the processes of refining, to diversify the useful by-products to be obtained from the refining of petroleum and to introduce them into general use, and these efforts have resulted to their

---

This paper is derived with extensive augmentation and amendment from Scherer (2008).

F. M. Scherer (✉)
John F. Kennedy School of Government, Harvard University, Cambridge, MA 02138, USA
e-mail: mike_scherer@harvard.edu

 Springer

great advantage as well as to the general benefit of the industry and the public at large …They have made great efforts to solve the problem of refining refractory oils and through the success of these efforts they have been able to utilize to their great advantage oils that otherwise were useless except for fuel purposes.[1]

Emphasized among Standard's innovative accomplishments was the Frasch-Burton process (as I shall argue, a misnomer) for deriving satisfactory illuminating oil (kerosene) from the high-sulfur oil found in the fields around Lima, Ohio.

In adjudicating the *Standard Oil* case, the courts could not ignore Standard's claims of superior entrepreneurship. The Supreme Court observed, for example, that:

> [I]n a powerful analysis of the facts, it is insisted [by Standard] that they demonstrate that the origin and development of the vast business which the defendants control was but the result of lawful competitive methods, guided by economic genius of the highest order, sustained by courage, by a keen insight into commercial situations, resulting in the acquisition of great wealth, but at the same time serving to stimulate and increase production, to widely extend the distribution of the products of petroleum at a cost largely below that which would have otherwise prevailed, thus proving to be at one and the same time a benefaction to the general public as well as of enormous advantage to individuals.[2]

Nevertheless, both the Circuit Court of first instance and the Supreme Court manifestly failed to address and resolve the contending claims. The Supreme Court at least admitted the task's difficulty:

> [T]o discover and state the truth concerning these contentions both arguments call for the analysis and weighing …of a jungle of conflicting testimony covering a period of 40 years, a duty difficult to rightly perform and, even if satisfactorily accomplished, almost impossible to state with any reasonable regard to brevity.[3]

Instead, asserting from historical and legal reasoning "an obvious truth" that individuals should not be allowed to secure monopolies by wrongful means, the Circuit Court concluded summarily, "Nor can arguments of reduced prices of product, economy in operation, and the like have weight," commencing its remedial order only two paragraphs later.[4] The Supreme Court affirmed, stressing in its precedent-setting rule of reason analysis how Standard's "acts and dealings" revealed the intent to "drive others from the field."[5]

One might speculate that the courts in *Standard Oil* attempted no balancing of the evidence on innovation and cost reduction because the job had been done for them, despite the evident lack of judicial gratitude, in a massive study that the Bureau of Corporations completed 2 years before the Circuit Court delivered its opinion. The

---

[1] Brief for Defendants on the Facts, *U.S. v. Standard Oil Company of New Jersey*, vol. I, pp. 109, 104.

[2] *Standard Oil Company of New Jersey et al. v. United States*, 221 U.S. 1, 48 (May 1911).

[3] Ibid.

[4] *U.S. v. Standard Oil Co. of New Jersey*, 173 Fed. 177, 196 (1909).

[5] Supra note 2 at 76. In his dissent, Justice Harlan criticized the majority for articulating its "rule of reason" to adjudicate monopolization cases without any evident basis in Congressional intent.

Bureau's staff observed inter alia that by far the largest declines in the margin between crude petroleum prices and refined product prices occurred between 1866 and 1872, "before the Standard can be said to have exercised any influence,"[6] that in the first decade of the 20th Century there was very little difference between the unit costs of Standard refineries and those of its larger rivals (who, it argued, would have been even larger and joined by others but for Standard's restrictive practices),[7] and, on technological innovation:[8]

> It is a familiar fact that whenever any absolutely new industry springs up, particularly one of a complex character, the costs at the outset are exceedingly high and are rapidly reduced with the first few succeeding years ... It is doubtless true that the Standard Oil Company ...was able to secure economies somewhat greater than could have been secured by a number of smaller concerns. It is, however, absurd to contend that no further economies in the industry would have been brought about after 1873 in the absence of the Standard or a similar combination ...The reduction of cost, even by small concerns, has been due to the natural development of the industry and to the general progress of science and invention—not to the enormous aggregation of capital.

2 A New Analysis of Patenting Trends

Support for the Bureau's inferences on innovation is provided by an analysis of data the Bureau staff failed to consider (presumably because it was not fashionable in economics to do so at the time, as it is now). From Jacob Schmookler's (undated) compilation of U.S. patents issued in various fields, Fig. 1 shows the number of petroleum refining patents issued during five-year periods between 1850 and 1929, along with the amount of crude oil produced in the United States during the same periods.[9] The plot is in logarithmic form, so a straight line implies a constant annual growth rate. The growth of patenting is most rapid before Standard Oil was incorporated and began absorbing competitors in 1870. By 1880, Standard had acquired at least 80% of U.S. refining capacity. During its period of dominance, patenting shows no growth and is at lower absolute rates than in 1865–1869. After the dissolution of the New Jersey Standard Company in 1912, there is new growth and a substantial increase in the level of patenting.

More detailed scrutiny suggests that the core components of Standard Oil generated only a small share of the 443 refining patents identified in Schmookler's tabulation for the years 1875–1899. A search was conducted in the Patent Office's annual *Index of Patents* covering those 25 years for any patent assignment to an entity with the name "Standard Oil ..." along with 50 subsidiaries named for various time periods in

---

[6] U.S. Commissioner of Corporations (1907, Part II, "Prices and Profits," p. 625).

[7] Ibid. pp. 650–655.

[8] Ibid., pp. 625–626.

[9] Schmookler (undated, Part II, for Patent Office classes 325 through 332).

🖄 Springer

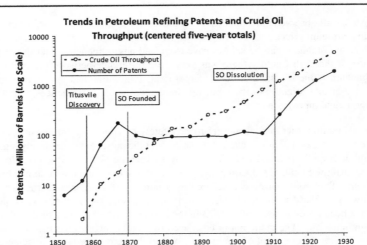

Fig. 1 Trends in petroleum refining patents and crude oil throughput (centered five-year totals)

Moody (1904).[10] Patents that pertained to barrel-making, can-sealing, and petroleum applications inventions were excluded to maintain consistency with the Schmookler definitions. With the benefit of the doubt resolved in cases of imperfect name matches in favor of counting patents as Standard-originated, from 48 to 54 patents, or at most 12% of the comparable Schmookler count, had origins in Standard companies.

It is possible that some inventions made by Standard employees were not assigned to the parent, and indeed, several instances were found in which employees assigned some patents to Standard units and retained individual rights to others. However, in 1871 U.S. law was revised to allow companies to require assignment of employee-made inventions, so Standard clearly had the right to mandate assignment, and 16 Standard units were found to have received assignments during the sample period.[11] Comprehensive data on patent assignments to corporations during the Standard monopoly period are sparse. The earliest data, derived from *Historical Statistics of the United States* (1960, p. 607), appear to be for 1901. From then to 1911, the number of U.S. patents assigned at the time of issue to U.S. corporations rose from 4,370 to 7,580, i.e., from 17.1 to 23.1% of all patent issues. Thus, although much less prevalent that in recent times, assignments were both common and rising in the latter years of Standard's monopoly.

During the period in question, Standard had an expressly articulated policy of rejecting unpatented inventions brought to its attention by independent inventors, but screening the patents of outside inventors and acquiring rights to those it considered

---

[10] The search utilized the *Index of Patents* volumes located in the Patent Office's public search room, which were found to be in seriously deteriorated condition, and the better-maintained volumes (missing 5 years) in the Boston Public Library.

[11] See May and Sell (2006, p. 123). The count of Standard subsidiary assignees here includes several inventions on non-refining inventions, of which numerous cases were found. In 1878 William Rockefeller, John D. Rockefeller's brother and business associate, took personal assignment on a non-refining invention.

attractive. See Hidy and Hidy (1955, p. 288). Given this, one might argue that Standard at least expressed a "demand pull" toward would-be petroleum process inventors, spurring their efforts, and perhaps acquiring many of the patents that my survey shows to have been assigned (i.e., at the time of issue) to independents. On this, very little information exists, although Hidy and Hidy report (1955, p. 288) that no proposed outside improvement to the Frasch refining methods was considered worth pursuing. To the Frasch contribution we now turn.

3 The Frasch Process

Standard's lawyers' briefs and the consensus of historians suggest that inventions by Hermann Frasch were the most important technological contribution by Standard during the last three decades of the 19th Century. Allan Nevins (1953, vol. 2, p. 101) views the story of Frasch's invention as "one of the romances in the Standard annals." Unfortunately, the many historical accounts are often quite inconsistent. Nevin's complaint (1953, vol. 2, p. 443) that "A biography of Frasch yet remains much needed" continues even now to be valid. My analysis here attempts to make sense of the conflicting evidence.[12]

Demand-pull for the Frasch inventions emerged when John D. Rockefeller chose in the 1880s, contrary to his prior policy, to invest heavily in crude oil properties—notably, in the vicinity of Lima, Ohio. But the oil that began flowing from Lima wells proved around 1886 or 1887 to have a sulfur content quite unsuitable for refining into Standard's principal profit-earners—illuminating oil, or kerosene, and lubricating oil. Lima-based kerosene burned with an offensive "skunk oil" smell and blackened the glass surrounding lamp flames, reducing their illuminating efficiency. Standard initially temporized by stockpiling Lima crude and then cultivating a demand for fuel oil, but that was a less profitable use of Ohio oil than refining kerosene would be—if the technology necessary for sulfur elimination were at hand. Standard's internal attempts to solve the problem were unsuccessful.

Hermann Frasch, born in Germany in late 1851, emigrated to the United States in 1868.[13] He studied and obtained a laboratory assistant's job in the Philadelphia College of Pharmacy and is said to have been fascinated by chemistry in general and the emerging petroleum technology in particular. He saved enough money to establish his own chemical laboratory around 1873, pursuing inventions of his own choosing and also doing contract work for Philadelphia companies. This work led inter alia to inventions underlying U.S. patent no. 205,792, applied for in August 1877 and issued in 1878. Its focus was the "separation and treatment of oils," emphasizing what is now considered conventional fractional distillation. It claimed the elimination of undesirable odors from volatile ingredients, but not with methods that resembled Frasch's later desulfurization inventions.

---

[12] It taps works listed in the References, several biographies of Frisch and of William Burton that can be found on the Worldwide Web, and an analysis of individual Frasch patents.

[13] His name was Anglicized to Herman during his U.S. residence.

 Springer

Frasch's petroleum invention came to the attention of Standard Oil, and Frasch was apparently enlisted as a chemist in a Standard subsidiary in Cleveland, to which he migrated around 1877.[14] The nature of his duties in Cleveland has not been pinpointed in any of the definitive sources. He made and patented several inventions from his Cleveland base, one on the "fractional distillation of oil" and one on the manufacture of waxed paper—the wax coming from petroleum-based paraffin. None of the inventions was assigned to Standard Oil or any known affiliate of Standard; all but one went to Frasch personally without prior assignment.[15] Reminiscing on his experiences upon receiving the Perkins Medal in chemistry for 1912, Frasch makes no mention of his early tenure as a Standard employee (Frasch 1912).

Frasch's Cleveland work relationship apparently ended around 1885. In what might best be characterized as a biographical novel claiming to draw upon private communications with co-workers, Heiss (1942, pp. 36–40) suggests that John D. Rockefeller was outraged when he realized later that Frasch's superiors failed to recognize the chemist's genius and had not made every effort to retain him and put him to work on problems critical to Standard Oil.[16]

What is well established is that around 1885 Frasch purchased oil production and refining properties in Ontario and moved to London, Ontario.[17] The purchase was made at bargain prices because the Ontario oil proved to have a high sulfur content, leading to product failures and expensive law suits. Frasch went to work and solved the problem, proposing an array of metal oxides to absorb the sulfur and precipitate it from the refined oil. On his invention he obtained, in addition to Canadian patents, a basic U.S. patent no. 378,246, applied for February 21, 1887, and issued in February 1888. The invention quickly came to the attention of Standard Oil, which was urgently seeking solutions to its high-sulfur Lima problem. Standard purchased Frasch's company, Empire Oil, along with its desulfurization patent, apparently in an exchange of Standard Oil stock for Empire stock, from which Frasch is said to have become quite wealthy. It also induced Frasch to return to Cleveland—some accounts say at a considerable salary, some with compensation in Standard stock. Most sources put the date of this transfer as 1886, which is inconsistent with the fact that U.S. patent

---

[14] Frasch's first Cleveland-based patent was applied for in August 1877.

[15] The exception was assigned to J. B. Merriam of Cleveland. Whether Merriam had a connection to Standard Oil is unknown.

[16] An analogy to the history of AT&T is suggested. Lee de Forest's triode electron tube (circa 1906) is widely considered one of the greatest inventions of all time, at least prior to conception of the transistor. In 1899 and 1900 de Forest was employed in the laboratories of Western Electric, AT&T's manufacturing subsidiary. His spare time work on wireless (radio) technology enraged his supervisor, who, according to de Forest's diary, exclaimed, "Look here, de Forest. You'll never make a telephone engineer. As far as I am concerned you can go to hell, in your own way. Do as you damn please!" De Forest reports that he "took him at his word, turned to my little corner where I had my spark gap and responder parts, and thereafter spent eight hours a day at my own delectable tasks, totally oblivious to the telephone work going on about me and for which I was supposed to be paid." Maclaurin (1949, p. 72). De Forest left for another job a month later.

[17] Williamson and Daum (1959, vol. 1, p. 616) apparently err in stating that Frasch was hired by the Imperial Oil Company of Canada. They may have been confused (as I was initially) by the name of Frasch's Ontario company, Empire Oil, since there was also at the time a Standard Oil affiliate in Canada named Empire Refining Co. Ltd.

378,246 lists Frasch's residence as London, Ontario, which must have been true at least at the February 1887 date of application. That the underlying inventions were made independently and not under Standard employment is shown by the fact that Rockefeller paid a handsome price to acquire the Frasch properties and bring Frasch back into the Standard fold.

Frasch did begin intensive work on the sulfur problem. Early results were disappointing, but by October 1888, the Frasch process yielded merchantable kerosene. Work continued on alternative processing methods—i.e., testing alternative metal oxides and means of recycling them, gaseous versus liquid processing, and many equipment design variants—improving yields and reducing costs.[18] Expenditures of approximately $200,000 on "the Herman experiment" were reported by Hidy and Hidy (1955, p. 165)—a sum equivalent to more than $2 million at year 2000 wholesale price levels. They yielded large returns to the Standard Oil companies, increasing the value of Lima oil, and were extended from the Lima refinery to Standard's giant new refinery at Whiting, Indiana, built in the early 1890s.[19]

One of the many curiosities in the Frasch story is the choice of the name Frasch-Burton process in Standard Oil's defense against monopolization charges. William M. Burton, who received his Ph.D. in 1889, did work briefly as Frasch's assistant in Cleveland, but only beginning in 1890, after the Frasch process had been proven successful. Burton's main contribution appears to have been demonstrating to skeptical large-volume buyers that kerosene refined from Ohio oil was as free of sulfur as kerosene from Pennsylvania oil. Or the designation could have been political, since Burton rose rapidly in the Standard organization and by 1895 was superintendent of its Whiting refinery.

Frasch apparently continued to be employed by Standard Oil through much of the 1890s, assigning between 1891 and 1899 a total of 19 petroleum refining patents to Standard affiliates (mostly to Solar Refining, under which the Lima refinery operated)—more than a third of all the patents traced to Standard Oil in my search covering the years 1875 through 1899. His conditions of employment must have been sufficiently flexible that, in the early 1890s, he began working on a problem well outside the articulated interests of Standard—mining sulfur from swampy deposits in Louisiana. From this research came a string of patents, the first three issuing in 1891, on what eventually came to be known as the Frasch process—i.e., for extracting liquified

---

[18] The first U.S. patent resulting from Frasch's new work in Ohio was number 448,480, applied for in October 1889 and issued in March 1891. It narrowed the set of oxides to copper and lead and reflected extensive experimentation.

[19] A remarkable fact difficult to reconcile with Alfred Chandler's emphasis on Standard Oil's success in securing economies of scale was that the Whiting, Indiana, refinery was designed to have 80 crude oil stills in order to achieve an unprecedented total capacity of 36,000 barrels per day. (One barrel = 42 gallons.) See Hidy and Hidy (1955, p. 164). A major source of petroleum refinery scale economies comes from the operation of the "two-thirds rule" in scaling up *individual* stills. Best-practice modern refineries operate stills with a daily throughput of 200,000 barrel s. Stills like those at Whiting in 1892 processing 450 barrels per day fell far short of this later condition. Compare Chandler (1990, pp. 21–25 and 93–96); with Scherer (1996, pp. 113–116).

sulfur from underground deposits through the injection of steam at high pressure.[20] All were issued to himself and not assigned to Standard Oil.

In his Perkins Medal address (1912, p. 138), Frasch reports that his early inventing and field experiments in Louisiana were "merely a hobby, the bulk of my time devoted to my Standard Oil work." In 1892, while still employed by Standard Oil, he organized the Union Sulphur Company, of which he became president. Union Sulphur soon became the leading supplier of sulfur in the United States, displacing imports from Sicily and Japan almost entirely.

4 Evaluation

The evidence on what Standard Oil attorneys considered the company's most noteworthy technological accomplishment—the Frasch process—yields a mixed verdict on Standard's leadership. The precipitating invention was made outside the Standard organization. Standard did show good insight in buying the basic Frasch patent, and it plowed what were for the time substantial sums into perfecting the process. My broader survey shows that relatively few patented inventions emerged from inventors who chose to assign, or whom Standard required to assign, their inventions to the company. While the petroleum industry was expanding rapidly, the number of petroleum refining process patents stagnated, resuming a growth trajectory only after the divestiture of Standard into 34 segments following the Supreme Court's 1911 decision.

A more important negative indicator is the invention that was almost neglected. While the Standard Oil monopolization case was proceeding, the petroleum refining industry was subjected to two technological revolutions. The demand for kerosene illuminating oil—Standard's principal early product—was threatened by the advent of electric illumination; and the emergence of the automobile created demand for gasoline, which until then had been a nearly worthless by-product of the refining process. In 1907, 8.0% of American homes were wired for electricity; by 1912, the figure had doubled and continued rising to 34.7% in 1920. In 1907, 43,000 passenger automobiles were produced; in 1912, 3,56,000; and after the first million-car year in 1916, factory sales reached 1.9 million in 1920.

Using traditional methods, petroleum refiners were hard-pressed to extract enough gasoline to meet the burgeoning demand. A new process for obtaining a much higher fraction of gasoline from a barrel of crude oil—thermal cracking—was invented around 1909 by William Burton, Frasch's former assistant and in 1909 head of production at Standard Oil Company of Indiana. Indiana Standard applied to Standard headquarters in New York for authorization to spend $1 million developing and installing thermal crackers. The request was turned down; the invention was considered too risky.[21] Only when Standard of Indiana became independent in 1912 could the project go forward. The Burton process was widely licensed. Between 1913 and 1920, when competing

---

[20] The first patent resulting from Frasch's desulphurization work at Lima also issued in 1891.

[21] See Yergin (1991, pp. 111–112); and Gibb and Knowlton (1956, pp. 116–117).

cracking processes began to emerge, 91 million (42 gallon) barrels of gasoline had been refined using the Burton process.[22]

References

Chandler, A. D. (1990). *Scale and scope: The dynamics of industrial capitalism*. Cambridge: Harvard University Press.
de Chazeau, M. G., & Kahn, A. (1959). *Integration and competition in the petroleum industry*. New York: Yale University Press.
Dictionary of American biography. (1931). New York: Scribner.
Enos, J. L. (1962). *Petroleum progress and profits: A history of process innovations*. Cambridge: MIT Press.
Frasch, H. (1912). Address of acceptance. *Journal of Industrial and Engineering Chemistry, 4*, 134–140.
Gibb, G. S., & Knowlton, E. (1956). *History of Standard Oil Company: The resurgent years 1911–1927*. New York: Harper.
Hawthorne, R. (1999). Biography of Herman Frasch. In J. Garraty & M. Carnes (Eds.), *American national biography*. New York: Oxford University Press.
Heiss, L. (1942). *Der Schwefelkoenig von Louisiana (The Sulfur King of Louisiana)*. Reutlingen, Germany: Ensslin & Laiblin.
Hidy, R., & Hidy M. (1955). *Pioneering in big business*. New York: Harper.
Maclaurin, W. R. (1949). *Invention and innovation in the radio industry*. New York: Macmillan.
May, C., & Sell, S. (2006). *Intellectual property rights: A critical history*. Boulder, CO: Lynne Rienner.
Moody, J. (1904). *The truth about the trusts*. New York: Moody Publishing Co.
Nevins, A. (1953). *Study in power: John D. Rockefeller, industrialist and philanthropist* (Vol. 2). New York: Scribner.
Scherer, F. M. (1996). *Industry structure, strategy, and public policy*. New York: HarperCollins.
Scherer, F. M. (2008). Technological innovation and monopolization. In W. D. Collins (Ed.), *Issues in competition law and policy* (Vol. 2, pp. 1033–1069). Chicago: American Bar Association.
Schmookler, J. (undated). *Statistics of patents classified by industry, United States, 1837–1957*. Privately published at the University of Minnesota.
U.S. Bureau of Corporations. (1907). *Report of the Commissioner of Corporations on the petroleum industry*. Washington.
U.S. Bureau of the Census. (1960). *Historical statistics of the United States: Colonial times to 1957*. Washington.
U.S. Patent and Trademark Office. (1875–1899). *Index of Patents*. Washington, annually.
Williamson, H. F., & Daum, A. (1959). *The American petroleum industry: The age of illumination*. Evanston: Northwestern University Press.
Yergin, D. (1991). *The prize*. New York: Simon & Schuster.

---

[22] Enos (1962), Appendix Table 1a.

🍃 Springer

3

BNA, Inc.

Antitrust & Trade Regulation
REPORT

Volume 84 Number 2090

Friday, January 24, 2003

ISSN 1523-2824

Page 65

Analysis & Perspective

Monopolization

Microsoft and IBM in Europe

Enforcement

F.M. Scherer is Aetna professor emeritus at the John F. Kennedy School of Government, Harvard University, and lecturer in the Woodrow Wilson School of Public and International Affairs, Princeton University. Between 1974 and 1976, he served as Director of the Bureau of Economics in the Federal Trade Commission. His most significant publications on antitrust are collected in a volume, "Competition Policy, Domestic and International" (Edward Elgar: 2000).

There are remarkable parallels between the *Microsoft* case currently pending before the competition policy authorities of the European Union and the action against IBM pursued by the European Commission during the early 1980s. There are also valuable lessons for responding to Microsoft conduct that almost surely will be found to violate EU competition law.

Unlike the U.S. Department of Justice complaint against Microsoft, which targeted Microsoft's conduct during the mid- to late 1990s, the European investigation appears to be focusing upon two still-contemporary issues: Microsoft strategies that, by keeping certain interface information and programming tools secret, give its workgroup server operating systems a significant advantage over independent server software writers attempting to achieve inter-operability with ubiquitous Microsoft desktop computer operating systems; and the bundling of Microsoft's audio and video playing software with its desktop operating systems.

The European Commission's investigation of IBM during the early 1980s also emphasized bundling and non-disclosure of interface information. Beginning in the late 1960s, IBM experienced increasing competition from "plug-compatible" manufacturers (PCMs). Some like Telex, Memorex, and StorageTek built peripheral equipment such as tape storage drives, disc drives, and add-on memory units that plugged into the standard interfaces used on IBM System 360 and then System 370 mainframes. Others, such as Amdahl (founded by the principal designer of IBM's System 360), Fujitsu, and IPL Systems, produced main frames (i.e., central processing units) that could be used interchangeably with IBM computers, but offered higher performance and/or lower cost. To combat these threats, IBM among other things began bundling peripheral equipment control functions into mainframe hardware. It also departed from what had previously been a full disclosure policy, keeping operating system software source code secret, reducing the amount of information disclosed on interface specifications, and delaying interface disclosures until they came too late to be of use by PCMs trying to design compatible equipment.

In response to complaints by several American computer manufacturers, the European Commission's competition policy directorate commenced an investigation of IBM's bundling and disclosure policies. After the U.S. Department of Justice abandoned its 13-year-old antitrust suit against IBM in January 1982, William F. Baxter, then head of the U.S. Antitrust Division, contacted the director of the European Commission's competition unit and "expressed concern" over continuation of the European action. The Europeans persisted, however, and were on the verge of issuing a formal complaint when IBM agreed in August 1984 to an "undertaking" accepted tentatively by the EC in lieu of an official mandate.

In the undertaking, IBM agreed to disclose within four months of the announcement of a new System 370 product, or at the time a product became generally available, if earlier than the four-month deadline, interface information sufficient to allow both hardware and software manufacturers to attach their offerings to IBM main frames and to its Systems Network Architecture. It also agreed to sell within the European Common Market unbundled System 370 computers with no more main memory than what was required for testing purposes. Violation of the undertaking, an EC official announced at the time, could lead to reinstatement of formal case proceedings. The undertaking was to remain in force until at least January 1990. In fact, it was discontinued in July 1994.

The undertaking reflected a compromise between IBM and EC authorities. Originally, the EC staff sought disclosure of interface specifications within 30 days of product announcement; the compromise settled on 120 days. The staff also sought disclosure of underlying operating system source code, but this provision was not covered by the undertaking. No guidelines were provided for compensation to be paid by PCMs receiving the IBM information, and so IBM in fact was able to charge what one PCM veteran said to the author was "quite a bit of money."

One moral of the history is that the European Commission sought to remedy perceived competition policy problems even though the U.S. Department of Justice chose to abandon its antitrust case and urged the Europeans similarly to withdraw.

In interviews, two former U.S. plug-compatible manufacturer executives expressed to the author differing views on the impact of the European undertaking. One important rival of IBM stated that, given the secrecy policies IBM had previously implemented, the undertaking "was absolutely essential to our ability to compete." Another former PCM executive said that the settlement had little effect, mainly because by the mid-1980s IBM had such a huge base of computers in use by customers that it was forced to standardize its interfaces and keep their specifications relatively constant. He distinguished the situation in the 1980s from current Microsoft disputes, observing that software operating system interfaces can be changed much more easily, and with more debilitating consequences for rivals attempting to maintain compatibility, than the hard-wired interfaces embodied in IBM main frames.

From the European IBM case experience, several lessons to help inform impending European decisions on Microsoft can be extracted. First, unbundling remedies are not unprecedented in the information technology realm. Second, timely disclosure of interface specifications is crucial to the attainment of inter-operability. Prompt reporting of post-announcement software modifications that affect interfaces is equally essential. An IBM competitor reported that following the 1984 undertaking "IBM was pretty good in disclosing bug fixes." Third, interviewees made it clear that although they were able to function without access to underlying IBM source code, they could have achieved even better plug compatibility with relevant source code information. Fourth, the question of compensation for timely disclosure of interface and source code information cannot be overlooked. It would not be inappropriate for the European Community authorities to reduce the fines they might otherwise levy and correspondingly require that Microsoft disclose information at zero monetary cost to firms developing Microsoft-compatible software. Finally, in view of Microsoft's perennially uncooperative stance toward antitrust inquiries and remedies, the European Union would be well advised to issue a formal order mandating desired behavioral changes rather than accepting, as it did in the IBM case, an undertaking enforceable only in cases of non-compliance with a substantial and deleterious time lag.

Bibliography

"IBM Shocks the Plug-Compatibles," Business Week, June 18, 1979, p. 107.

"I.B.M. Faces Europe on Antitrust Charge," New York Times, January 19, 1981.

"IBM's Mimics Struggle To Keep Pace," Business Week, September 20, 1982, p. 93.

"Europeans Aim Action at I.B.M.," New York Times, April 27, 1984.

"Under the Gun: Common Market Officials Are Still Watching IBM Closely, Although Perhaps Not Close Enough," Datamation, September 1, 1984, pp. 42-48.

Organisation for Economic Co-operation and Development, Competition Policy in OECD Countries: 1984-1985 (Paris: 1987), pp. 253-254.

[4]

ABUSE OF DOMINANCE BY HIGH TECHNOLOGY ENTERPRISES: A COMPARISON OF U.S. AND E.C. APPROACHES

*Frederic M. Scherer**

Abstract

This paper compares how the United States and the European Community dealt with competition policy challenges by two firms operating at the frontiers of technology: Microsoft and Intel. The U.S. Microsoft case was broadly targeted but largely unsuccessful in implementing remedies once violation was found. The European case was more narrowly focused, failing in its media player unbundling remedy but fighting hard to implement its interoperability information remedy. The European case on Intel was also tightly focused, leading to the highest fine in E.C. competition policy history and a mandate to avoid quantity-linked rebates. The newest U.S. settlement regarding Intel poses difficult monitoring problems with respect to its ambitious claim for remedies. The paper ends with critical comments on E.C. adjudication procedures.

Keywords: innovation, antitrust, dominant firms

Parole chiave: innovazione, antitrust, imprese dominanti

Jel classification: L4

Received: 20.9.2010
Final revision received: 3.11.2010

* Harvard University, John F. Kennedy School of Governement; Mike_Scherer@harvard.edu.

Economia e Politica Industriale - Journal of Industrial and Business Economics
2011 vol. 38 (1): 39-62

F.M. Scherer   *Abuse of high technology dominance in the E.C. and U.S.*

Introduction

European Community competition policy has advanced by leaps and bounds since it was first authorized in the 1957 Treaty of Rome. Recently it has moved to the frontier of difficulty: dealing with alleged abusive conduct by enterprises dominating the high technology fields in which they operate. The most prominent thrusts are the cases involving Microsoft and Intel. This paper examines and compares the approaches taken by the United States, a veteran of high technology competition actions, and the European Commission in their handling of the Microsoft and Intel challenges.

1. Microsoft

Microsoft presented the first set of challenges, addressed initially by U.S. authorities.[1] I begin with some background. Created in the 1970s to write software for primitive early personal computers, Microsoft leapt to prominence by being chosen to provide a borrowed operating system, MS/DOS, for the IBM personal computer introduced in August 1981. Up to that time, personal computers were regarded as little more than hobbyists' toys. IBM's entry into the PC field gave them business legitimacy, precipitated rapidly increasing sales, and as applications software writers targeted their creations first toward the IBM PC and the MS/DOS operating system it embodied, a snowball effect ensued. On the theory, see Katz and Shapiro (1994). By far the largest number of applications were written for the MS/DOS operating system, leading most personal computer buyers to choose a system, either from IBM or numerous imitators, resting upon MS/DOS. This "applications barrier to entry" helped Microsoft gain the lion's share of the PC operating system market. The main challenger was Apple with its Macintosh, launched at demand-limiting premium prices with a revolutionary graphical user interface (GUI) in 1984. Asked by Apple to write applications software for Macintosh, Microsoft learned the Mac's internal architecture and launched its own GUI operating system, Windows 1.0, in November 1985. Versions of Windows up to the year 2000 operated atop an MS/DOS foundation, and so Microsoft was able to offer users both backward compatibility with their old software and the advantages of GUI. But the early versions were clunky and crash-prone. Not until May 1990 did Microsoft succeed in offering an attractive version of Windows, Windows 3.0, and from that time on, Microsoft dominated personal computer operating system markets overwhelmingly.

1. There is of course a huge literature. My approach is based upon Offenhauer and Scherer (1999); Scherer (1996, chapter 7); Scherer (2008).

Microsoft, however, had a vulnerability. During the first two decades of personal computing, the dominant model was for applications programs to be stored within the desktop box. When the World Wide Web first became publicly accessible during the mid-1990s, it was accessed from desktop computers by means of another applications program, a browser, the most important of which, Netscape Navigator, was widely distributed beginning in late 1994. See figure 1.

Figure 1 – Desktop applications use in the mid-1990s

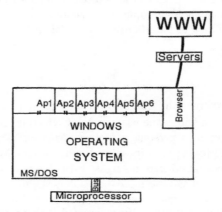

Microsoft soon saw that the alternative model characterized by figure 2 threatened its dominant position. A user might employ a browser to access applications programs located on a server anywhere on the World Wide Web. And almost simultaneously, Sun Microsystems introduced a new potentially universal programming language, Java, whose compiler could be placed on any computer. An applications writer was able to write its program not specifically for Windows but for Java, and if such programs proliferated on the World Wide Web, users would be freed from their reliance upon Windows-based applications and could therefore equip their desktop computers with operating systems – perhaps skeletal – other than Windows.

Microsoft perceived this threat in 1995, licensed a browser from a company (Spyglass) that had evolved from the same University of Illinois base as Netscape, and offered the browser, renamed Internet Explorer, as a separate free complement to its Windows operating systems. At nearly the same time it approached the leaders of Netscape and offered them financial assistance conditional upon their writing Navigator only for old versions of Windows and not for the new Windows 95 introduced in August 1995. Netscape refused Microsoft's offer and was threatened that Microsoft would "cut off their air supply". Microsoft did take retaliatory action, delaying until October 1995 the provision of interface information Netscape needed to make their Navigator

F.M. Scherer   *Abuse of high technology dominance in the E.C. and U.S.*

software fully compatible with Windows 95. Internet Explorer thereupon moved ahead of Navigator in software magazine quality ratings and began to challenge Navigator for market share. To blunt the figure 2 threat even more, Microsoft agreed to offer a fully compatible version of Sun's Java compiler on Windows programs but in fact introduced an incompatible version which forced software writers to develop distinct Microsoft-compatible versions.

Figure 2 – Microsoft's nightmare vision of future computing

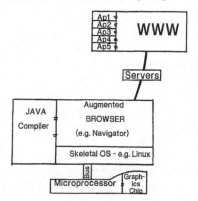

From a position of slight market share inferiority relative to Navigator in 1997, Microsoft's Internet Explorer surged ahead of Navigator in 1998 when Microsoft launched new Windows versions with the Internet Explorer fully bundled into and undetachable from the Windows operating system. If the operating system already included a well-functioning Microsoft browser, why bother separately installing Navigator? Microsoft also brought pressure to bear upon personal computer system assemblers and Internet service providers to emphasize Internet Explorer at the expense of Navigator.

1.1. The U.S. antitrust cases

The U.S. Department of Justice Antitrust Division reacted to Microsoft's bundling decision with a narrowly-targeted complaint.[2] When District Court

2. An earlier antitrust suit challenged Microsoft's policy of requiring computer assemblers to pay Microsoft a fee for each operating system they installed, whether it was Windows or that of a rival. A settlement was negotiated in July 1994. When District Court Judge Stanley Sporkin attempted to broaden the terms, he was reversed and removed from the case by an Appellate Court. See U.S. v. Microsoft Corporation, 56 F. 2d 1448 (1995). Sporkin's ill-fated attempt to broaden the remedy was in part informed by the excellent Wallace and Ericson (1992) book.

F.M. Scherer   *Abuse of high technology dominance in the E.C. and U.S.*

Judge Thomas P. Jackson's December 1997 order to unbundle Internet Explorer was reversed by an Appellate Court, the Department of Justice escalated its attack, filing a broad complaint accusing Microsoft of monopolization, attempted monopolization, and illegal tying (i.e., bundling) and citing a wide array of practices used by Microsoft to thwart competition from rival operating systems and browsers. After an accelerated trial attempting to avoid the manifold delays plaguing the earlier U.S. antitrust case against IBM, Judge Jackson ruled in November 1999 that Microsoft had violated the Sherman Antitrust Act on numerous grounds.[3] Judge Jackson then commissioned Appellate Court Judge Richard Posner to mediate a settlement. When the settlement talks failed – largely on Microsoft's unwillingness to make its computer codes more widely available – Judge Jackson ordered in June of 2000 that Microsoft be broken into two parts, an operating systems company and an applications company, and required that it cease a variety of other restrictive practices.

Microsoft of course appealed to higher authority, and from that point on, the government's challenge faltered. In late 2000, George W. Bush prevailed over Al Gore in a contest for the U.S. presidency, thanks in part to a U.S. Supreme Court decision overturning a State of Florida Supreme Court decision requiring the recount of challenged ballots – a recount that was widely expected to give Gore a narrow victory, both in Florida and the nation as a whole. Microsoft's appeal was heard by the District of Columbia Appellate Court. The choice of attorneys to plead the Department of Justice side was as always delicate. Normally such appeals are handled by staff of the solicitor general, but on complex cases, it is not unusual for the appeal to be argued by the principal Antitrust Division attorney. Quite atypically, the Microsoft prosecution had been led for the Department of Justice by a prominent private sector trial attorney, David Boies.[4] But Boies was also principal attorney for Al Gore in his appeal of the Florida presidential election outcome before both the Florida and U.S. Supreme Courts. Would a new Republican Department of Justice, led by an Attorney General to whose failed senatorial election campaign Microsoft had contributed 19,500 dollars, choose Boies to argue the appeal? Not surprisingly, the choice went to the Solicitor General staff. The author listened to the proceedings on the radio and concluded, as did *Business Week* the following week,[5] that attorneys for the government simply did not understand the complex economics of the case.

3. U.S. v. Microsoft Corporation, 84 F. Supp. 2d 9 (1999). For blow-by-blow accounts of the Department of Justice suit and its forerunners, see Auletta (2001) and Heilemann (2001). I participated in the early Department of Justice deliberations and prepared as a consultant for Sun Microsystems a detailed chronology of Microsoft's strategic actions.
4. On Boies' reputation as a litigator, see Kaplan (2010, pp. 81-95).
5. Prasso (2001, p. 14).

F.M. Scherer   *Abuse of high technology dominance in the E.C. and U.S.*

The Appellate Court ruled that Microsoft had in fact monopolized the PC operating system market and thereby violated the Sherman Act, but overturned several other counts of Judge Jackson's decision, including his finding that Microsoft's bundling was a per se Sherman Act violation. The Court invited the government to readdress the question of whether the bundling constituted a rule of reason violation.[6]

The Department of Justice chose not to pursue the Appellate Court's invitation on bundling, but instead negotiated with Microsoft what was generally considered a mild set of behavioral remedies, notably, avoidance of secret discounts to Windows licensors and disclosure of information sufficient to allow interoperability between Windows and writers of "middleware" software, i.e., browsers, Java translators, and e-mail programs. Dispute continued for several years over details of the disclosure obligations and the charges Microsoft was allowed to levy on those who received interoperability information. Eventually, the royalty rates demanded by Microsoft were substantially reduced as a result of Antitrust Division objections.

1.2. The European Commission case

Despite being put on notice in 1997 that it risked antitrust challenges through strategic bundling, Microsoft in May 1999 physically bundled its Windows Media Player, cloned from a predecessor offered by Real Networks and previously provided as a separate software package, into its Windows operating systems. Having branched into the provision of computer server operating systems along with PC operating systems, Microsoft advertised that its servers interoperated more seamlessly with the ubiquitous Windows desktop operating systems than those of rival work group server software developers due to Microsoft's superior knowledge of the required intercommunication protocols.

The latter problem was apparently the initial impetus for a European Commission investigation, following a complaint from server provider Sun Microsystems. The investigation was broadened in February 2000 to include Microsoft's physical bundling of the Windows Media Player, apparently on the basis of complaints inter alia from Microsoft rival Real Networks. On August 1, 2000, an initial statement of objections focusing on the interface disclosure problem was issued; it was amended to include the bundling issue on August

---

6. U.S. v. Microsoft Corporation, 253 F. 3rd 34 (2001). In fact, Judge Jackson's decision included careful support for a rule of reason violation. The Appellate Court also criticized Jackson for discussing the ongoing trial with a reporter and for failing to hold hearings on the Department of Justice's proposed remedial measures. On remedies, see the lengthy Amici Curiae brief by Litan *et al.* (2000), submitted on invitation by Judge Jackson.

30, 2001. Following further proceedings, the Commission adopted in April 2004 a lengthy, carefully-argued decision concluding that Microsoft had violated the European Community law against abuse of a dominant position through its media player bundling and its biased disclosure of server interoperability data.[7] Microsoft was fined 497 million euros, ordered to offer a version of Windows with the media player unbundled, and required to provide information sufficient to allow other firms' server software to interoperate seamlessly with Windows desktop operating systems. Microsoft appealed to the European Court of First Instance for a stay of the remedies, but following a two-day hearing in Luxembourg, its appeal was rejected,[8] and in September 2007 the Court of First Instance broadly upheld the Commission's 2004 decision.[9]

Following the rejection of its petition for a stay of execution on remedies, Microsoft did offer a version of Windows with the Windows Media Player unbundled from the operating system. The measure was an abject failure, however, because the Commission allowed Microsoft to sell the unbundled system at the same price as the bundled system, and in the first nine months of availability, only one buyer out of 20,000 chose the unbundled version.[10] The Commission took a much tougher stance on the disclosure of interoperability information. Technical experts reported repeatedly that the information supplied by Microsoft was insufficient for smooth interoperability, and in 2006, the Commission began levying noncompliance fines eventually cumulating to 1.18 billion euros before Microsoft's disclosures were judged adequate. Although it deferred to Microsoft on the pricing of an unbundled Windows Media Player, it rejected Microsoft's demands for a 5.95% royalty on software benefitting from its information disclosures and eventually imposed a maximum royalty rate of 0.4%.

In May of 2008 at a conference in St. Gallen, Switzerland, Judge Bo Vesterdorf, retired Chief Judge of the European Court of First Instance and presiding judge at the Microsoft appeal, expressed surprise at the magnitude of the non-compliance fines levied on Microsoft and warned that «one should be careful» not to encroach too much on patent rights «by a too-zealous enforcement of competition law». He warned further that such encroachment could «create legal uncertainty for the holders of intellectual property rights, thereby perhaps diminishing the incentives to sometimes desirable but very expensive research and development».[11] His concern presumably turned on both the

---

7. Commission of the European Communities, decision, case COMP/C-3/37.792 (4.21.2004).
8. Order of the President of the Court of First Instance, 12.22.2004. I appeared before the Court as a witness on behalf of Real Networks.
9. Microsoft Corporation v. Commission, case T-201/04, 9.17.2007.
10. Meller (2005, p. C-16).
11. From a Reuters news dispatch 5.22.2008, by David Lawsky, read on the American Antitrust Institute web site.

F.M. Scherer   *Abuse of high technology dominance in the E.C. and U.S.*

compulsory licensing of Microsoft's patents and Commission intervention in requiring royalty rates much lower than those sought by Microsoft.

Although Judge Vesterdorf's fears were in theory warranted, they (and the records supporting both the U.S. and European Microsoft proceedings) ignored important truths. First, the compulsory licensing of key patents had been ordered in settlement of more than a hundred U.S. antitrust cases. Despite complaints that such compulsory licensing threatened investments in innovation, careful investigations revealed that at least among well-established corporations, the compulsory licensing decrees had little or no discernible adverse effect on the subject companies' R&D investments.[12] Second, although Microsoft invested prodigiously in research and development and the provision of erratically reliable software packages, its record as a true innovator left much to be desired. See table 1.

Table 1 – Precursors to Microsoft's principal software innovations

Microsoft program	*Precursors*
Basic for Altair "computer"	Dartmouth College Basic program (written by Kemeny and Kurtz)
Excel spreadsheet	VisiCalc (written by Harvard Business School Student), Lotus 1-2-3
Word word processor	WordStar, WordPerfect
PowerPoint	Purchased from Sunnyvale, CA, start-up firm's "Presentation" program
Windows	Adapted from Apple's Macintosh operating system
Internet Explorer	Leased from Spyglass, cousin of Netscape's Navigator
Windows Media Player	Adapted from Real Networks' Real Player

Source: author's personal knowledge.

Most of its "innovations", it seems clear, were cribbed and then expanded upon from the efforts of others. Requiring it to license information needed to make its software function seamlessly with others' offerings hardly seems likely to dampen the vigorous pace of innovation that has characterized the computer software industries.

12. See Scherer (1977, pp. 59-78) and Scherer (2008), especially the discussion of Xerox at pp. 1054-1057.

2. Intel

The integrated circuit, emerging in the late 1950s, was without doubt one of the greatest inventions made during the 20th century.[13] That step alone, however, would have been relatively unimportant had it not been for incessant design and production process improvements making possible astonishing increases in integrated circuit density and speed characterized by "Moore's Law", first articulated by Gordon Moore, a founder of the Intel Corporation.[14] Also crucial to the emergence of powerful high-speed computers, including personal computers, was the microprocessor, often called in its early years the "computer on a chip". Credit for the 1971 invention generally goes to Ted Hoff of the Intel Corporation, although Hoff himself has said that the advancing state of the art made the invention virtually inevitable, and if he had not taken the honors, «somebody else would have».[15]

Rapid improvements in the power and speed of microprocessors and complementary dynamic random access memory chips (DRAMs) set the stage for the advent of personal computers in the late 1970s. A key event, as observed earlier, was the introduction of the IBM Personal Computer (PC) in August 1981. IBM chose among three contenders the Intel 8086 microprocessor to run its Microsoft MS/DOS operating system. With this choice, a software compatibility bandwagon effect made Intel, like Microsoft, the greatly preferred basis for personal computer operation. After first using Motorola and then IBM microprocessors, Apple eventually also switched to the Intel architecture for its Macintosh personal computers. In choosing Intel as its microprocessor supplier, however, IBM was wary of becoming locked into a single source. It therefore demanded as a condition for buying Intel's microprocessors that Intel establish a fully competitive second source. Advanced Micro Devices (AMD), which at the time produced specialized processors, was chosen as the second source, and in its contract with Intel AMD was given full access to Intel's intellectual property, its circuit architecture, and (crucially) the information needed to produce new versions of the Intel processor. Its competitive efforts succeeded beyond Intel's expectations, so that by the mid 1980s it had gained nearly half of so-called I-86 (also called X-86) microprocessor orders. The royalty scheme worked out between the two firms turned out to be disadvantageous to Intel, since it was based upon the companies' proprietary chip complexity rather than sales volume, and the Intel chips sold unexpectedly in much larger quantities than AMD's specialized offerings.

13. On the early history, see Scherer (1996, pp. 202-204).
14. See Flamm (1993, 2007). Moore predicted in 1965 that integrated circuit density would double annually, a figure he later revised to every 18 months.
15. Anonymous (1993, p. 47).

F.M. Scherer   *Abuse of high technology dominance in the E.C. and U.S.*

Intel was not pleased.[16] The first versions of the Intel chips chosen by IBM processed data in 16-bit chunks. Intel's management decided to move up to 32-bit microprocessors and took a conscious decision not to notify AMD, as it was contractually obliged to do, of its plans. The first Intel 32-bit processor, the I-80386, was rolled out commercially in September 1986. When AMD finally learned of Intel's plans, it was well behind any schedule it could have achieved even if Intel provided the necessary architectural information. And Intel refused to provide any design information, requiring AMD to begin ab initio in developing its own Intel-compatible chip. Meanwhile, AMD invoked the arbitration clause in its contract with Intel, eventually winning on most counts, including rights to imitate the Intel architecture.[17] AMD introduced its first 32-bit clone, the AMD-386, only in 1991. It was joined as a competitor in 1992 by another firm, Cyrix, which also launched challenges against Intel under the U.S. antitrust laws,[18] but failed to sustain market momentum and was taken over eventually by a Taiwanese company, Via.

After AMD and Cyrix entered the market with X-86 compatible microprocessors, Intel pursued a variety of strategies to counter them. The pace of Intel's chip innovation accelerated significantly after inter-chip rivalry began, as figure 3 reveals.[19]

Figure 3 – Time trend of Intel microprocessor introductions

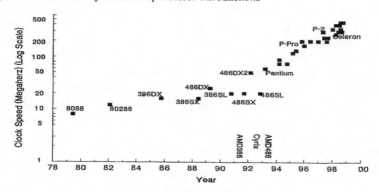

Source: author's research for Federal Trade Commission.

16. This paragraph is based upon the author's personal knowledge gained as a consultant to AMD in AMD's arbitration and competition policy disputes with Intel during the 1990s.
17. See Pollack (1992, p. C1) and (on judicial affirmation) Hill (1995).
18. See Wilson and Warren-Boulton (1995).
19. The time break is highly significant statistically, with an F-ratio of 21.71. For a similar conclusion based upon later behavior, see Nosko (2010). The diagram was prepared but not

Up to about 2005, the main focus of rivalry among microprocessor vendors was chip speed, measured in millions of clock cycles (megahertz) per second, and with three firms competing to offer Intel architecture, Intel was forced to accelerate the rate at which it introduced faster chips.

Along with innovating more rapidly, Intel pursued several other strategies to thwart its rivals. It intoduced "fighting brands" such as the Celeron (i.e., chips based upon prior designs, but with some functionality impaired so they could be sold at lower prices). It brought patent infringement suits in situations where rival rights were unclear. In the early stages of a new chip's life cycle, quantities were limited, and computer assemblers who were loyal to Intel were given first access to chip supplies, disadvantaging computer makers who split their business between Intel and rivals. Similar disparities were sustained on access to advance information about microprocessor interfaces, needed to design new computer models. Under its "Intel Inside" program, it granted computer makers advertising discounts, conditional upon displaying the popular "Intel Inside" logo only on computer lines using Intel chips exclusively. Other discounts were structured to reward loyalty to Intel.

To understand Intel's discount strategy, which was the central focus of the European Commission's case against Intel, one must delve more deeply into the economics of semiconductor production, a digression that, alas, was not taken in the European Commission's otherwise admirable Intel case decision.

Semiconductors represent the classic learning curve industry.[20] At least in the early stages of production, one learns "by doing" how to avoid defective chips and increase volume as additional chips are produced. Typically, each doubling and redoubling of cumulative chip volume reduces unit batch costs by 20 to 30%. Learning curves tend to be linear on doubly logarithmic coordinates, and their "slope" is stated to be 100 minus the percentage by which costs are reduced with each doubling of cumulative output. This leads among other things to a phenomenon often ignored in the economics literature: because each batch causes learning that reduces future batch costs, marginal costs, taking into account both current costs and the impact on future costs, are

used in connection with the author's work as principal economic consultant for a Federal Trade Commission case narrowly focused on Intel's data disclosure practices with respect to chip buyers who challenged its patents. The case was settled before trial in 1999. In the matter of Intel Corporation, FTC docket 9288, consent order (1999). The diagram was included in the author's testimony before the Court of First Instance in the Microsoft case. AMD's first 32-bit microprocessor was the AMD-386. The AMD-486 was a similar microprocessor coupled with a math co-processor, which previously had been sold separately.

20. See Flamm (1993, chapters 6 and 7) and Scherer (1996, chapter 6). For a basic theoretical contribution, see Spence (1981).

far below current batch costs, more so when the future cost impact is not discounted to present value, as compared to when the impact of learning on future costs is discounted.

Figure 4 provides a fairly typical example, using DRAM volumes experienced during the late 1980s.[21] At cumulative production of 100,000 chips, for instance, batch costs are 6.75 dollars while discounted marginal costs are only 3.03 dollars. According to information compiled by the author during the 1990s, the curves bottom out somewhere between cumulative "good" chip volumes of 5 and 50 million. Learning curve data are extremely confidential, so it is unclear whether these relationships persist into the 21st century. The existence of a substantial discrepancy between average batch and marginal costs and the advantages of augmenting current volume for future cost efficiency give rise among other things to tendencies for very aggressive pricing in the early stages of learning.[22] That these dynamics continue into the 21st century is suggested by the aggressive pricing that emerged during the so-called "dot.com" recession of 2000-2001, precipitating price fixing agreements that led to U.S. and European antitrust interventions against DRAM (and also flash memory) producers.[23]

Figure 4 – DRAM learning curve with 72% slope

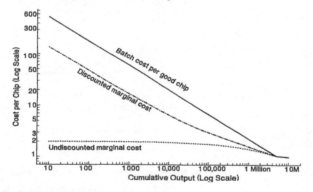

Source: author's computations.

There is more. Figure 4 focuses only on what might be called variable batch costs. In addition, huge front-end costs are incurred to devise and lay out new cir-

21. It is drawn from Scherer (1996, p. 211), using sales timing information published in Flaherty (1992).
22. See Scherer (1996, pp. 212-214).
23. See (on the U.S. case) Flynn (2003) and (on the European case) Kanter (2010). Fines of 331 million euros were levied in the latter case.

cuit architecture, test it, and prepare the tooling required to produce a new generation of circuits. Ignoring the billions of dollars spent to build and equip a fabricating facility (a "fab"), it has been estimated that the front-end sunk costs incurred for a new generation of microprocessors amount to hundreds of millions
of dollars.[24] Figure 5 combines average variable batch cost curves, assuming a
relatively conservative 80% learning curve slope and falling (since microprocessors are more complex and costly than DRAMs) to 50 dollars per chip (dot-dot-
dash line), with an average fixed cost curve (dotted line), assuming setup costs
for a new line to be 300 million dollars. Average total cost (solid line) is found to
fall all the way out to a cumulative volume of at least 20 million chips, showing
what is in effect a natural monopoly condition. And even at very high volumes,
batch costs are substantially below average total costs. These are conditions under which, if there are several rivals rather than a single natural monopolist, aggressive price wars can be expected, absent strong oligopolistic coordination.[25]

Figure 5 – Approximate life cycle cost curve for microprocessor production

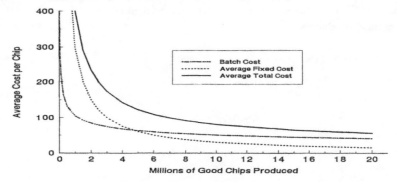

* learning curve slope = 80%; fixed costs = 300 million dollars.
Source: author's computations.

The natural monopoly state of microprocessor production, at least at volumes
up to 20 million chips, argues for concentrating production in a single firm. But
the technological rivalry effect shown by figure 3 argues for competition, at least
among two or a handful of firms. A difficult tradeoff is required. The author's
own judgment is that, at least for higher-volume chips, more rapid innovation
should trump natural monopoly cost considerations, but on this, reasonable observers could disagree. No such tradeoff was attempted in the European Commission case with respect to Intel, which will be described more fully in what follows.

24. U.S. Federal Trade Commission (2009, paragraph 43).
25. See for historical comparison Jones (1920). See also Scherer and Ross (1990, pp. 294-308).

F.M. Scherer   *Abuse of high technology dominance in the E.C. and U.S.*

Figure 6 abstracts from front-end fixed costs to consider the kind of pricing that might be expected in microprocessors with one and then two firms and learning-by-doing that persists out to 10 million chips produced. It assumes that Intel leads the way into a new generation of microprocessors and advances rapidly down its 80% learning curve before AMD responds with its own version.

With a much smaller market share, AMD advances only slowly down the batch cost learning curve LL', with progress denoted by quarter-year marks (e.g., Q1, Q2, etc.). Without competition, Intel pursues a typical monopoly pricing strategy, below cost initially to stimulate demand and then increasingly above cost.[26] However, when AMD progresses at quarter 2 far enough to have costs below Intel's monopoly price, Intel initiates what its staff during the late 1990s called "the waterfall", reducing its price in one step along AB to a level below AMD's costs and holding it there until AMD has produced a cumulative total of a million good chips. In this way, profitable competition by AMD was rendered difficult even if not impossible.

Figure 6 – Timing of AMD's progression down an 80% learning curve

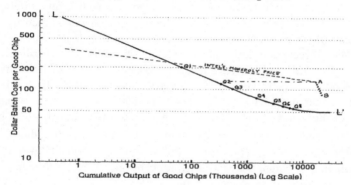

Source: author's computations.

There was a possible escape hatch for AMD – accelerated innovation, with which AMD minimized its technological lag vis a vis Intel or even took the lead. At first, as AMD struggled to catch up, this was difficult. AMD's first early technological lead came soon after its move into 32-bit processors when it introduced chips that consumed less power than Intel counterparts.

These were particularly advantageous for use in battery-powered laptop computers and were therefore widely successful in Taiwan, where most of the

26. See Flamm (1993, chapter 6).

world's laptops were produced. Intel's response was a patent infringement suit against AMD's Taiwanese customers, which was eventually thwarted through an antitrust investigation by the Taiwan Fair Trade Commission.[27] AMD subsequently moved ahead of Intel with faster chips, 64-bit Intel-compatible chips, and multiple core chips (generating less heat relative to processing power).

With AMD emerging as a more potent even if limited-line rival, Intel needed new strategies. One that it adopted was to offer computer assemblers (and in some cases computer retailing chains) rebates conditional on allocating the lion's share of their X-86 (i.e., Intel) architecture microprocessor purchases to Intel. Actual data are not available because the European Commission chose not to disclose them.

Consider, however, the following simplified but plausible illustration. Assume that the total demand for a particular computer assembler's microprocessor usage is 1,000 units at a price of 100 dollars per chip. Total chip sales will be 100,000 dollars.

If Intel normally takes 90% of the business, its sales will be 90,000 dollars and AMD's sales will be 10,000 dollars. Suppose now that Intel offers its customers 10% rebates beginning with unit one conditional upon their purchasing at least 90% of their X-86 product line chips from it. If the purchaser meets the quota, it receives a discount of 10%, or 10% times 90,000 dollars = 9,000 dollars. For AMD to match this rebate in absolute volume, it would have to refund 9,000 dollars, or 90% of its sales if it gains only 10% of the sub-market but a smaller percentage of its sales if by matching the rebate it can win a share of the market greater than 10% (e.g., 45% of its sales if it can increase its market share to 20% while maintaining a list price of 100 dollars).[28]

Needless to say, given strong product differentiation in favor of Intel's broader line of chips, this is a difficult challenge for AMD to meet.[29] For an even wider array of outcomes, see figure 7.[30]

27. In March 1994 the author testified on behalf of AMD before the Taiwan Fair Trade Commission.

28. In fact, the evidence suggests that AMD had to sell its chips at lower list prices than Intel's.

29. See for example Helft (2010, p. B1), in which Intel's CEO refers to Dell as «the best friend money can buy». Between 2003 and 2007, Intel's rebates to Dell totalled 4.3 billion dollars. Wyatt (2010, p. 1).

30. Viewing the possibilities encompassed by figure 7, one is tempted to develop a mathematical model "solving" AMD's problem on price and quality dimensions. But to do so would require empirically unsupported assumptions about cross price elasticities, whether list pricing conformed to cooperative or non-cooperative norms, alternative discount strategies, and cross elasticities with respect to individual product qualities.

F.M. Scherer   *Abuse of high technology dominance in the E.C. and U.S.*

Figure 7 – Challenger's rebate percentage relative to market share won

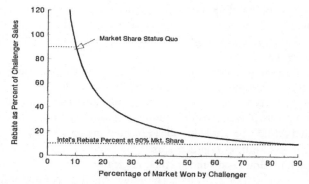

° assumes 10% rebate with 90% loyalty.
Source: author's computations, from a suggestion by Mark Fagan.

2.1. The European Commission case

It was such a conditional rebate scheme that drew a challenge from the European Commission, prompted by complaints to the Commission by AMD in October of 2000 and November 2003 and to the German competition authority in July 2006. The Commission launched investigations in two main stages, focusing first on Intel's discounts to computer assemblers and then on its discounts to a German retailer, Media-Saturn-Holding GMBH. On 5.13.2009, the Commission held that Intel had violated article 82 of the European Community Treaty by virtue of its volume-dependent rebates.[31] It levied a fine of 1.06 billion euros, the largest front-end fine imposed on a single company in EC history. Although the fine was large in absolute amount, it was roughly equivalent to six weeks of Intel European sales, said by the Commission to be approximately 30% of total company annual sales. Intel was also ordered to refrain from any «act or conduct having the same or equivalent object or effect» (i.e., to cease granting exclusionary volume-linked rebates).

Intel was reported to control in the ten-year period 1997-2007 approximately 70% of what the Commission said was the relevant market, defined as the worldwide market for microprocessors based upon Intel X-86 architecture. Ignored therefore were sales of specialized microprocessors used mainly in servers, specialized graphical data processors, and the very large set of special-purpose microprocessors for such applications as cell phone operation and

31. Commission decision, case COMP/C-3-37990-Intel (May 13, 2009), provisional non-confidential version, accessible (like other Commission decisions) on the World Wide Web.

F.M. Scherer   *Abuse of high technology dominance in the E.C. and U.S.*

automobile engine and industrial machine control. This is no doubt a defensible backward-looking market definition, but it is likely to become increasingly questionable in the future as late-generation multi-function smartphones and computers such as the Apple iPad, introduced in 2010, compete with traditional computing devices.[32]

The Commission's decision was consistent with the dim view it had taken in prior cases of volume-linked rebates and discounts that encourage recipients to deal exclusively or nearly exclusively with dominant firms. It recognized the important role played by innovation in focusing consumer demand and acknowledged AMD's recent leaps ahead of Intel in clock speed, 64-bit X-86 architecture,[33] and multi-core processors.

The Commission pioneered methodologically in the use of what it called an "efficient competitor analysis". The issue was how volume-related rebates by a dominant firm affected the price-cost competitiveness of smaller rivals forced to match the rebates to retain or gain sales. The question was, does the absolute rebate, spread over the "contestable" sales the smaller rival could reasonably expect to achieve, bring the net per-unit price realized by the smaller rival below the smalller rival's "average avoidable cost"? If so, the Commission reasoned, the rebates could render the smaller rival unprofitable at the margin and therefore jeopardize its longer-run viability. This approach is a detailed variant of the "average variable cost" test for predation proposed by Areeda and Turner (1975).[34] Although the decision is not completely clear because of numerous data excisions, the Commission apparently estimated the costs of an "efficient competitor" by focusing on the average variable cost of Intel itself. This approach, as the Commission recognized in paragraph 1037 of its decision, is conservative and "more favourable to Intel", since AMD's costs were presumably higher than those of Intel because, at least in the early stages of non-pioneer production, it operated farther up its learning curve than its larger rival, a phenomenon acknowledged only obliquely by the Commission. If volume-linked rebates brought net prices for the rival below the variable costs of Intel, they almost surely had an even greater deterrent impact on smaller AMD. The Commission admitted considerable difficulty obtaining re-

32. See e.g. Parloff (2010, p. 21); Vance (2010a, p. B2); Vance (2010b, p. B1).
33. However, it failed to recognize Intel's earlier mistake, developing at huge cost a 64-bit chip, the Itanium, incompatible with prior Intel architecture.
34. The Areeda-Turner rule was argued to be analytically deficient by several economists, including a recent Nobel Prize laureate. For a review of the debate, see Scherer and Ross (1990, pp. 468-479). The diligent reader is cautioned that figures 12.2(a) and (b) in Scherer and Ross were transposed. In Matsushita Electric Industrial Corporation v. Zenith Radio, 475 U.S. 574 (1986), at pp. 584-585, the U.S. Supreme Court observed that «there is a good deal of debate on what cost is relevant in [alleged predation] cases» but chose not to resolve the debate.

liable data on "average avoidable cost". The only estimate made public (paragraph 1043) by the Commission was derived from Intel's aggregate public financial statements, showing that its "cost of goods sold" was 35% of its average selling price. The decision apparently relied significantly upon that figure, given conflicting estimates from expert witnesses.

2.2. The U.S. Federal Trade Commission case

Issuance of an antitrust complaint by the U.S. Federal Trade Commission in December 2009, only seven months after the European Commission's Intel decision, might be viewed as an example of regulatory "piling on".[35] The complaint, which, before a negotiated settlement was reached in August 2010,[36] was scheduled to be tried on a "fast track" schedule allowing only one hundred and sixty-one courtroom hours for each side to present its case, is distinguishable from the European Commission action on several counts.

First, the Intel conduct at issue was specified to commence beginning only in 1999. This exclusion, not explained in the Commission's complaint, was presumably dictated by the fact that the Federal Trade Commission concluded in 1999 through consent settlement a previous case against Intel focusing mainly on Intel's actions taken toward customers who sued it for patent infringement.

Second, the relevant (worldwide) product markets proposed by the Federal Trade Commission were broader than those of the European Commission: they spanned both central processing units (CPUs, i.e., microprocessors) for personal computers and servers (but excluded cell phone processors); plus graphics processor units (GPUs), which, the Commission asserted, «are adding more CPU functionality with each product generation» and hence «are a threat to Intel's monopoly in the relevant CPU market» (paragraph 15).[37] Intel was said to hold market shares of 75 to 85% in the alleged CPU markets and «in excess of 50%» in the GPU markets.

35. In the matter of Intel Corporation, docket No. 9341 (12.16.2009). The case was brought under section 5 of the Federal Trade Commission Act, condemning "unfair methods of competition". Section 5 had been interpreted in earlier Supreme Court decisions to encompass Sherman Act violations. Only a month earlier, AMD settled its own private antitrust suit against Intel by accepting 1.25 billion dollars in alleged damages (which made up nearly all of AMD's reported 2009 profits). In November 2009, the State of New York also launched an antitrust suit against Intel (presumably stimulated by the ongoing construction of a large AMD-linked plant in upper New York State).
36. In the matter of Intel Corporation, docket No. 9341, decision and order, 8.4.2010.
37. See note 31 supra. On the use of both Nvidia GPUs and Intel chips in the world's "fastest supercomputer" race, see Vance (2010c, p. B9).

Third, the Federal Trade Commission complaint encompassed a much wider array of conduct than the European Commission case. It challenged volume-dependent rebates, as did the European Commission case. However, it also reached inter alia discounts granted by Intel to computer assemblers for delaying the launch of rival products, preferred access to chips during periods of shortage, variation in marketing support to reward more faithful customers, the manipulation of software and interfaces to degrade the performance of rival processors, misrepresentation of performance benchmark reports on competitor as compared to Intel products, discriminatory access to Intel intellectual property, and through both design changes and information suppression, impeding the interoperability of rival GPU chips with Intel microprocessors.

Fourth, the Federal Trade Commission proposed to prohibit all the conduct of which it complained. This seems an eminently logical step. In practice, however, it faces formidable difficulties. When conduct is prohibited, the prohibitor bears the burden of monitoring the respondent's actions in subsequent years to ensure that it does not recur. The varieties of conduct singled out by the Federal Trade Commission as contrary to law were so vast and so complex, and the remedy negotiated in August 2010 was so correspondingly far-reaching that, for effective monitoring, a substantial and technically proficient compliance staff would be required into the future (with a six year horizon set in the negotiated settlement). The great difficulties the U.S. Department of Justice and the European Commission competition authorities experienced monitoring Microsoft's compliance with relatively narrow information disclosure mandates suggest even greater problems in monitoring a much broader array of Intel conduct. From my own experience as head of the Federal Trade Commission's Bureau of Economics during the 1970s, I know that the FTC did not possess such monitoring capability then. The Commission apparently recognized its inability to do the monitoring job on its own. The negotiated settlement requires Intel to pay up to 2 million dollars to compensate technical consultants hired by the Federal Trade Commission for purposes of monitoring and judging inevitable conflicts as to whether e.g. disclosure of interfaces has been sufficient and whether changes in Intel designs strategically degrade the functioning of complementary chips. Whether this will be sufficient remains to be seen. Doubts intrude when one recognizes that, at a 500 dollars per hour fee typical for experts at the time, expert advisor time of only about seventeen normal working weeks per year over six years would be compensated under the arrangement. The tasks may prove to be more difficult than provisions for their support assume.

It has long been a philosophical maxim in competition policy circles that proven abuses of monopoly power can be combatted in either of two ways: through conduct remedies that channel a dominant firm's actions into desired patterns, or through structural remedies that render industry structure more competitive and hence more likely to function workably, guided by the "invisible hand".[38] Structural remedies are to conduct remedies as surgery is to sustained pharmaceutical therapy. With surgery, there is pain in the short run, after which, one hopes, the patient will live healthily ever after. Pharmaceutical therapy on the other hand requires continuing application and monitoring to ensure that dosages are correct and resistance has not emerged. In the Federal Trade Commission's Intel complaint, one sees no evidence that the structural alternative was considered.[39]

The agreed-upon Intel conduct remedies may be the most complex ever attempted in U.S. antitrust history. Monitoring conduct in detail is highly regulatory. One must be apprehensive, however, about imposing the pain of alternative structural remedies upon a company that has performed as efficiently and innovatively as Intel.[40] In terms of plant structure, Intel does not pose the single-unit difficulties that deterred Judge Wyzanski from fragmenting the United Shoe Machinery Corporation in 1953[41] and complicated possible structural reorganization of Microsoft (with most of its software-writing operations concentrated at the time in a single Redmond, Washington, campus).[42] As of the late 1990s, Intel had 61 production facilities in the United States and 25 overseas. And it had at least three well-staffed chip development groups (one in California's Silicon Valley, one in Oregon, and one in Israel). Splitting Intel into three viable units would almost surely have been feasible.

However, I have emphasized earlier the natural monopoly character of microprocessor development and production, at least at the individual chip gen-

38. The belief is so deeply and long-ingrained that I am no longer able to provide citations to definitive literature sources. For an anticipation, see Kaysen and Turner (1959), especially p. 96. It should be noted that structural remedies include not only breakup of a single firm into multiple entities, but also such actions as merger controls and the compulsory licensing of patents or other intellectual property undergirding monopoly positions. Intel already had patent licensing agreements with its three main competitors, but the Commission's final order recognizes that changes in the future could impair their effectiveness.

39. For an explicit attempt to weigh structural vs. conduct remedies in the U.S. Microsoft case, see Litan *et al.* (2000). It should be noted that the Federal Trade Commission has rarely sought divestiture in non-merger cases. And a congressional budgetary bill rider during the late 1970s expressly prevented it from ordering structural divestiture of breakfast cereal manufacturers.

40. However, Intel has been remarkably dependent upon other organizations' basic architectural concept innovations. See Flamm (2007, figure 12).

41. U.S. v. United Shoe Machinery Corporation, 110 F. Supp. 295 (1953), affirmed at 347 U.S. 521 (1954). On the subsequent difficulties, see Scherer (2008, p. 1050, note 67).

42. See again Litan *et al.* (2000).

eration level even if not at the level of a multi-design, multi-plant production operation. Scale economies might be lost, and with a more fragmented industry structure whose marginal costs are low relative to average total costs, there is a danger of cut-throat price competition during recessions. The remedy decision was exquisitely difficult, with arguments on one hand as compelling facially as those on the other hand. It cannot be said confidently that the Federal Trade Commission erred in its choice of a highly regulatory approach, despite its inconsistency with the general trend of U.S. government-industry interactions during the past half century.

3. Adjudication problems

When one compares the U.S. and European Commission approaches to the Microsoft and Intel challenges, one finds good reason to applaud the E.C.'s performance. The European approach to dominant firm abuse problems has tended to be more tightly focused, targeting two main facets of Microsoft's practices and conditional discounts in two sectors of Intel's marketing, as compared to the broader array of practices addressed in the U.S. Microsoft and Intel cases. The European Commission of course took the lead in challenging Intel, although it lagged on Microsoft. And the European Commission was much tougher in following through on Microsoft, insisting that its disclosure mandates be satisfied. It is too early to assess the Federal Trade Commission's performance with respect to Intel.

Some aspects of the European Commission's performance, however, cry out for criticism. It is awkward for an American to advance the critique, but it must be done, and I have not seen it done by European economists.

We who have worked on competition policy in the United States have had drilled into our heads the mantra that the task of the government enforcement agencies is to protect the process of competition, not to protect competitors. Among other things, although we were not unwilling to entertain complaints and information from aggrieved competitors, we tried hard to treat such interventions skeptically, recognizing the mixed motives of the complainants, and marshall our own analysis and evidence presentation rather than relying on third-party expert witnesses.

The European Commission openly admits in its decision documents that the Microsoft case was initiated following a complaint from Sun Microsystems and the Intel case following a complaint from AMD. At the Court of First Instance hearing on Microsoft in Luxembourg in October 2004, I appeared as a witness explicitly on behalf of Real Networks; engineers for Real Networks also testified; and there was additional testimony from representatives of other aggrieved software companies.[43] The legal argumentation was to be sure carried by the Commission's attorneys, but there was no expert testimony from the Commission's economics staff. This, I believe, conveys the wrong image of what competition policy is, or at least should be, all about. The Commission should use its own staff as expert witnesses rather than relying on those of aggrieved competitors. And when the necessary expertise is lacking internally, the Commission should do as the American antitrust agencies do, hiring outside experts, supporting their preparation, and presenting them as their own witnesses, not as representatives of third parties.[44]

Also, the adjudication process underlying a European Commission decision to issue statements of violation and remedy tends to be a star chamber proceeding, in which evidence is presented at a forum open to neither the public nor to counsel for accused parties. The parties affected are to be sure heard, but not in direct confrontation with opposing witnesses and counsel. In its 5.13.2009, decision, the Commission makes the remarkable admission (paragraphs 28-29) that Intel attorneys were given access to the complete case file, including confidential documents and testimony, on only three days (7.31.2007, 7.23.2008, and 12.19.2008).

Presumably, Intel counsel were allowed to bring a copying machine with them, but on this, the record is silent. And disclosure of the information obtained beyond Intel's counsel and economic advisers was prohibited. Intel's February 2009 request for an oral hearing before Commission staff concerning the Commission's supplementary statement of objections was denied. Technically, the Commission's proceedings did not anticipate criminal liability, and Intel arguably is not a human person, so the proceedings fall outside the scope of United Nations Universal Declaration of Human Rights (1948) Article 10, which states that: «Everyone is entitled in full equality to a fair and public hearing, in the determination of his rights and obligations and of any criminal charge against him».

Nevertheless, in view of the substantial penalties assessed, it would appear proper that a more even-handed and more open approach to adjudicating such major competition policy issues should be adopted.[45]

43. Sun Microsystems was originally scheduled as a complainant but settled its own private treble damages suit against Microsoft in the United States for 1.9 billion dollars and withdrew from the European proceedings.
44. In the U.S. Federal Trade Commission's remedial approach to the Intel case, continuing intervention by Intel rivals seems inevitable if Intel deviations from the agreed-upon conduct rules are to be monitored.
45. See also the leader, Anonymous (2010, p. 15), asserting in the wake of the Intel case that «enforcement of competition law in Europe is unjust and must change». See also concerning a new European Commission inquiry on Microsoft, Meller (2006, p. C2).

F.M. Scherer   *Abuse of high technology dominance in the E.C. and U.S.*

A complement to the closed form of Commission hearings is the failure to disclose in decision documents the identities of those who have testified as expert witnesses. The Commission's 5.13.2009 decision on Intel reveals that Intel presented reports from at least two economic experts, but the individuals are designated in the non-confidential version only as «Professor [...]» or in one instance as an unnamed Professor of Management in the Graduate School of Business at Stanford University (paragraph 1044). Open publication of one's views is a critical aspect of credibility for academics. Having one's views open to criticism by peers is an important incentive for doing the best job one can and constantly aspiring to the goal of *veritas*. The European Commission would be well advised to reform its witness confrontation and disclosure standards to follow the maxim on the basis of which President Theodore Roosevelt created the predecessor to the U.S. Federal Trade Commission as a corrective for the perceived misdeeds of the so-called "trusts":[46] «Publicity is the only sure remedy which we can now invoke... The first requisite is knowledge, full and complete, knowledge which may be made public to the world».

References

Anonymous. 1993. Modern wonders: the thinker. *The Economist*, December 25.

Anonymous. 2010. Prosecutor, judge and jury. *The Economist*, February 20.

Areeda P., Turner D.F. 1975. Predatory pricing and related practices under section 2 of the Sherman act. *Harvard Law Review*, 88 (4): 697-733.

Auletta K. 2001. *World War 3.0: Microsoft vs. the U.S. Government*. Random House: New York.

Flaherty M.T. 1992. Manufacturing and firm performance in technology-intensive industries: U.S. and Japanese DRAM experience. *Review of Industrial Organization*, 7 (3/4): 273-294.

Flamm K. 1993. *Mismanaged Trade? Strategic Policy and the Semiconductor Industry*. Brookings Institution: Washington.

Flamm K. 2007. The microeconomics of microprocessor innovation, *University of Texas Working Paper*.

Flynn L.J. 2003. Samsung to pay large fine in price-fixing conspiracy. *New York Times*, October 14.

Heilemann J. 2001. *Pride Before the Fall: The Trials of Bill Gates and the End of the Microsoft Era*. HarperCollins: New York.

Helft M. 2010. Dell in talks to settle Intel inquiry with S.E.C. *New York Times*, June 11.

Hill C. 1995. State court ruling protects AMD rights to clone, sell older line of Intel chips. *Wall Street Journal*, January 3.

46. From *Addresses and Presidential Messages of Theodore Roosevelt 1902-1904*, p. 294.

Jones E. 1920. Is competition in industry ruinous. *Quarterly Journal of Economics*, 34 (3): 473-519.

Kanter J. 2010. An old chip cartel case is brought to a swift end. *New York Times*, May 20.

Kaplan D.A. 2010. Corporate America's No. 1 gun for hire. *Fortune*, November 1.

Katz M., Shapiro C. 1994. Systems competition and network effects. *Journal of Economic Perspectives*, 8 (2): 93-115.

Kaysen C., Turner D.F. 1959. *Antitrust Policy: An Economic and Legal Analysis*. Harvard University Press: Cambridge (Mass.).

Lawsky D. 2008. Ex-judge in Microsoft/EU case surprised at fine. *Reuters*, May 22.

Litan R., Noll R., Nordhaus W.D., Scherer F.M. 2000. *Remedies Brief of Amici Curiae*. In re U.S. v. Microsoft Corporation, published online.

Meller P. 2005. Microsoft in European court says 2004 ruling is a failure. *New York Times*, December 23.

Meller P. 2006. Microsoft accuses Europe of colluding with rivals. *New York Times*, March 3.

Nosko C. 2010. Competition and quality choice in the CPU market, *NBER Working Paper 16507*.

Offenhauer P., Scherer F.M. 1999. *Microsoft on Trial*. John F. Kennedy School of Government case CR14-99-1522.0.

Parloff R. 2010. Has Intel finally met its match?. *Fortune*, 162: 21.

Pollack A. 1992. Intel rival is favored in ruling. *New York Times*, February 25.

Prasso S. (ed.) 2001. Upfront: did Microsoft catch a break?. *Business Week*, March 12.

Scherer F.M. 1977. *The Economic Effects of Compulsory Patent Licensing*. New York University School of Business Administration Monograph 1977-2: New York.

Scherer F.M. 1996. *Industry Structure, Strategy, and Public Policy*. HarperCollins: New York.

Scherer F.M. 2008. Technological innovation and monopolization, in Collins W.D. (ed.) *Issues in Competition Law and Policy*, volume II: 1033-1068. American Bar Association (ABA): Chicago.

Scherer F.M., Ross D. 1990. *Industrial Market Structure and Economic Performance*. Houghton Mifflin: Boston.

Spence A.M. 1981. The learning curve and competition. *Bell Journal of Economics*, 12 (1): 49-70.

Vance A. 2010a. Start-up aims to slay chip Goliath. *New York Times*, August 16.

Vance A. 2010b. British chip maker quietly builds on niche in low-power devices. *New York Times*, September 20.

Vance A. 2010c. Chinese wrest supercomputer title from U.S. *New York Times*, October 28.

Wallace J., Ericson J. 1992. *Hard Drive: Bill Gates and the Making of the Microsoft Empire*. Wiley: New York.

Wilson R.W., Warren-Boulton F. 1995. Riding the wave: exclusionary practices in markets for microprocessors. *International Journal of the Economics of Business*, 2 (2): 241-262.

Wyatt E. 2010. Dell to pay $100 million in settlement. *New York Times*, July 23.

PART II

MERGER POLICY

Review of Industrial Organization (2006) 28:327–341
DOI 10.1007/s11151-006-9105-9

© Springer 2006

A New Retrospective on Mergers

F. M. SCHERER
Harvard University Emeritus, 601 Rockbourne Mills Court, Wallingford, PA 19086, U.S.A.
e-mail: fmscherer@comcast.net

Abstract. This paper is based on my keynote address given at the 2006 International Industrial Organization Conference in Boston, April 8, 2006. I survey long-run trends in mergers, review the debate over the economic success of mergers generally, and examine the changing treatment that business schools have accorded mergers over the past five decades. A final section is a time series analysis of links at the U.S. macroeconomic level between changes in merger activity and labor productivity growth.

Key words: business schools, efficiency, mergers, productivity.

I. Introduction

They say a perpetrator always returns to the scene of his crime. I have returned more than once – in this case, to the question of mergers and their effect on X-efficiency. Thirty-six years after my first published struggle with the issue, I have three itches that still need scratching. First, during the past year merger activity has revived strongly and bids fair to reach the highest levels ever recorded. It is time to take a new look at the trends. Second, the debate over the success of mergers continues. And third, I have become intrigued about how mergers and their consequences are being treated in business schools. This paper addresses all three themes.

II. Recent Trends

After a brief slump connected with the 2001–2002 stock market crash, merger activity appears to be resuming. Figure 1 extends a statistical series begun in the first (1970) edition of my industrial organization textbook. It is a series of splices, beginning with Ralph Nelson's series for 1895–1920 and then extending the series, expressed in billions of constant 1972 dollars, with adjustments for Tobin's Q and data source coverage.[1]

---

[1] For the most detailed description of splicing methodology, see Scherer (1980, p. 120). Data following discontinuation of the Federal Trade Commission large manufacturing and

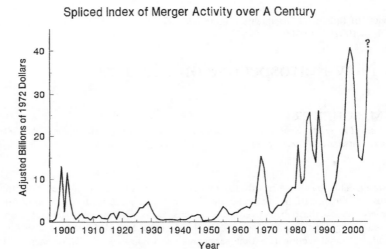

Figure 1.

Thus, more than a century of U.S. merger activity is tracked. One sees clearly the great merger wave in the early years of the 20th Century, the more modest 1920s boom, the largely conglomerate wave of the 1960s, the resurgence in the 1980s and, after a brief lapse, the continuing growth during the 1990s and the early 21st Century.

Even more striking is the extent to which companies have disappeared through merger from periodic lists of the largest 100 U.S. "industrial" (preponderantly, manufacturing and mining) corporations. Figure 2 presents the figures for eight discrete time intervals covering most of the 20th Century.[2] After a long hiatus influenced at first by the Great Depression and World War II (evidently, there are some things more important than making mergers – such as winning a war) and then by vigorous antitrust enforcement, large-firm exits through merger rose sharply during 1980s and then climbed to the record-setting level of 1.9 exits on average per year between 1993 and 2002.

Footnote 1 continued

mining merger series after 1988 are spliced, with considerable downward adjustment, from various issues of the W.T. Grimm & Co. *Mergerstat Review*, combined with Q-ratio data kindly provided by Professor Tobin.

[2] Disappearance data for the first five time intervals are from Collins and Preston (1961). They are supplemented by my own tabulations using *Fortune* magazine's largest corporation lists. Banking, insurance, trade, and other service sector companies have been systematically excluded from the tallies.

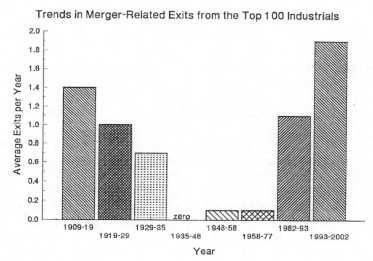

Figure 2.

III. Efficiency Effects?

My most systematic attempt to assess the efficiency effects of mergers was the book with Ravenscraft, *Mergers, Sell-offs, and Economic Efficiency* (1987). It was in my opinion the best single scholarly work I have published during my long career. I take pride in it because it addressed an important topic – the massive merger wave that peaked during the 1960s; because it exploited the most comprehensive, narrowly disaggregated accounting data ever brought to bear on the question of merger causes and effects – 4 years of Federal Trade Commission Line of Business data, supplemented by 15 case studies; and because I was fortunate to have an especially able co-investigator, Ravenscraft. We worked on the project for more than 3 years, estimating from our combined results that manufacturing sector inefficiencies following in the wake of the conglomerate merger wave reduced the growth of U.S. real gross national product between 1968 and 1976 by between 0.074 and 0.101 percentage points per year.[3]

Yet by and large, our research has been ignored, especially by the people who do much of the research on mergers – the corporate finance specialists. Being ignored is one of the worst things that can happen to a scholar. It is worse than being criticized. There was a brief period, before the book was published, when finance economists regularly took pot shots at our results, but that attention atrophied after the book itself was published – in my

---

[3] Ravenscraft and Scherer (1987, pp. 202–203).

prejudiced judgment, because the book's results were bullet-proof. Over the two decades between 1985 and 2005, one can find in the *Social Sciences Citation Index* 525 articles with the word "merger" in their title. But our book was cited in only 81 articles, including only 13 articles published in journals specializing in corporate finance questions. Compared to the frequency with which some of my other works have been cited, this is a miserable performance, especially when one takes the relative quality of the merger book into account.

There are some plausible explanations for the neglect the Ravenscraft–Scherer merger research has experienced. Each merger wave in American history had unique characteristics. The wave of the 1960s, which left among other things a legacy of sell-offs during the 1970s and 1980s, was preponderantly conglomerate, bringing together entities in quite different lines of business. By the time our book appeared, conglomerate mergers had fallen out of fashion, in part because they were on average so disappointing.

The new wave of 1980s involved a much higher fraction of horizontal and vertical mergers, facilitated in part by more lax antitrust enforcement. One might expect opportunities for cost saving and benefits from complementarity to be much stronger for horizontal and vertical mergers than for conglomerates, and so the record of widespread failure we documented may simply have become irrelevant. It is without doubt that some mergers, perhaps many, yield significant efficiencies. It is also clear, however, that many mergers fail – sometimes because the acquirers experienced a winner's curse and bid too much, sometimes because of corporate culture mismatches, incentive failures, or clumsy implementation. What is uncertain is where the balance lies. In my principal publication returning more recently to the merger question, I summarized several large-scale studies, some by management consulting firms, that found widespread disappointment and failure in the record of more recent mergers.[4] In a survey earlier this year,[5] *The Economist* recalled that the only one of its weekly covers to be selected in an American editors' poll as one of the 40 best magazine covers of the past 40 years was one from 1994 headed "The Trouble with Mergers" and showing two camels in *flagrante delecto*.[6] According to the more recent (2006) survey:

---

[4] See Scherer (2002, p. 5). A more detailed survey of the same literature by Pautler (2002) concluded that "Mergers and acquisitions are risky undertakings that achieve the primary goals of the surveyed managers substantially more than half the time, but are only successful in a more quantitative financial sense (i.e., raising shareholder value relative to pre-deal levels) about 30–55% of the time."

[5] "A Survey of the Company," *The Economist*, January 21, 2006, p. 8.

[6] "The Trouble with Mergers," *The Economist*, September 10, 1994.

The article that went with it explained why most mergers go wrong. But mergers have become no more extinct than camels. Last year was a bumper one for cross-border acquisitions in Europe, and in America the value of telecoms deals alone was over $100 billion. Nevertheless, it remains extremely difficult to make mergers work.

Similarly, a leading German newspaper, calling attention to the new boom in merger activity, asked rhetorically, "Have not managers learned? Have not dozens of studies shown that in truth two out of three mergers only destroyed value?"[7] It seems clear that the problem of failed mergers has by no means disappeared since the period on which Ravenscraft and I focused.

Another reason for the neglect of our work by financial specialists is that we inhabit separate, distinct, and scarcely communicating methodological worlds. Ravenscraft and I analyzed accounting data. They have their difficulties, to be sure, but we deployed a substantial array of controls to adjust for systematic biases. The finance specialists emphasize "event studies," determining how stock market investors respond in a typically short time window around the announcement of a merger. The most typical finding has been that the stock of the target company rises significantly, largely because a takeover premium is expected, while the stock price of the acquiring company changes insignificantly. A plus added to a zero is a plus, signifying the enhancement of economic value. And if antitrust enforcers are doing their job properly, the change cannot be attributed to enhanced monopoly power, so the gains must stem from the realization of efficiencies and/or complementarities.

There are two main problems with this approach, which I have explored at greater length in a (2002) article. Finance specialists live or die on the basis of their belief in efficient markets, asserting that at any moment in time markets impound all the information available on the evolution of future events.[8] If combined stock prices rise in the few days surrounding a merger announcement, it must be because rational stock market investors anticipate future earnings gains. Skepticism toward this view is suggested inter alia by evidence from numerous studies that over the longer run of one to 3 years after major mergers, the "abnormal" returns of the merged firm tend to decline.[9] Finance specialists who defend mergers as value-enhancing tend to dismiss these results as an anomaly, non-causal,

---

[7] "Jeden Tag ein neuer Deal" ("Every Day a New Deal"), *Die Zeit*, March 9, 2006, p. 23 (my translation). The article goes on to observe, "These are the questions of yesterday" due to new rules of the game, including "cool and systematic" pre-merger calculations.

[8] See, e.g. Jensen (1988, p. 26).

[9] See, e.g., the survey by Mueller (2003).

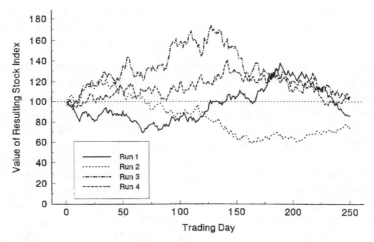

Figure 3.

or (in a startling non sequitur) as inconsistent with the axioms of market efficiency combined with the assurance that mergers are value-enhancing.

The other problem is that the company leaders who decide whether to initiate mergers believe, or at least claim to believe, that stock markets are not so efficient that they cannot be outwitted through superior analysis or insider information. It is almost universally accepted that stock prices follow random walks. Figure 3 shows four simulated random walks, adhering closely to random walk parameters defined by Black (1986) in his presidential address to the American Finance Association.[10] If a would-be acquirer in Firm 1 can see through the random walk and recognize that his firm's stock is randomly overvalued at 200 days after the simulation began and that Firm 2's stock is randomly undervalued, the makings of a profitable acquisition exist. The key question is whether real-world decision-makers can see through random valuation errors to engage in such analyses. Abundant clinical evidence suggests that they do, or at least believe that they can. Finance specialists disagree, and therein lies a fundamental methodological disagreement.

IV. What Business Schools Teach and Why

When the IIOC organizers invited me to present this paper, I began to puzzle actively over something that had been subliminal for a long-time.

---

[10] Details are provided in Scherer (2002).

I received my MBA from the Harvard Business School (HBS) in 1958. Reflecting on my 2-year course of study, I could recall only one case study (assigned in the second-year core Business Policy course) focusing mainly on a merger – the merger between Merck and Sharpe and Dohme in 1953. Consulting with colleagues from that era, I found that they recalled no formal merger cases and certainly no emphasis on mergers in the overall curriculum. Perhaps we have reached an age at which we remember little from our ancient past. But to juxtapose the possibly imperfect recollection of our past experience against the present, I first searched the list of case study titles in the HBS's computerized list of the case studies it had available in 2005. Thirty-one had titles containing the word "merger;" 11 the word "takeover;" 37 "acquisition;" and seven "M&A." Three courses offered during the 2005–2006 academic year focused directly on M&A-like questions: "Acquisitions and Alliances," "Creating Value through Corporate Restructuring," and "Negotiating Complex Deals and Disputes." Several other courses had clear M&A components. A friend on the faculty of the Stern School of Business at New York University reported that the mergers and acquisitions course was one of the most popular electives, offered in two distinct flavors, one taught by an experienced merger-maker and one by a scholar.

Memories deceive, so I sought more solid quantitative evidence on trends. One of the few textbooks we used in our first year at the HBS was a collection of case studies, *Case Problems in Finance*. We purchased for use in our studies the 1955 revised edition, edited by HBS faculty members Hunt and Williams. The collection has been updated under diverse editors, typically with HBS affiliations, through 12 editions. Figure 4 shows various collections' content devoted to mergers and acquisitions as a percentage of total pagination (counted up to the first index page). Merger content rose from 3.7%, expansively defined,[11] in the 1955 edition to a peak of 22.6% in the 2005 edition. The only break in the series is the decline for the 1981 edition, following a merger slump, from the higher value for 1972 in the wake of 1960s conglomerate merger boom.

In the 1958 edition of the authoritative Paton and Dixon accounting textbook, only $3\frac{1}{2}$ pages out of 792, or 0.4%, dealt with merger and acquisition accounting. There was a vast increase in the number of pages devoted to merger questions between the fourth edition of the *Accountant's Handbook*, published in 1956, and the ninth edition, published in 1999.

The increased orientation of business schools toward M&A activity pleases students, and indeed, it may reflect sensitivity to students' demands in the tough competition among business schools for attractive students.

---

[11] If a case study concerning an involuntary sell-off required under the Public Utilities Holding Company Act is excluded, the figure falls to 2.8%.

334   F. M. SCHERER

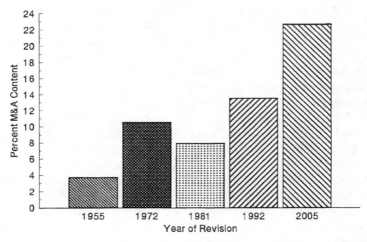

Merger & Acquisition Content in Editions of a Leading Finance Casebook

Figure 4.

Some quotations from Ridgway (2005) on the aspirations, studies, and work experiences of undergraduates at Pennsylvania's Wharton School – ranked consistently as the top undergraduate business program – are indicative:

> [The students] quickly discover that the only thing more prestigious than becoming an investment banker is becoming an investment banker at the most elite of deal-making houses – Goldman Sachs (p. 31) ... Goldman has been a leader in advising mergers and acquisitions (p. 32) ... Lazard was renowned for its legendary advice on mergers and acquisitions (p. 41) ... Parr embodied the type of banker that Jessica dreamed of becoming ... the man credited for sparking and executing more mergers and acquisitions than anyone else in the industry's history (p. 45) ... . When the economy started picking up in the mid to late 1990s, concentrations in finance and entrepreneurial management, with all their promise of power and the American dream, quickly became intoxicating to many Wharton students. Investment banks were prospering, raking in billions of dollars in fees for huge mergers and acquisitions (p. 95) ... "I want to be the first woman to run mergers and acquisitions at some large bank," she proclaimed (p. 117) ... "Investment banking is unparalleled in terms of the amount of responsibility you get at such a young age," she said. "Plus there's an adrenaline rush. I want to pick up the *Wall Street Journal* one day and see a deal that I did" (p. 119).

Studying finance in particular, said by Ridgway (2005, p. 26) to be the major favored by two-thirds of Wharton undergraduates, was seen to be the leading pathway into M&A work. In sharp contrast, and quite consistent with my experience at Harvard, is Whyte's (1956, pp. 75, 68) characterization of business students' aspirations a half century ago:

> Those who mark down finance as a choice are also staff-minded. Few ever mention speculating or investing in stocks and bonds. Their interest in finance is administrative rather than accumulative; they are primarily interested in credit, mortgage loan work, trust and estate work, and financial analysis ... Placement officers find that of the men who intend to go into business ... less than 5% express any desire to be an entrepreneur. About 15–20% plan to go into their fathers' business. Of the rest, most have one simple goal: the big corporation.

Attitudes have changed in part because opportunities and market demands have changed. But in addition, it must be admitted that M&A is one of the most interesting, intellectually challenging topics taught in business schools. When I think back upon my MBA studies, I realize that, although quite fundamental, the material we covered was humdrum – the basics of accounting, channels of distribution, how to choose effective advertising media, how top-level functional managers coordinate their activities, how to motivate subordinates, and – yes, we spent three hours on the matter – how to place a workpiece squarely in the jaws of a milling machine. How much more excitement there is in "doing the numbers" to estimate the internal rate of return from a big proposed merger, devising takeover strategies and financial incentives to force merger despite the reluctance of well-known corporate leaders, and structuring merger partners' payments to minimize taxes!

In this, I am not simply fabricating comparisons out of thin air. Recently Harvard's Kennedy School, whose reformed curriculum in the early 1970s was strongly influenced by business school models, surveyed thousands of alumni to ascertain their views on the quality of their educational experience.[12] On the excellence of their KSG training in relevant concepts and skills, those who graduated between 1984 and 1994 ranked "systematic thinking about problems" first, "economics" second, and "cost-benefit analysis" third. With the three lowest rankings among 23 categories were "managing people," "organizing/mobilization," and "leadership." It is easy to impress one's students about quantitative analyses that have crisp, definitive right and wrong answers. It is much harder to teach

---

[12] John F. Kennedy School (2005, p. 85).

336   F. M. SCHERER

the soft arts of leadership and motivation, although, I should add, some Kennedy School faculty members such as Ronald Heifetz do so superbly.

There is more to the story. In 1958, the year I received my MBA, 4,041 masters' degrees in business subjects, including 474 in accounting, were conferred by U.S. institutions of higher learning.[13] Those who received MBAs were an elite group. Those who took jobs in big business could expect to be put on the fast track, observed, and groomed for higher-level responsibilities by top management. In the year 2000, 112,258 master's degrees in business studies were awarded by U.S. schools. Receiving an MBA is far from an elite distinction, and although there is sorting based upon the much-publicized quality of the program from which a young person graduates, there are many more people one must overtake to move up in the corporate hierarchy. Working on an important acquisition helps one stand out.

A brief digression: from the numbers in the previous paragraph, one can calculate an average growth rate for MBA degrees of 7.92% per year. The comparable rates for master's degrees in some other fields of direct interest to business were as follows:

Engineering	3.62%
Physical sciences (incl. chemistry)	1.11
Mathematics	2.42
Biology and other life sciences	3.46%

In 1958, the number of business master's degrees was 35% of the combined number of masters degree recipients in these four S&E fields; in the year 2000, the proportion was almost exactly the reverse.[14] At least in part because business graduates' salaries tend to be higher than those of technically educated individuals, our nation has been increasing its stock of individuals trained in the techniques of business administration much more rapidly than it has been augmenting the number of people trained in the scientific underpinnings of the important things business firms do to satisfy consumer demands and raise productivity.[15]

Given the increased numerical competition among MBA holders, it is only sensible for business school students to study subjects that will win them high-visibility jobs immediately and/or bring them quickly to the

---

[13] The data are from the "earned degrees conferred" tables of the *Statistical Abstract of the United States* for 1960 and 2002.

[14] Degrees in the four S&E fields were 36% of the business master's degrees for the year 2000. If we add master's degrees in computer and information sciences – a category not counted separately in 1958 – the combined fraction for five S&E fields in 2000 rises to 49%.

[15] For an analysis of domestic and foreign science and engineering education trends, see Scherer (1999, Chapters 6 and 7).

attention of top managers. As we have seen from the Wharton School study, investment banking, whose forte is M&A, is one such fast track – a particularly well-paid one. (It was not so when I graduated from HBS.) If a new MBA joins a large non-financial corporation, the assignment most likely to bring one into the thick of conducting big, high-visibility projects and attract the attention of top managers is to work in a business development or finance group analyzing possible avenues to growth through mergers and acquisitions. Plodding away as an accountant, salesperson, foreign exchange specialist, advertising account assistant, or production foreman is a ticket to permanent obscurity as one of Whyte's (1956) "organization men."

Thus, we in the US have created a sizeable professional establishment that sees as a significant justification for its existence the making of mergers. Business school curricula emphasizing mergers are a reaction to corporate sector demand, but the supply in turn reinforces the demand. That would be troubling enough, if business program training provided the members of that establishment deep insight into the consequences of what they are doing. But there are grounds for skepticism. As Ridgway (2005, p. 114) quotes one interviewee in her Wharton study:

> "Investment banking is a narrow skill set," he explained. "It's crunching numbers and modeling. You do not get what is behind the numbers we're analyzing. The bottom line is that what you're doing is just working with numbers. You cannot see how they fit into the bigger picture. I personally feel that those numbers are worthless, especially with investment banking."

I believe that from all this I see why my book with Ravenscraft has received little attention from finance academics, most of whom are employed by business schools. Our finding that mergers during the 1960s and 1970s were on average efficiency-reducing and similar conclusions from other more recent studies challenge one their most popular educational offerings. It is like telling Ford Motor Company that its SUVs have a high propensity to roll over, or like telling Coca-Cola that its Coke Classic contributes to obesity and eventual diabetes. It can hardly expect to receive an enthusiastic reception.

V. Mergers and Productivity Growth

The emphasis of fast-track business school graduates on merger-making would be unproblematic if, in contrast to what Ravenscraft and I found, mergers of recent vintage were indeed efficiency-enhancing rather than merely boosting managerial egos and compensation.[16] I remain open to proof of that proposition. As one small step toward a further exploration of the issues, I used the century-long data series graphed in Figure 1 for a statistical test of relationships between aggregate merger activity and private nonfarm sector productivity growth.[17]

Merger activity was initially measured as year-to-year changes from the previous year's value. The series of year-to-year percentage changes is extremely noisy and skewed toward high values. Therefore, logarithms (to base 10) were taken of the merger level values in Figure 1 and year-to-year first differences $\delta LOGMERG_0$ were computed. (The zero subscript denotes a change from previous to current year merger activity.) The distribution of $\delta LOGMERG$ differed insignificantly from normal. The results reported here differ little when regressions were run in the unlogged variables. Because the U.S. economy was dominated by war production and subsequent inflation during World Wars I and II, the years 1917 through 1920 and 1940–1946 are excluded from all analyses.

We begin by addressing the classic hypothesis that merger cycles are positively correlated with, and presumably influenced by, stock market fluctuations. Where $\delta S\&P_0$ is the year-to-year percentage change in the Standard & Poor's stock price index and δGNP_0 is the percentage change in real gross national product (or in later years, real gross domestic product), the fitted regression equation is:

$$\delta LOGMERG_0 = -0.033 + 0.0036 \ \delta S\&P_0 + 0.0082 \ \delta GNP_0;$$
$$[1.12] \quad [1.99] \quad\quad\quad [1.25]$$
$$R^2 = 0.094; \ N = 97; \tag{1}$$

with t-ratios reported in subscripted brackets. The conventional wisdom is supported, although only weakly. When the data are limited to the post-World War II years 1947–2003, the GNP variable is statistically significant while the S&P variable, though positive, falls into insignificance.

We now focus on $\delta PRODY_0$, which is the percentage change in output per labor hour in the non-farm business sector or, prior to 1941, using the Kendrick series, for the private domestic economy. If mergers have a positive impact on productivity, it should take a year or so for it to materialize, so three prior years of the $\delta LOGMERG_0$ variable are used. There

---

[16] On compensation, see, e.g. Gretchen Morgenstern, "What Are Mergers Good For?" *New York Times Magazine*, June 5, 2005, pp. 56–62; and "Fat Merger Payouts for CEOs," *Business Week*, December 12, 2005, pp. 34–37.

[17] The productivity variable is spliced together from various editions of the *Economic Report of the President* and U.S. Department of Commerce (1966), p. 189. All first differences were computed between years from a continuous series.

might arguably be an impact in the year of merger, if for example lay-offs are effected shortly after mergers made during the earlier months of a calendar year. Here, however, we must be careful of confounding effects from another variable. It is well known under a phenomenon variously described as Verdoorn's law that productivity growth is higher when real GNP growth is higher.[18] We control for the contemporaneous Verdoorn effect with δGNP_0. To minimize an autocorrelation problem, all regressions are computed using a Cochrane–Orcutt correction.

For the entire data series (excluding wartime observations) with productivity data from 1899 to 2004, the fitted regression omitting current-year merger activity is:

$$\delta PRODY_0 = 1.62 - 0.52 \ \delta LOGMERG_1 - 0.004 \ \delta LOGMERG_2$$
$$[5.21] \ [0.41] \qquad\qquad [0.00]$$
$$-1.41 \ \ \delta LOGMERG_3 + 0.226 \ \delta GNP_0; \ R^2 = 0.112; \ N = 95$$
$$[1.19] \qquad\qquad\qquad [3.55] \tag{2}$$

where subscripts on the $\delta LOGMERG$ variables indicate the number of years lagged. The Verdoorn hypothesis is supported. All three signs on the mergers productivity effect are negative, but none is statistically significant. When the current-year merger variable is added, the regression is:

$$\delta PRODY_0 = 1.63 + 1.87 \ \delta LOGMERG_0 - 1.17 \ \delta LOGMERG_1$$
$$[5.07] \ \ [1.39] \qquad\qquad [0.84]$$
$$+0.28 \ \delta LOGMERG_2 - 1.26 \ \delta LOGMERG_3 + 0.201 \ \delta GNP_0;$$
$$[0.21] \qquad\qquad [1.03] \qquad\qquad [2.95]$$
$$R^2 = 0.101; \quad N = 93. \tag{3}$$

Now the signs alternate. Harmful collinearity between the $\delta LOGMERG_0$ and δGNP_0 variables is implied by the reduced t-ratio on δGNP_0 and the fall in R^2. The algebraic sum of the four merger impact coefficients is negative. When the four lagged merger terms were combined into a single rectangular lag variable, the regression coefficient was -0.78, with a statistically insignificant t-ratio of 0.37.

---

[18] See Verdoorn (1949) and (for an emphasis on short-run cyclical phenomena) Gordon (1979).

If we turn now to the data from 1947 to 2004 only, which may reflect a new and more enlightened era of merger-making, the analog of regression (2) is:

$$\delta PRODY_0 = 0.29 - 1.18 \ \delta LOGMERG_1 + 0.53 \ \delta LOGMERG_2$$
$$\qquad\qquad [0.77] \ [0.98] \qquad\qquad\qquad [0.43]$$
$$+0.98 \ \delta LOGMERG_3 + 0.615 \ \delta GNP_0; \quad R^2 = 0.504; \ N = 57.$$
$$\quad [0.83] \qquad\qquad\qquad [7.16] \tag{4}$$

The sum of the merger impact coefficients, all insignificant, is positive but small. The Verdoorn hypothesis is strongly supported. With a contemporaneous merger activity variable added, the regression is:

$$\delta PRODY_0 = 0.26 - 1.35 \ \delta LOGMERG_0 - 1.02 \ \delta LOGMERG_1$$
$$\qquad\qquad [0.68] \ [1.09] \qquad\qquad\qquad [0.82]$$
$$+0.39 \ \delta LOGMERG_2 + 0.93 \ \delta LOGMERG_3 + 0.64 \ \delta GNP_0;$$
$$[0.32] \qquad\qquad\qquad [0.78] \qquad\qquad\qquad [7.23]$$
$$R^2 = 0.502; \qquad N = 56. \tag{5}$$

Here the merger variables are more negative, but insignificant, as is a rectangular lag combining all four lagged merger variables.

In sum, the regression analysis provides no significant support for the hypothesis that more intense merger activity leads to higher productivity growth at the national level with a lag of zero to 3 years. To be sure, these results should not be the last word on a controversial subject. The level of aggregation is high, and both the merger and productivity series are the result of splices. Productivity is notoriously difficult to measure, and it is driven by multiple forces, most notably, by the research and technological development performed by scientists and engineers whose numbers have risen much more slowly than the number of MBAs. At most, the results can be read as a mild caveat to the assertion that mergers yield important productivity benefits to the U.S. economy.

VI. Conclusion

My return to the merger scene is not reassuring. The volume of merger activity has risen, and the disappearance of large industrial firms through merger has reached record levels. High levels of merger activity encourage students of business administration to emphasize merger-making skills in their training, and as they succeed in becoming leaders within the corporate hierarchy, a continuous feedback loop may operate, fostering an attitude that sustains and encourages vigorous merger activity.

One would like to believe that mergers bring substantial efficiency benefits to the economy, but on this point, the balance of evidence remains tenuous. Mainly through technological innovation based upon the human capital the US cultivates domestically and attracts from abroad, the 20th Century has been the American century. Continuation depends upon providing strong inducements for young people to pursue careers in science and engineering and maintaining sufficiently diverse centers of industrial initiative, allowing 100 flowers to bloom. For the new century, my task is to get out of the way. But I worry about what kind of economic environment we pass on to subsequent generations.

References

Black, F. (1986) 'Noise,' Presidential Address to the American Finance Association, *Journal of Finance*, **41**, 529–543.

Collins, N. R. and L. E. Preston (1961) 'The Size Structure of the Largest Industrial Firms,' *American Economic Review*, **51**, 986–1011.

Gordon, R. J. (1979) 'The 'End-of-Expansion' Phenomenon in Short-Run Productivity Behavior', *Brookings Papers on Economic Activity*, **10**, 447–461.

Hunt, P. and C. Williams (1955) *Case Problems in Finance*, revised edn. Canada: Irwin.

Jensen, M. (1988) 'Takeovers: Their Causes and Consequences', *Journal of Economic Perspectives*, **1**, 21–48.

John F. Kennedy School of Government, Harvard University (2005) *Report of the Teaching Programs Review Committee*. Cambridge, MA: JFK School.

Mueller, D. (2003) 'The Finance Literature on Mergers: A Critical Survey,' in M. Waterson, (ed.), *Competition, Monopoly and Corporate Governance*. UK: Edward Elgar, pp. 161–205.

Paton, W.A. and R.L. Dixon (1958) *Essentials of Accounting*. New York: Macmillan.

Pautler, P.A. (2002) 'The Effects of Mergers and Post-Merger Integration: A Review of Business Consulting Literature,' Draft paper, Federal Trade Commission.

Ravenscraft, D.J. and F. M. Scherer (1987) *Mergers, Sell-offs, and Economic Efficiency*. Washington, DC: Brookings Institution.

Ridgway, N. (2005) *The Running of the Bulls: Inside the Cutthroat Race from Wharton to Wall Street*. New York: Gotham Books.

Scherer, F. M. (1980) *Industrial Market Structure and Economic Performance*, 2nd edn. Chicago: Rand-McNally.

Scherer, F. M. (1999) *New Perspectives on Economic Growth and Technological Innovation*. Washington, DC: Brookings Institution.

Scherer, F. M. (2002), 'The Merger Puzzle,' in W. Franz et al. (eds.), *Fusionen*. Tuebingen: Mohr Siebeck, pp. 1–22.

U.S. Department of Commerce (1996) Bureau of the Census *Long-Term Economic Growth 1960–1965*.

Verdoorn, P. J. (1949) 'Fattori che regolano lo sviluppo della produttivita del lavoro,' *L'Industria*, **1**, 45–53.

Whyte, W. H. (1956) *The Organization Man*. New York: Simon & Schuster.

[6]

MERGER EFFICIENCIES AND COMPETITION POLICY

-- Note by Professor F. M. Scherer --

1.   Some OECD nations nations -- I do not know how many -- have incorporated an efficiencies defense into the evaluation of mergers that might otherwise be expected to reduce competition and raise prices. Adjudicating the tradeoff between efficiencies and anti-competitive effects is difficult. I address here some of the most important issues from the perspective of my own experience in actual U.S. cases. Efficiency defenses have at least in U.S. practice also been asserted against claims of excessive or abusive monopoly power -- e.g., in the 1911 Standard Oil case and the 1956 Cellophane case -- but brevity requires me largely to pass over the relevant experience.

1.   The Williamson tradeoff

2.   The tradeoff analyzed in 1968 by Oliver Williamson is well-known and will have been exposited by the conference organizers. I choose the risk of duplication here to highlight some caveats. The original Williamson analysis is summarized in Figure 1 below.[1] It is assumed that before merger the industry supply function, i.e., the envelope of individual producers' marginal cost curves -- is given by the curve S_1. Merger to monopoly reduces the marginal cost curve to MC_M, i.e., by $15 per unit. A tradeoff is required only if the merger enhances monopoly power so much that e.g. the new profit-maximizing solution entails equation of the now-lower marginal cost with marginal revenue MR, precipitating an increase in the price from approximately $139 to $149 per unit, corresponding with an output reduction of approximately 16 percent. The social loss normally attributable to this output reduction is the dot-shaded deadweight loss triangle in Figure 1. The social gain from the monopoly-based cost reduction is the vertically shaded gap between the old, higher supply curve and the new marginal cost curve. As Figure 1 is constructed, the cost-reduction gain is about four times the deadweight loss, and so by Williamson's reckoning, the merger might be justified under welfare economic criteria. Evoking (but not citing) a result demonstrated as early as 1890 by Alfred Marshall,[2] Williamson argues that many realistic combinations of demand elasticities and monopoly-based cost reductions could entail a net welfare gain.

3.   In 1984 the U.S. Department of Justice (DoJ) revised its merger guidelines to allow what appeared to be a Williamsonian efficiencies defense. The statement left important points unclear, however, and in an early case involving an already-consummated 1982 merger between Archer-Daniels-Midland (ADM) and Clinton (Iowa) Corn Processing Company, views on how the defense could be sustained clashed.[3] Department of Justice attorneys insisted that efficiencies could support a valid defense only if

---

1.   See Oliver Williamson, "Economies as an Antitrust Defense: The Welfare Tradeoffs," American Economic Review, March 1968, pp. 18-36. Less than a year before publication Williamson completed a one-year assignment as the second-ever U.S. Department of Justice Antitrust Division chief economist -- although the formal title differed then.

2.   Alfred Marshall, Principles of Economics (1890), p. 447, footnote 1.

3.   U.S. v. Archer-Daniels-Midland Co. et al., CCH 1991 Trade Cases para. 69,647. When the case was initiated, it was believed to be the first test of the new merger efficiencies defense. However, other cases moved ahead because of procedural delays. The first successful litigated defense known to me was in a

their cost-reducing effect led to a decrease in high-fructose corn syrup prices below the price that had prevailed (presumably, under more vigorous competition) pre-merger, or at least, to no price increase. In effect, the Williamson *tradeoff* between higher prices and lower costs was to be ignored. For the merging parties I submitted in 1987 a memorandum rebutting several points in the DoJ approach and strongly supporting the Williamson tradeoff. The memo is provided as a supplement to this report [4] (see Annexe 1 - DAF/COMP/WD(47)ANN1). Extensive support was added in court, but the presiding judge, fearful of treading on unexplored precedential ground, chose to approve the merger on more traditional grounds, thereby dodging the efficiencies question.

Figure 1. Illustration of Williamson Efficiencies Tradeoff

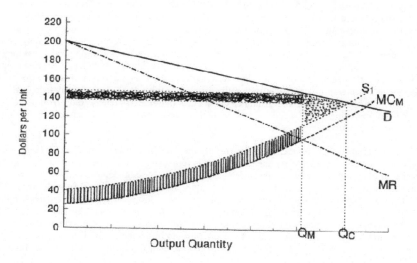

4.   Even though the Williamson tradeoff was originally advocated by the only competition enforcement agency chief economist to be honored with the Nobel Prize in economics, the U.S. agencies have continued to insist that no tradeoff be accepted. Rather, in the words of the joint agency Horizontal Merger Guidelines of August 19, 2010, section 10:

> ... *To make the requisite determination, the Agencies consider whether cognizable efficiencies likely would be sufficient to reverse the merger's potential to harm customers in the relevant market, e.g., by preventing price increases in that market....*

5.   By the Williamson analysis and by the arguments I advanced in my May 1987 memorandum, this policy is wrong. However, I have more recently begun to have doubts. When Williamson published his 1969 article, civilian sector unemployment in the United States was 3.5 percent. It was 6.2 percent in 1987.

---

hospital merger case, U.S. v. Carilion Health Systems et al., CCH 1989 Trade Cases para. 68,451. Details of what was achieved operationally by ADM and the legal issues addressed are found in John F. Kennedy School of Government case study 1126.0, "Archer-Daniels-Midland and Clinton Corn Processing" (1992).

4.   Originally reprinted in F. M. Scherer, Competition Policy, Domestic and International (Edward Elgar: 2000), Chapter 18.

DAF/COMP/WD(2012)47

At the time, most economists believed we had essentially conquered the business cycle and the scourge of unemployment. Now one is much less certain. The United States has experienced several years running with unemployment rates above 8 percent. For the Euro zone excluding Germany, the unemployment rate in 2012 averaged 12 percent, with youth (under age 25) unemployment rates of nearly 30 percent.

6.   Full employment can no longer be so readily assumed, and given this, two shortcomings of the Williamson tradeoff take on greater weight. First, the resources released through merger-based efficiencies -- the vertically shaded area of my Figure 1 -- enable social gains by releasing resources that will be used in other economic sectors to provide goods and services that enhance consumer welfare. At substantial levels of unemployment, this is no longer certain. Resource leakage is likely, and impact multipliers of less than unity are required. Second, the Williamson tradeoff analysis assumes in effect that Say's law operates. That is, in the first instance, monopoly price-raising adds profits at consumers' expense nearly equal to the curlicue-shaded rectangular area in Figure 1. Those profits are assumed to recirculate into effective demand for additional investment goods or, when distributed to shareholders, through incremental consumer demand. But in a world of liquidity traps, corporations are accumulating profits that they choose not to invest, and when the profits are distributed to typically wealthy shareholders, marginal propensities to consume are below unity in normal times and savings propensities are even stronger in troubled times. Ignoring stock ownership by operating corporations, nearly a third of all domestically-held U.S. common stocks are held by pension funds and insurance companies. Individuals increase their consumption little or not at all when the value of the securities held by their insurers rises. Thus, increased output is much less than equal to the resource savings achieved through mergers.

7.   Another difficulty is acknowledged briefly by Williamson (pp. 27-28). The curlicue-shaded rectangle in Figure 1 represents a transfer of what before merger was consumers' surplus to profit or producer's surplus and ultimately to the merging company's share-holders. Common stockholdings are disproportionately concentrated among the most wealthy families. If one believes with Alfred Marshall (1890, Book III, Chapter III) that the marginal utility of money diminishes as wealth increases, the effect of monopoly price-raising is to redistribute income from consumers with relatively high marginal utilities to shareholders with lower marginal utilities, implying a welfare loss.[5] This is an immensely controversial proposition, and it is no longer fashionable for economists to propound it. But it has become all the more relevant as the inequality of wealth holdings has increased, as it has in many if not most OECD nations during the past two decades.

8.   For these reasons, there is more force than I was once willing to admit for the argument that cost savings must be passed on to consumers if those savings are to be viewed as a justification for mergers. But the Williamson tradeoff could still work if a more sophisticated incidence analysis is appended. One must admit that such an analytic extension adds difficulty to the other challenges I will address shortly. Also, the less-than-full-employment problem that now plagues many (not all) OECD member nations is, one hopes, transitory. When it abates, the case for implementing a full Williamson tradeoff analysis gains strength.

2.   The with-or-without question

9.   We turn next to what operations researchers have long called the "with-or-without" question. That is, one attempts to compare performance <u>with</u> the intervention in question vs. what could be achieved using alternative feasible measures. In their August 2010 revised Merger Guidelines, the U.S. antitrust agencies stated the same concept as: "The Agencies credit only those efficiencies likely to be accomplished

---

5.   See also W. Blum and H. Kalven, The Uneasy Case for Progressive Taxation (University of Chicago Press, 1953); and F. M. Scherer, "A Note on Global Welfare in Pharmaceutical Patenting," The World Economy, July 2004, pp. 1127-1142.

with the proposed merger and unlikely to be accomplished in the absence of either the proposed merger or another means having comparable anticompetitive effects." Again, difficult "but for" analyses must be made.   Let me illustrate with the proposed 1998 merger between defense contracting companies Lockheed-Martin and Northrop-Grumman. I was part of the Department of Justice team addressing competitive effects and efficiency benefits. One benefit claimed by Lockheed was a consolidation entailing the closure of nearly 100 specialized research laboratories, with consequent cost savings. Analyzing the relevant data, I realized that nearly all of the laboratories proposed for closure had counterpart laboratories within the same company performing substantively similar research. So why was the merger needed? Why wasn't one laboratory in a field closed, with transfer if needed of critical personnel to a parallel laboratory? The surprising answer was that in 1993, perceiving that the United States was supporting more contractors than it could fully load with new programs in the future, Defense Secretary William Perry induced the U.S. Congress to pass a legislative loophole stating that contractors would be reimbursed for installation closure costs made in conjunction with a merger, otherwise, presumably not. So Lockheed-Martin waited for an appropriate merger to effect closures that it could have made, but at greater cost to itself, even if not to the public till, without merger. The question was, did these facts violate the "with or without" test? As events ensued, the efficiencies analysis was not needed, because decision-makers in the Department of Defense came to believe that they needed Northrop-Grumman as an independent center of technological initiative.[6]

10.   Two other illustrations reinforce this example, which, because of the special legislative context, may have been anomalous.

11.   In 1976 a U.S. Senate subcommittee held extensive hearings on a bill (S. 2387) proposed by its chairman, Senator Philip Hart, to initiate a divestiture program substantially reducing the vertical integration of market-dominating U.S. petroleum companies. Witnesses for the companies insisted that vertical disintegration would sacrifice substantial efficiencies. Drawing upon research I had done on the economics of multi-plant operation, including the petroleum industry, I then testified[7] that the principal advantages of vertical integration in petroleum stemmed critically from major imperfections in petroleum markets, including distortions imparted by a "percentage depletion" law for crude oil, the advantages integrated marketers drew from preferred access to gasoline supplies under the existing system of "two tier" price controls, and integrated company control of crucial pipelines. The bill was approved in subcommittee but died on the Senate floor. But the market distortions that gave integrated companies their main advantages were gradually eliminated, and more recently, several companies have verified the unimportance of integration in a more unrestrained market by voluntarily severing refining and marketing divisions from crude oil exploration and production.

12.   Here too, the market failures that made multi-plant integration profitable stemmed in part from misguided government interventions. A case absent government distortion arose in the proposed 1978 merger between Jones & Laughlin Steel and Youngstown Steel, the seventh- and eighth-largest U.S. steel producers. Although the antitrust agencies had not yet adopted efficiencies defense guidelines, efficiency consequences and others were weighed in view of a crisis U.S. steel makers were experiencing at the time. Advising Attorney General Griffin Bell on the matter, I detailed the parties' claims that they would derive

---

6.   In a new paper, "Mergers and Innovation in the Pharmaceutical Industry," William S. Comanor and I have proposed that a similar test be applied to pharmaceutical mergers. The Defense Department's decision might have been an historical anomaly. For the first time in 1998, the Department had an Undersecretary for Acquisitions, Jacques Gansler, trained in economics (specifically, defense economics) rather than engineering or business. Gansler recognized, as engineers were unlikely to, the value of having diverse independent centers of technological initiative. Much to Lockheed's surprise, Gansler's view was strongly supported by the colonels who play a key role in defense acquisition decision-making, and so Lockheed voluntarily abandoned the merger.

7.   The testimony is not reproduced as an OECD file, but can be found in Scherer, Competition Policy, Domestic and International, Chapter 20.

DAF/COMP/WD(2012)47

benefits from cross-shipment of their iron ore, coking coal, finished coke, and unfinished steel shapes.[8] I asked, however, why those benefits could not also be realized by arm's-length purchase and sale transactions. The would-be acquirer replied that "Short of merger, J&L has no interest in YS&T's survival. Therefore, absent unusual circumstances ... J&L would not enter into contracts with YS&T because of competitive concerns." Viewing this attitude as an indicator of market failure, I responded that "it is a sad commentary on the US steel industry that its members are willing to cooperate in lobbying for governmental protection against imports but not to engage in mutually advantageous market transactions that reduce costs and improve their competitiveness against foreign producers."

3.   The tendency toward erroneous evaluations

13.   The Jones & Laughlin - Youngstown merger also illustrates what is perhaps the most serious barrier to introducing efficiency defenses in proposed merger evaluations -- the difficulty of making accurate projections about necessarily uncertain future events, including both costs and, at least as hard, prices. My work on the cost implications of that merger provides a concrete example, since I revisited the facts several years later and learned that I had been excessively pessimistic in assessing the potential benefits.[9]

14.   In my 1978 analysis for Attorney General Bell, (see Annexe 2 - DAF/COMP/WD(47)ANN2) I observed that Youngstown's most modern plant, at Indiana Harbor on Lake Michigan, had been unprofitable. I observed that "What Indiana Harbor needs to serve the nation well is good management and an infusion of capital." I expressed doubts whether J&L's management, depleted as a result of turnover following previous mergers, was up to the task and noted that J&L, like Youngstown, was severely cash-constrained. My retrospective revealed that these were indeed the core of Youngstown's problems. However, I was wrong in my skepticism about J&L's ability to fill the gap. I failed to realize that the problem with Youngstown's conglomerate parent (ascertained in later interviews) was profound ignorance of how to operate a steel mill rather than unbreakable cash constraints. And relying upon paper documentation rather than face-to-face meetings with J&L managers, I underestimated their competence. I was probably biased in this judgment because four years earlier I had visited J&L's newest steel works and found it appallingly badly managed in comparison to a directly comparable Japanese plant I visited a month earlier. J&L reassigned able managers to Indiana Harbor and invested funds among other things in spare parts for the Indiana Harbor hot strip rolling mill -- a key bottleneck, raising its output from 68 percent of capacity pre-merger to nearly full capacity and thereby permitting a substantial expansion of ancillary product finishing mill output.

15.   In the longer run, however, those measures proved insufficient. Further mergers by J&L experienced significant indigestion problems. The industry was plunged again into crisis by a severe recession and intensified import competition. J&L's parent filed for bankruptcy. A series of reorganizations followed. The remaining Youngstown, Ohio, plant was permanently closed. Youngstown's more modern Indiana Harbor plant operated under diverse ownership constellations until it was acquired by Arcelor-Mittal, which had also acquired what was once the Inland Steel Corporation. Since 2005, therefore, the two major Indiana Harbor works, separated by a canal's width, became an integrated entity owned by the Mittal interests.[10]

---

8.   My memorandum has been reproduced and placed on the OECD web site. It was published in Scherer, Competition Policy, Domestic and International, Chapter 17.

9.   The later analysis was one of 15 case studies presented in my book (with David Ravenscraft), Mergers, Sell-offs, and Economic Efficiency (Brookings 1987), especially pp. 275-279. My retrospective is included with permission as "Youngstown Sheet & Tube" on the OECD web site.

10.   Note that in my 1978 report to Attorney General Bell, I recommended that, absent acquisition by a Japanese steel maker, an alternative superior to acquisition of Youngstown's Indiana Harbor works by LTV would be consolidation with Inland Steel (see Annexe 2 - DAF/COMP/WD(47)ANN2).

4. Coping with uncertainty: I

16. For me, the Youngstown - J&L experience was humbling. I erred significantly in forecasting improvement prospects for an industry on which I had unusually deep insight. This raises the broader question, how should competition policy enforcement agencies cope with the uncertainties attending claims that mergers will yield significant efficiencies?

17. The Clinton Corn Processing acquisition, it must be reiterated, took place eight years before the government's challenge was resolved judicially. The lag was attributable in part to uncertainty over whether the transaction was a merger rather than a long-term lease and then to procedural delays. Archer-Daniels-Midland began implementing efficiency improvements on the day it took the Clinton, Iowa, plant over, and by the time a formal trial was held in late 1990, a clear performance record had been established and few relevant uncertainties remained. Among other things, it was possible to show that ADM made many investments that Clinton's prior management had not contemplated, had achieved productivity far superior to other industry members, and even that its average prices were lower than those of competitors.

18. Most merger challenges do not enjoy this historical luxury, in part, at least in the United States, because before the antitrust agencies were granted power under the 1976 Hart-Scott-Rodino Act to delay mergers pending settlement or judicial approval, it proved difficult to unscramble eggs that had already been scrambled.[11] Had divestiture been required eight years after the Clinton Corn Processing merger, the efficiencies achieved in that virtually free-standing plant could probably have been sustained, despite the absence of Archer-Daniels-Midland management's cost-sparing obsession. The main new costs would have come from the need for Clinton to develop its own field sales force, from cessation of access to the parent's operating know-how and specialized enzymes, and from the sacrifice of modest inter-plant peakload-balancing advantages. But for other mergers, especially those contemplating substantial multi-plant coordination and reorganization, restoring the status quo ante several years after a hold-separate order could be difficult. To the extent that this is true, a three-way tradeoff among ex ante prediction uncertainty, the delay of efficiency-increasing measures until legal uncertainty is achieved, and breakup costs if the merger is retroactively disapproved, must be faced.

19. One possible solution would be to weigh these tradeoffs in a preliminary judicial or administrative hearing. If substantial long-term reorganizations between acquirer and acquired firm operations are contemplated, it is probably necessary to accept the uncertainties of predicting efficiency consequences in a front-end "go - no go" decision. But if predicted operational changes are expected to occur mainly within the acquired entity with only modest multi-plant interaction, a two-stage approach might be adopted, with the enforcement authority allowing the merger for a limited (e.g., three-year) period and then revisiting the facts after experience has resolved remaining uncertainties. The emergence of companies that specialize in divesting segments of existing organizations, reorganizing them, and then offering new equity shares for them in public capital markets might add to the two-stage approach's feasibility.[12]

---

11. See Kenneth Elzinga, "The Antimerger Laws: Pyrrhic Victories," Journal of Law & Economics, April 1969, pp. 43-78.

12. During the 1980s, those firms were called leveraged buyout specialists. Their functioning is analyzed in Ravenscraft and Scherer, supra. More recently, private equity companies perform similar functions. Bain & Co., in which U.S. presidential candidate Mitt Romney gained most of his business experience, is one example.

DAF/COMP/WD(2012)47

5.   Coping with Uncertainty: II

20.   If efficiency claims must be evaluated ex ante, i.e., before a proposed merger is consummated, the question remains, who should analyze the claims on behalf of the enforcement agency?

21.   My natural, possibly prejudiced, assumption is that economists on the enforcement agency's staff or retained by the agency as consultants would perform the necessary analyses. But on this, I have serious misgivings. Presumably, many of those staff economists focused their Ph.D. studies in the academic field known as "industrial organization." (Later) Nobel laureate Wassily Leontief once said in a Harvard University lecture that an industrial organization economist "is a person who has never been inside a factory." The remark was made in jest, but it reflected a touch of reality. And since Leontief uttered it in 1960, its truth has increased. Up to the 1960s, there was a tradition that students completing their Ph.D. studies in the field of industrial organization would submit as their thesis a book-length in-depth study of how some industry functioned. To the best of my knowledge, that tradition has almost totally ebbed. Now industrial organization dissertations emphasize econometric analysis of some data set or theoretical derivations, not hands-on industry analysis.[13] And the economist who hasn't wrestled with the recalcitrant facts of industry production processes is likely to have difficulty sorting out uncertain efficiency predictions.

22.   Once upon a time, the ability of economists to deal with real-world industry production and marketing questions was strengthened through the completion of substantial industry studies by the staff of enforcement agencies. The Federal Trade Commission and its predecessor, the Bureau of Corporations, compiled a brilliant record of performing such studies, which among other things laid a foundation for major U.S. antitrust cases against Standard Oil of New Jersey (1911), the American Tobacco Co. (1911), the United States Steel Corporation (1920), and antibiotic manufacturers (1958), among others. But such efforts appear to have been abandoned in the 1980s and not resumed since then.[14] The United Kingdom Monopolies Commission published many excellent industry studies in earlier decades. Whether the U.K. tradition has continued, or been extended by other nations' competition agencies, I do not know. A resurrection of the industry study tradition, in academia or the enforcement agencies or both, would contribute significantly to the knowledge base on the basis of which merger efficiency claims are evaluated and also to the training of economists who understand in depth how cost savings are achieved in real-world industries. Also worth encouraging are new multi-industry comparative studies of the sources of industrial scale economies like those performed in the past by Joe S. Bain, Clifford Pratten of Cambridge University, Gunnar Ribrandt of Stockholm, and the collaborators in my study on The Economics of Multi-Plant Operation.[15]

23.   If economists default in evaluating merger efficiency claims, an alternative solution might be for merger law enforcement agencies to contract with specialists in consulting firms or working as independent consultants. Here too there are problems. Management consulting firms in particular earn most of their bread through their continuing relationships with the firms making mergers. Bias could be difficult to avoid, and deep understanding of industrial processes is often lacking. My most recent litigation consulting experience, for example, has focused on the muddle left when a prominent company followed the erroneous production technology advice of a leading U.S. management consulting firm. Among other things, the staff of such firms is often recruited predominantly from top graduates of leading MBA

---

13.   Studies of government regulation's impact on specific public utility industries may be an exception.

14.   See F. M. Scherer, "Sunlight and Sunset at the Federal Trade Commission," Administrative Law Review, Fall 1990, pp. 461-487.

15.   On Europe, see Commission of the European Communities, Research on the "Cost of Non-Europe (the so-called Cecchini Report), especially volume 2, "Studies on the Economics of Integration" (1988).

programs. Most such programs provide relatively little exposure to complex problems of production management and emphasize training in the field of corporate finance. To the extent that this is true, serious biases can intrude. The finance literature stresses the stock market consequences of mergers, which are correlated at best loosely with real operational efficiency effects.[16] If I were retaining a management consulting firm to assist in efficiencies claim evaluation, I would insist that the retained principals have their primary educational background in operations research or industrial engineering rather than business finance. Similarly, I would look to such academic specialists rather than traditional business school faculty in choosing individual merger evaluation consultants.

6.   Conclusion

24.   In sum, solving the merger efficiencies question correctly is important. Some mergers -- from my own experience, a minority -- yield substantial efficiency gains that benefit consumers and advance economic growth. Separating the wheat from the chaff is difficult. Uncertainties are particularly great when predictions must be made before mergers are actually consummated. Inviting would-be merger makers to present an efficiencies defense is on balance a desirable policy not only to facilitate good enforcement agency decisions, but also to concentrate would-be merger makers' minds on the important operational consequences of their strategies -- a focus that in my experience is all too frequently absent when stock market arbitrage possibilities must be exploited quickly. Enforcement agencies need to work hard to ensure that they can perform the evaluation task competently and minimize error.

---

[16].   My most recent of numerous writings on this theme is "A New Retrospective on Mergers," Review of Industrial Organization, June 2006, pp. 327-341.

[7]

ON THE PATERNITY OF A MARKET DELINEATION APPROACH

F. M. Scherer
John F. Kennedy School of Government
Harvard University

In June 1982, the Antitrust Division of the Department of Justice announced in a published brochure new merger guidelines which were to replace guidelines issued in 1968. The 1982 Guidelines laid out innovative approaches to the antitrust analysis of proposed mergers. Despite periodic revisions, the core of the Guidelines has been maintained to the present day. Among the innovations was a new approach to delineating the relevant market that might be affected by a merger. The essence of the approach was characterized (1982, p. 4) as follows:

> Taking the product of the merging firm as a beginning point, the Department will establish a provisional product market. The Department will include in the provisional market those products that the merging firm's customers view as good substitutes at prevailing prices.... The Department will add additional products to the market if a significant percentage of the buyers of products already included would be likely to shift to those other products in response to a small but significant and non-transitory increase in price. As a first approximation, the Department will hypothesize a price increase of five percent and ask how many buyers would be likely to shift to the other products within one year....

An analogous approach was proposed (pp. 7-8) for delineating economically meaningful geographic markets.

Given Washington's love affair with acronyms, the test entailing a Small but Significant and Non-transitory Increase in Price became known as, and is still known as, the SSNIP test.

The 1982 Guidelines provide no citations to a prior economic literature on the intellectual origins of the SSNIP approach. Insight into the foundations upon which the Guidelines were constructed has emerged in a series of retrospectives. The first known article articulating the Guidelines' rationale, published just a year later by an Antitrust Division staff economist "intimately involved" in the development of the guidelines, cited no intellectual precedents for the SSNIP test.[1] Indeed, author Gregory Werden asserts at p. 515 that "economists have contributed little to market delineation in the antitrust context," citing among other things George Stigler's lament that "this battle on market definitions ... has received virtually no attention from us economists."[2] An earlier

---

1. Gregory J. Werden, "Market Delineation and the Justice Department's Merger Guidelines," Duke Law Journal, (June 1983), pp. 514-577, at p. 514. The preliminary abstract characterizes the Guidelines approach to market delineation as "Perhaps the most innovative and important aspect of the Guidelines..."

2. From George J. Stigler, "The Economists and the Problem of Monopoly," American Economic Review, Papers and Proceedings, vol. 72 (May 1982), pp. 1-11 at p. 9. My contemporary interpretation of the Stigler assertion was that it was "sour grapes" reflecting Professor Stigler's defeat in an attempt to define gasoline markets as nationwide in

Werden article on shortcomings in market delineation methods used previously also contains no precedential insights on SSNIP.[3]

In a retrospective published two decades after the Guidelines were first issued, Dr. Werden casts his net broader and identifies several antecedents.[4] Most importantly, he shows that Morris Adelman of Massachusetts Institute of Technology, an eminent industrial organization economist, published a prescient formulation in a 1959 article analyzing an early Celler-Kefauver Act case:[5]

> No matter how the boundaries may be drawn in terms of products or areas, there is a single test: if, within the purported market, prices were appreciably raised or volume curtailed, would supply enter in such amounts as to restore approximately the old price and output? If the answer is "yes," then there is no market, and the definition must be expanded. If the answer is "no," the market is at least not wider. ... Any other scheme of definition is not so much "wrong" as meaningless.

Clearly, Adelman has the best first mover claim. Werden goes on to identify three other formulations from which one might infer the SSNIP approach: a 1977 treatise by Lawrence Sullivan, the first (1978, vol. 2) edition of the treatise by Philip Areeda and Donald Turner, and a 1978 Department of Justice report to Congress on the coal industry.[6] The first of these, Sullivan's, states *inter alia* at p. 41:

> ... To define a market in product and geographic terms is to say that if prices were appreciably raised or volume appreciably curtailed for the product within a given area, while demand held constant, supply from other sources could not be expected to enter promptly enough and in large enough amounts to restore the old price or volume. If sufficient supply would promptly enter from other geographic areas, then the "defined market" is not wide enough in geographic terms; if sufficient supply would promptly enter in the form of products made by other producers which had not been included in the product market as defined, then the market would not be wide enough in defined product terms....

Sullivan provides no citations to prior literature for his concept, but only a page later in a related context he cites the 1959 Adelman paper, suggesting an inference that he was influenced by

---

Marathon Oil Co. v. Mobil Corporation et al., N.D. Ohio, 530 F. Supp. 315 (1981). See note 19 infra.

3. Gregory J. Werden, "The Use and Misuse of Shipments Data in Defining Geographic Markets," Antitrust Bulletin, vol. 26 (Winter 1981), pp. 719-737.

4. Werden, "The 1982 Merger Guidelines and the Ascent of the Hypothetical Monopolist Paradigm," Antitrust Law Journal, vol. 71 (2003), pp. 253-269, at p. 253.

5. M. A. Adelman, "Economic Aspects of the Bethlehem Opinion," Virginia Law Review, vol. 45 (1959), pp. 684-696, at p. 686.

6. Lawrence A. Sullivan, Handbook of the Law of Antitrust (1977); Phillip Areeda and Donald F. Turner, Antitrust Law (1978), para. 518 at p. 347; and U.S. Department of Justice, Antitrust Division, Competition in the Coal Industry (May 1978).

Adelman's seminal construction.

Both the Areeda-Turner and coal analyses define markets as economic spaces within which monopoly price-raising would be feasible and presumably profitable, and thus encompass much of what emerged in the 1982 Guidelines. Werden admits that at the time he drafted the market definition section of the coal industry report, he "at the time had read neither Adelman nor Sullivan (and Areeda and Turner was not yet available)."[7]

In a similar two-decade retrospective, Lawrence J. White, chief economist of the Antitrust Division at the time the Guidelines were formulated and issued, observes that:[8]

> Prior to that time the conceptual basis for market delineation was, at best, limited. Most industrial organization economists understood that the definition of markets rested on cross-elasticities of supply and demand.... Market delineation for merger analysis and enforcement by the Division and by the FTC was largely ad hoc.

He adds in a footnote (2) that "(as of 1982) there was no one at the Division who knew of Adelman's suggestion."

Neglected Insights

My dormant curiosity on the paternity of the SSNIP test was piqued through a still more recent retrospective by Professor White on which I was asked by the author to comment.[9] The original basis for my puzzlement was testimony I presented in Federal District Court for the Eastern District of Michigan during April 1972 concerning a proposed preliminary injunction against acquisition of the Associated Brewing Company by the G. W. Heileman Brewing Company.[10] My appearance in the proceeding -- my first experience as a witness in a litigation -- was precipitated by an interview I conducted a year earlier with the president of Associated and my distress that what seemed an eminently sensible rescue of a fading, if not failing, firm was being opposed by the government. The interview was one of 125 conducted as part of research for my book, The Economics of Multi-Plant Operation, which required me to become familiar inter alia with the

---

7. Supra note 4 at 256, note 9.

8. Lawrence J. White, "Present at the Beginning of a New Era for Antitrust: Reflections on 1982-1983," Review of Industrial Organization, vol. 16 (2000), pp. 131-149, at p. 132.

9. "Economics, Economists, and Antitrust: A Tale of Growing Influence," in John Siegfried, ed., Living Better Through Economics (Harvard University Press: forthcoming).

10. CCH 1972 Trade Cases para. 74,080. I no longer have the transcript, but memorialized parts in a book cited in note 12 *infra*. My testimony complemented that of Kenneth Elzinga, who emphasized the incoming and outgoing shipments test introduced in Elzinga and Thomas Hogarty, "The Problem of Geographic Market Definition in Antimerger Suits," Antitrust Bulletin, vol. 18 (Spring 1973), pp. 45-81.

4

Loeschian economics of geographic space.[11] My testimony, presented *pro bono* two days after the initial contact by Associated, offered evidence on the magnitude of transportation costs in shipping beer from one part of the country to another -- e.g., eight cents per dollar of f.o.b. plant value to ship 350 miles -- and the ability of identified third parties to ship from locations outside the individual states and eight-state territory alternatively alleged by the government to be relevant markets for antitrust purposes. Explaining why the eight-cent cost and distance evidence was relevant, I engaged in the following colloquy:[12]

Q: What does an economist look at when he is trying to evaluate the nature of competition? ... Strictly from an economist's standpoint, not a lawyer's standpoint?

A: What an economist looks at when he examines a situation that may contain a monopoly is the ability to raise prices; that is, to raise prices above the cost of doing business. That is what the whole thing is about.

Q: How does that tie into our case?

A: In trying to define what the relevant market is one has to ask, does a seller in some territory, or do a group of sellers in some territory, have the ability to raise prices above their cost of doing business and keep those prices there? That is the relevance to the question of market definition. That is what we are interested in. We are interested in defining the market in such a way as to answer the question: can the sellers in the territory, if they get a large enough share of the territory's sales, can they, by virtue of their large share of those sales, raise prices above the cost of doing business? That is the key question.

Q: How did you answer that question in relation to what the government has defined as the geographic market?

A: The relevance is this. At any moment in time, say the year 1971, which I believe is the year on which Mr. Dobson's memorandum focused, it may well be that certain sellers have a large share of some state's sales. That is an important thing to look at. That is an interesting thing to look at. But the problem of market definition is this: suppose they do get a large share of the sales in, let us say, a state. Does that give them the ability to raise prices above the cost of doing business? That is what market definition is all about. It seems to me that the state-wide definition is really too narrow in this case.

Consider, for example, the state of Illinois. I don't know who the leading sellers are in the state of Illinois. I suspect from Mr. Dobson's memorandum that whoever the top four are, they have a pretty high share of the market. What if they tried to exploit their high

---

11. With Alan Beckenstein, Erich Kaufer, R. D. Murphy, and Francine Bourgeon-Masssen (Harvard University Press: 1975).

12. It and additional segments of my testimony are reproduced in Scherer, Competition Policy, Domestic and International (Edward Elgar: 2000), pp. 233-238.

share of Illinois sales by raising prices? That is the key question.

Here we have 15 companies all pretty well able to penetrate various states in this whole eight-state area in response to some kind of price stimulus. If the price is raised, that will stimulate, let us say, Memphis to start shipping beer more and more to the north in response to that profit opportunity. That will stimulate maybe Falstaff on the far border of Iowa to ship beer into Illinois. It will certainly stimulate Duquesne or Pittsburgh Brewing Company to begin shipping more beer westward in response to that price stimulus.

Thus, in that critical respect, when there are brewers with quite feasible shipping radii who are able, even though they don't sell currently, as soon as firms try to raise the price the Illinois sales territory becomes interesting, and one transports beer in response to that price stimulus.

As soon as somebody tries to raise the price, that will bring beer flowing toward the raised price and create a competitive situation that will make it difficult to sustain the increased price.

The next section of my testimony was qualified by referring to raising the price "significantly" above the cost -- i.e., the eight percent value associated with 350-mile shipments.

Presiding over the Associated proceedings, District Judge de Mascio observed that "defendants offered sophisticated economic testimony to dispute the government's contention that its [single-state or eight-state] area is a relevant market."[13] He ruled the testimony unpersuasive, however, citing the Supreme Court's acceptance of similar markets in the Blatz-Pabst case and other mergers.[14] The merger was nevertheless allowed to proceed (with later minor brand divestitures) because of Associated's precarious financial condition -- the first reversal of a string of brewing company merger prohibitions that included but also predated the Supreme Court's acceptance of a single-state market definition in the Pabst-Blatz case.

To me, the Associated testimony seemed a distinct intellectual precursor to the 1982 SSNIP rule. But there was no reason to assume that the team drafting the 1982 Merger Guidelines was aware of it. Douglas Dobson, the Justice Department economist who testified at the 1972 Associated Brewing trial, moved shortly after the trial to the Federal Trade Commission Bureau of Economics, presumably taking his accumulated knowledge with him. Therefore, as I explained when I published excerpts from my Associated Brewing testimony in a collection of my papers on competition policy during 2000, at which date I remained unaware of the Adelman and other earlier formulations:[15]

---

13. U.S. v. G. Heileman Brewing Co. et al., 1972 CCH Trade Cases, Para. 74,080 at 92,463 (1972).

14. U.S. v. Pabst Brewing Co. et al., 184 U.S. 546 (1966). See also Kenneth Elzinga and Anthony Swisher, "The Supreme Court and Beer Mergers," Review of Industrial Organization, vol. 26 (May 2005), pp. 245-267.

15. Supra note 12 at p. 7.

I have seen no clear chain of causation running from my testimony to the <u>Merger Guidelines</u>, but the approach makes compelling analytic sense, and correct analytical concepts must sooner or later triumph. The most I can claim is that following my testimony the approach was 'in the air' for the taking.

Professor White's most recent retrospective led me to look back and see whether I had suggested a SSNIP-like approach in other pre-1982 testimony or writings. In fact, three examples surfaced.

In June 1975, I testified pro bono as initial economist witness in the U.S. v. International Business Machines Corporation monopolization case.[16] My remit was to lay out broad principles to guide the trial of a monopolization case, including principles for market definition. My testimony, somewhat disorganized after only one day of preparatory coordination with government counsel, included the following:[17]

> ... [I]n defining economically meaningful markets we are really interested in defining the boundaries within which competition takes place or does not take place.... A monopoly situation is believed to exist when a firm has the power to elevate price and to hold it above cost.... [W]e want in defining an economically meaningful market -- let's deal with the seller's side of it -- we want to include that set of sellers ... who can be expected to respond to changes in price... [W]hen we define an economically meaningful market ... we are concerned on the one hand with defining the geographic bounds of the market, and secondly, we are concerned with defining the product bounds ... [I]n terms of geographic space the key variable is transportation cost ... [W]e are interested in how much must the price be elevated in order to draw a supply from greater and greater distances.

The testimony went on to deal with the more complex problem of product market definition, with the anti-friction bearings industry (one of my multi-plant study foci) taken as an illustration. Excerpts included:[18]

> ... [F]or the producer of tapered bearings for railroad wheel applications -- it would be necessary for him to raise his price very substantially before railroad car manufacturers found it less costly to substitute ball bearings for tapered bearings.... In making fractional horsepower electric motors, ball bearings seem to have a very substantial technological advantage, and ... the manufacturers of ball bearings would have to raise their prices very substantially above cost before it would be possible for tapered bearings to make significant

---

16. At the time I was chief economist at the Federal Trade Commission, and testified as an independent individual on leave from my Commission duties.

17. United States v. International Business Machines Corporation, 69 Civ. 200 (June 16, 1975), Trial Transcript, pp. 2312-3, 2316, 2317, 2318.

18. *Supra* note 21 at 2321, 2322.

> inroads into that particular application.... So what I have suggested is that there may be some applications in which one physically different product has such a significant technological advantage that its price would have to be raised very much above cost before the other technologically discrete type could make significant inroads. On the other hand, there are other applications where the two may substitute one for the other on rather narrow terms without significant [price] differentials.

Further illustrations were presented for energy resources. No attempt was made to apply the basic concepts to computers, on which I had done no prior research, nor had I analyzed discovered documents.

The IBM case was, of course, one of the most important antitrust initiatives of its time. The government's economic team, however, was separate from the main group of Antitrust Division economists, and so it is possible Antitrust Division economists were unaware what their own agency was presenting in court.

I revisited the market definition problem again in 1981 for the Marathon - Mobil merger case. Given its unusual size and charges that, following sharp increases in crude oil prices, the major oil companies were "drilling for oil on the floor of the New York Stock Exchange," the case was followed closely in the business press. I argued for Marathon Oil that the market should be defined regionally; Professor Stigler proposed for Mobil that the market was nationwide.[19] Asked by counsel for Marathon what factors I as an economist would take into account in determining the relevant geographic market, I testified inter alia:[20]

> [H]ere you have to ask the question as follows: What happens if the price -- what happens if the price, say, the price of gasoline in Cleveland is raised -- because of say some breakdown of competition among the sellers of gasoline in Cleveland? What happens if the price is raised? Who are the people who might move into this gap to supply more product, to offer more product on the market and bring down that price until the price has [been] competed back down to the competitive level? So you really want to know who the relevant people are in a position to compete down the price. That in turn depends in an industry like gasoline, or the other petroleum products, that depends critically on transportation costs.

There followed an extensive analysis of transportation costs, including comparative truck, water, and pipeline costs; the locations of petroleum pipeline terminals and limitations on pipeline access; and of both historical and contemporary differentials in gasoline prices and their persistence across narrowly-defined geographic areas. My analysis showed that price differentials on the order of one to two cents per gallon persisted across many terminal points and metropolitan areas. I testified further that a one-cent differential amounted to roughly five percent of the refiner's processing plus

---

19. *Compare* note 2 *supra.*

20. Marathon Oil Company v. Mobil Corporation et al., Civil Action No. C81-2193, November 23, 1981, approximately p. 225 of the trial transcript (page numbers on copy illegible).

transportation cost margin, net of crude oil costs, and "in a good year" 25 percent of the refiner's net profit margin. Presiding Judge John Manos concluded that the magnitude of intercity price differentials was in fact "significant when compared to a petroleum company's profits" and provisionally, pending the presentation of more detailed evidence, that states could be viewed as meaningful markets.[21] The criterion he accepted for a "significant" price differential entailed a much lower price elevation than the five percent value adopted as "a first approximation" in the 1982 Merger Guidelines, but given the economic facts in petroleum refining, it made good economic sense. Following further proceedings adverse to Mobil,[22] a merger between Marathon and United States Steel Corporation was consummated. Many years later the merger was voluntarily reversed, and Marathon Oil continues to be an independent participant in U.S. petroleum product markets.

It is possible, of course, that the persons drafting the 1982 Merger Guidelines were unaware of this testimony, as they might also have been unaware of my Associated Brewing and IBM testimony. On reading Professor White's most recent retrospective, the question occurred to me for the first time, might I have presented a similar conceptualization in another venue with more widespread visibility? The main possibility was my industrial organization textbook, which I then scrutinized for DNA clues.[23] In the first edition, my treatment of market definition methodology focused on traditional shibboleths: cross elasticities of demand and Joan Robinson's search for a "clear gap in the chain of substitution." But to my surprise (one does forget what one has written!), the 1980 revision had been decisively influenced by my Associated Brewing and IBM experiences. The relevant passage (p. 60) read:

> The ideal definition of a market must take into account substitution possibilities in both consumption and production. On the demand side, firms are competitors or rivals if the products they offer are good substitutes for one another in the eyes of buyers. But how, exactly, does one draw the line between "good" and "not good enough" substitutes? The essence of the matter is what happens when price relationships change. If the price of product A is raised by a small percentage and as a result consumers substitute product B for product A in significant quantities, then A and B are good substitutes and ought to be included under a common market definition.

The discussion then proceeded to deal with possible implementation problems -- notably, what has come to be known as "the Cellophane fallacy," under which a firm with monopoly power in some product line raises its price near, but not all the way up to, the level at which alternative products become significant substitutes, causing an analyst applying the price increase rule to infer that the market is competitive when in fact it is not.

There is considerable parallelism between the last two sentences of my textbook formulation quoteabove and the language of the 1982 Merger Guidelines: the relevant market should be

---

21. 530 F. Supp. 315, 322 (1981).

22. Marathon Oil Company v. Mobil Corporation et al., 669 F. 2d 378 (1981).

23. F. M. Scherer, Industrial Market Structure and Economic Performance, 1st edition 1970, 2nd edition 1980.

expanded "if a significant percentage of the buyers of products already included would be likely to shift to those other products in response to a small but significant and non-transitory increase in price." One might reasonably accept the alternative hypothesis of independent (even though not simultaneous) invention. But there is evidence that Department of Justice staff were at least aware of my textbook approach. In his nearly contemporary exposition of principles underlying the 1982 Merger Guidelines, Gregory Werden identifies the Herfindahl-Hirschman (HHI) index as the variable chosen to measure concentration. He observes in a footnote that there are many other such measures of the size distribution of sellers, and advises, "*See generally* F. SCHERER, INDUSTRIAL MARKET STRUCTURE AND ECONOMIC PERFORMANCE 56-59 (2nd ed. 1980)."[24] What is striking about this nearly contemporary reference is that the 1980 textbook pages explicitly cited are followed only one page later by my statement articulating "the ideal definition of a market." It seems plausible that, reading those previous pages as a general authority on concentration indices, Werden also became aware of my "essence of the matter" principle for defining relevant markets one page later.

Conclusion

To be sure, one cannot conclusively rule out simultaneous but independent invention of the SSNIP approach to market definition. What is undeniable is that there were other antecedents not cited by Drs. Werden and White in their retrospectives. I clearly was not the first inventor. If there were business methods patents at the time, my friend Morris Adelman would have been accorded provisional priority. Sullivan, Areeda and Turner, and Werden -- works unknown to me until recently -- were significant late movers. But under U.S. patent precedents, "invention" depends both upon conception of the idea and diligent reduction to practice. Had I challenged Morris Adelman's priority by claiming due diligence in reducing the concept to practice, I might have won the patent. Obviously, there are no patents and there will be no legal challenge. But standards of scholarship demand that all relevant priority claims be recognized.

---

24. *Supra* note 1 at 517, note 13. From a search of prior references, I have been unable to find any that used the exact words "Herfindahl-Hirschman Index" to name the index before my 1980 edition did so.

[8]

Journal of Health Economics 32 (2013) 106–113

Contents lists available at SciVerse ScienceDirect

Journal of Health Economics

journal homepage: www.elsevier.com/locate/econbase

Mergers and innovation in the pharmaceutical industry

William S. Comanor [a,*], F.M. Scherer [b,*]

[a] University of California, Los Angeles, Santa Barbara, United States
[b] Harvard University, United States

ARTICLE INFO

Article history:
Received 28 October 2011
Received in revised form 14 August 2012
Accepted 22 September 2012
Available online xxx

JEL classification:
L1
L4
O3

Keywords:
Pharmacuetical mergers
Innovation

ABSTRACT

Conflicting trends confound the pharmaceutical industry. The productivity of pharmaceutical innovation has declined in recent years. At the same time, the cohort of large companies who are the leading engines of pharmaceutical R&D has become increasingly concentrated. The concurrent presence of these trends is not sufficient to determine causation. In response to lagging innovation prospects, some companies have sought refuge in mergers and acquisitions to disguise their dwindling prospects or gain R&D synergies. On the other hand, the increased concentration brought on by recent mergers may have contributed to the declining rate of innovation. In this paper, we consider the second of these causal relationships: the likely impact of the recent merger wave among the largest pharmaceutical companies on the rate of innovation. In other words, have recent mergers, which may have been taken in response to lagging innovation, represented a self-defeating strategy that only made industry outcomes worse?

© 2012 Elsevier B.V. All rights reserved.

The pharmaceutical industry has encountered a period of dramatic structural change. The first manifestation has been a productivity shock, as the number of new molecular entities approved for introduction into the United States market between 1970 and 2010 grew only slightly despite an increase in inflation-adjusted research and development expenditures at a rate of roughly seven percent per year.[1] As a result, the R&D cost of an average new molecule has skyrocketed – from roughly $40 million at year 2000 price levels in clinical testing costs alone for drugs introduced during the 1980s to $280 million for 1990s drugs, and even more recently.[2] This has occurred despite the emergence of radically new means to discover candidate molecules – DNA analysis combined with gene splicing – and the growth of a new biotech industry oriented around those techniques. Third, because of the expiration of key patents without commensurate replacement, legal changes, and insurance mandates, generic fulfillment of prescriptions has risen from 17 percent in 1980 and 30 percent in 1990 to upwards of 70 percent by number in 2009.[3] Post-patent-expiration price competition has become more intense, compelling main-line drug companies either to innovate or fade away. Fourth, and not unrelated to these trends, the traditional pharmaceutical industry has experienced a wave of mergers, causing the disappearance of many companies that once were at or near the industry's innovative vanguard.

While industry leaders explain their mergers as a response to these shocks and a partial solution to the declining productivity problem, this paper advances the reverse hypothesis: that instead of enhancing R&D productivity, the merger wave has jeopardized it.[4] Our central thesis emphasizes the uncertainties inevitably encountered in new drug discovery and development and the role of "parallel paths" – i.e., the pursuit of multiple approaches to solving any given medical problem – in coping with those uncertainties.

1. The merger wave

Before starting our analysis, we present evidence on the contours of recent "Big Pharma" merger activity. Our attention was directed to this phenomenon most dramatically by two massive mergers consummated in 2009: the acquisition of Wyeth Laboratories, fifth-ranked on *Fortune* magazine's 2008 list of U.S.-based pharmaceutical firms, by Pfizer, even before the merger the largest U.S. pharmaceutical producer[5]; and the acquisition by Merck, fourth-ranked on *Fortune*'s list, of eighth-ranked Schering-Plough. In 2008, Pfizer invested $7.9 billion for pharmaceutical R&D across

---

* Corresponding authors.
E-mail address: comanor@ucla.edu (W.S. Comanor).

[1] Scherer (2013).
[2] Scherer (2010, 554), summarizing evidence compiled by Joseph DiMasi, Henry Grabowski, and others.
[3] Generic Pharmaceutical Association, press release of May 7, 2009.

[4] For another analysis reaching similar conclusions but employing a different methodology, see Munos (2009).
[5] Pfizer lagged Johnson & Johnson on *Fortune*'s sales ranking for 2008 (May 4, 2009, p. F-56), but nearly two-thirds of J&J's sales were in non-pharmaceutical lines.

0167-6296/$ – see front matter © 2012 Elsevier B.V. All rights reserved.
http://dx.doi.org/10.1016/j.jhealeco.2012.09.006

W.S. Comanor, F.M. Scherer / Journal of Health Economics 32 (2013) 106–113

107

Table 1
Recent history of large pharmaceutical mergers (survivors are ranked by 2010 worldwide sales).

1.	Pfizer 2009: Acquired Wyeth (which resulted from 1994 merger of American Cyanamid and American Home Products). 2003: Acquired Pharmacia (which acquired Upjohn in 1995). 2000: Acquired Warner-Lambert.
2.	Johnson & Johnson (no major mergers).
3.	Novartis 2011: Acquired Alcon. 1996: Resulted from merger of Ciba Geigy and Sandoz.
4.	Roche 2009: Consolidated 1990 acquisition of Genentech. 1995: Acquired Syntex.
5.	Bayer (no major mergers).
6.	Merck 2009: Acquired Schering-Plough.
7.	Sanofi-Aventis 2011: Acquired Genzyme. 1999: Name changed after merger of Rhone-Poulenc and Hoechst. 1995: Hoechst acquired Marion Merrell Dow. 1995: Rhone-Poulenc acquired Fisons. 1990: Rhone-Poulenc acquired Rorer.
8.	Glaxo SmithKline 2000: SmithKline Beecham merged with Glaxo. 1995: Wellcome merged with Glaxo. 1989: Beecham merged with SmithKline.
9.	Abbott (no major mergers).
10.	Astra Zeneca 1999: Zeneca Group merged with Astra AB.
11.	Eli Lilly (no major mergers).
12.	Bristol-Myers Squibb 2001: Acquired duPont Pharmaceuticals. 1989: Bristol-Myers and Squibb merged; name change.

its world-wide operations while Wyeth spent $3.4 billion, for a total of $11.3 billion. This sum was 22 percent of the worldwide R&D spending by members of the Pharmaceutical Research and Man- ufacturers of America (PhRMA) (including 14 entities with home bases overseas).[6] In 2008 Merck expended $4.8 billion on R&D and Schering-Plough $3.5 billion, for a combined total of $8.3 billion, or 17 percent of the PhRMA universe total. Thus, the four merged entities together accounted for 39 percent of PhRMA members' 2008 outlays, and hence must be considered a major element in the progress of pharmaceutical technology.

These mergers were only the high point in a broader trend. Table 1 summarizes the principal mergers completed in recent years by the world's twelve leading pharmaceutical producers, ranked by worldwide sales in 2010. Altogether, those firms' posi- tions in 2011 were influenced by 19 significant mergers and acquisitions from 1989 to 2011, not including various smaller con- solidations.

The eight largest pharmaceutical sellers, including both domes- tically and foreign-owned companies, accounted for 36 percent of "pharmaceutical preparation" factory sales in the United States in 1987 and 54.2 percent in 2007 – the latest year for which

Census data are available.[7] Five significant mergers since 2007 have undoubtedly increased the degree of concentration, which is understated as a measure of how technological initiative is struc- tured because the U.S. Census Bureau tally includes the (rapidly increasing) sales of generic drug producers, most of whom perform relatively little R&D. For an alternative way of quantifying these structural changes, one can compare *Fortune 500* sales listings for 1998 and 2011. In each year, the domestic *Fortune* listings included 12 pharmaceutical manufacturers. In 1998, the four sales leaders accounted for 56 percent of the 12 listed companies' sales. In 2011, the four leaders' combined sales share had risen to 70.7 percent.

2. Parallel paths and the dispersion of technological initiative

When concentration ratios are analyzed by economists, the con- ventional rationale is that sufficiently high concentration of sales among the four or eight largest companies in well-defined product line segments can lead to cooperative oligopolistic pricing. This was apparently the principal but not sole focus of U.S. antitrust agencies when they evaluated the most recent Pfizer and Merck mergers, among others.[8] Here we take a different approach. Our central argument is that technological innovation is characterized by major uncertainties, so that it is usually unclear ex ante whether a partic- ular initiative will be successful. Some firms will hesitate to invest at all in R&D; while others may support technical approaches that prove worthless in the end. Technological progress is best achieved in a field like pharmaceuticals when there is widespread dispersion of R&D initiatives both across companies and within them through the exploration of multiple technical paths. In the literature of oper- ations research and (less so) economics, the investment strategies embodying this dispersion of initiatives are called "parallel paths" strategies.[9]

Some history provides perspective. The oldest known conscious use of a parallel paths strategy was the famous British Longitude Prize, announced in 1714, for which many individuals competed to devise a means by which naval ships could determine, short of crashing onto shoals, how far east or west they had travelled. Introducing the prize approach to the British Parliament, Isaac Newton identified five specific technical avenues plus variants. One he considered unpromising – a clock capable of keeping exact time relative to the Greenwich meridian – eventually won the prize for Joseph Harrison, but only after the prize committee was "besieged" with proposals (Sobel, 1995, pp. 52–55). During World War II, fearing that Germany might be developing an atomic weapon, the United States Manhattan Project supported five alternative

---

[6] R&D expenditures within the United States by PhRMA members in 2007 – the last year for which comparable U.S. Census data are available – were nearly 77 per- cent of pharmaceutical industry expenditures measured in a U.S. National Science Foundation survey.

[7] U.S. Bureau of the Census, Census of Manufactures, *Concentration Ratios in Man- ufacturing: 2007* (retrieved from the Census Bureau web site).
[8] Consistent with Horizontal Merger Guidelines amended periodically, most recently section 6.4 of the August 2010 version, the U.S. antitrust agencies also ana- lyze whether a merger is "likely to diminish innovation." Divestitures of narrowly defined competing lines or patents have sometimes been required before allowing mergers to go forward. For example, in the Pfizer-Wyeth case, some overlapping assets in the animal health area were voluntarily divested. In addition, Merck and Schering Plough were required to divest certain household pet and (human) nau- sea therapies. For a list of nine pharmaceutical mergers between 1980 and 1998 on which compulsory licensing of narrowly selected potentially blocking patents was required, see Preis (2005, pp. 108–110). The authors of this paper submitted in February 2009 a memorandum to the Federal Trade Commission on the Pfizer merger, emphasizing the same points as those analyzed in the present paper. There is no evidence that the Commission pursued the kind of broad analysis suggested here.
[9] A pioneering contribution was Nelson (1961). The concept was developed qualitatively by Peck and Scherer (1962, Chapter 9) and extended in numerous dimensions by Scherer (1966, 2007). For still another approach, see Abernathy and Rosenbloom (1969).

methods of separating the needed fissionable material as well as two completely different approaches to bomb design – the uranium gun-barrel and a plutonium implosion device.[10] The five separation approaches, if carried through to a full technological demonstration, were expected together to cost $500 million, which at the time was one-third percent of annual U.S. GDP. A decade earlier, du Pont synthesized 81 different polyamide molecules before coming up with five that best satisfied the prerequisites for its nylon synthetic fiber. And Thomas Edison explored 1600 different materials before embracing the carbonized filament used in his first incandescent lamps – a solution displaced later by tungsten filaments.

Less well known is the history of one of the 20th century's most important inventions, the integrated circuit.[11] Recognizing the desirability of packing many more transistor functions into a given cubic volume, the U.S. military services issued a dozen parallel R&D contracts to induce a solution. None succeeded, but seeing the demand for such a product, two companies, Fairchild and Texas Instruments, developed complementary solutions to the integrated circuit concept. The predecessor company to Fairchild had made numerous unsuccessful efforts to win one of the military contracts to support its work, but its staff had to go forward with Fairchild's funds and achieve a winning concept.[12]

3. Uncertainties in pharmaceutical discovery and testing

The essential rationale for parallel paths strategies depends upon two conditions: (1) uncertainty about the correct solution among numerous possible approaches to a technological challenge; and (2) the desirability of achieving the rewards from solving the problem earlier rather than later. The second mandate is clear in pharmaceuticals: effective new drugs are profitable to their originators and even more valuable to the population whose ills they alleviate. The first condition is readily verified. The development of a new drug is typically characterized by a series of activities – first discovery of promising molecules, then testing for safety in animals, and then increasingly expensive "phases" in which safety is first explored with human patients (Phase I), then early indications of therapeutic efficacy are sought through small-scale human trials (Phase II), and finally, statistically reliable proof of efficacy and safety is sought through Phase III trials involving hundreds to thousands of patients. As these phases are pursued, uncertainties decline.

At the discovery phase, it is not uncommon for only one molecule in one hundred, or even more, to reveal enough promise to be carried into human testing. Uncertainties ebb only as the process continues. Studies by DiMasi et al. (2003, p. 162) reveal that in recent experience, only 21 percent of the drug candidates tested in Phase I on average survive all three phases of testing to receive regulatory approval for general therapeutic use in the United States. The highest attrition rate is at Phase II, from which only about 44 percent of target molecules carried into that phase progress further. And of the roughly 21 percent of drugs that survive all three testing phases, only about one-third achieve sufficient commercial sales and profits to pay back the capitalized value of their R&D investments. See Grabowski et al. (2002). Thus, there is substantial uncertainty as to whether any specific drug candidate is in fact therapeutically effective and whether successful drugs can achieve sufficient commercial success in the market to be profitable.

There is, to be sure, an alternative to a strict parallel paths strategy in coping with R&D uncertainty – the so-called series strategy. With the latter, investment is directed to one set of options (or an initial set in parallel), and if that thrust fails, additional options are pursued sequentially until success is achieved. Given uncertainty, a pure series strategy option usually takes much longer than a parallel paths strategy. If the benefits conditional upon R&D success are substantial, and if, as in drug testing, time lags are appreciable, waiting until success is achieved through a sequential series of R&D thrusts is economically unacceptable.

4. A simple example

At this point, we illustrate a relatively simple parallel-only example, adapted from Scherer (1966, 2007). We assume that decision-makers are unable to discern ex ante which of diverse contending molecules has a higher probability of success, i.e., single-approach success probabilities P_S are assumed homogeneous.[13] The probability of success for the aggregation of all N parallel approaches is P_{SN}, or $1 - (P_F)^N$, where P_F is the probability of failure on a single approach ($= 1 - P_S$) and N is the number of parallel approaches. The optimal strategy depends not only upon success probabilities but also crucially on the benefits, or in the case of private firms, quasi-rents, i.e., the surplus of annual sales revenues over variable production and distribution costs, attainable when success is achieved. We further assume that these quasi-rents $Q(t)$ continue over time from the first year T_S after at least one successful molecule is approved to a future time horizon H. Future quasi-rents must of course be discounted to present value at a discount rate r. The decision-maker therefore chooses the number of paths N expected to maximize the surplus of discounted quasi-rents minus R&D costs, where the latter is N times the cost of a single approach $C(RD)$:

$$\text{Max} \int_{T_S}^{H} P_{SN} Q(t) e^{-rt} dt - N C(RD). \tag{1}$$

The model was evaluated for five diverse probabilities of single-approach success, ranging from 0.01 (one in one-hundred, most closely approximating the situation in early pre-clinical drug research) to 0.3, which approximates the historical odds of emerging from Phase I and Phase II clinical trials with a molecule that warrants further (more expensive) Phase III testing. To repeat, it is assumed that all approaches have the same a priori success probability expectation.

Numerical solutions for this model are graphed in Fig. 1. To approximate most closely conditions in Phase II clinical testing, Fig. 1 assumes that testing costs for a single approach are $50 million, assumed (oversimplifying) to be incurred in a single year.[14] If success is achieved, further Phase III tests must be conducted, with a probability-weighted expected cost of $P_{SN} C_3$ discounted to time 0. That Phase III cost C_3 is assumed here to be $200 million. Benefits begin flowing in at the conclusion of Phase III tests, assumed to be at $t = 5$ and continue for 14 years out to year 19. With this

---

[10] See Baxter (1947, pp. 433–436).

[11] See Scherer (1996, pp. 203–204).

[12] From a conversation by co-author Scherer with Victor Jones, a member of the Schockley Semiconductor Laboratory staff and later professor of solid state physics at Harvard University.

[13] Significantly differing a priori success probabilities for alternative approaches tilt one's strategy in the series direction. See Scherer (1966). In a homogeneous-probability analysis lacking the Phase III time lags assumed here, Scherer (2007) shows that combining parallel with series strategies tends to yield higher profits, e.g., by roughly 20 percent in a low success-probability case, with the number of paths explored per period declining by as much as one-half. However, the total number of paths planned ex ante for exploration in this case, conditional upon no early success, tends to be higher than in the all-at-once case.

[14] In these numerical calculations, the model has been modified for the sake of realism from analogous versions presented in Scherer (1966, 2007). The cost and timing assumptions are adapted from Scherer (2013).

W.S. Comanor, F.M. Scherer / Journal of Health Economics 32 (2013) 106–113

Optimal Parallel Paths Choices

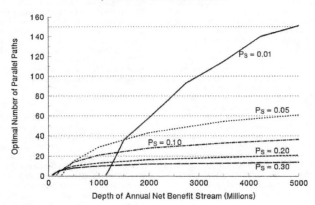

Fig. 1. Optimal parallel paths choices.

modification, Eq. (1) above includes an additional term $-200P_{SN}$. The horizontal axis in Fig. 1 measures the depth of the realized quasi-rent stream. Quasi-rents range in Fig. 1 from $50 million per year to $5 billion per year – the latter figure somewhat below the quasi-rents realized by the best-selling drug in history, *Lipitor*, in 2011. Again, benefits continue to accrue at a constant level for 14 years, i.e., to $H = 19$. A discount rate of 0.10 is used.[15] Shorter benefit inflow durations, higher discount rates, and higher R&D costs would mandate fewer parallel paths, all else being equal.

Fig. 1 arrays the profit-maximizing parallel paths choices for various success probability and benefits stream values. For prospects with success probabilities of only 0.01, as in pre-clinical drug discovery, profits are maximized by supporting as many as 150 parallel paths for the most lucrative prospects, assuming that a sufficient number of alternative equal-probability approaches can be identified. The profit-maximizing solution is highly sensitive, however, to the depth of the quasi-rents stream.[16] With success probabilities of 0.3, at the other extreme, from two paths (at annual quasi-rent flows of $100 million) to 14 parallel paths are warranted, depending upon the depth of the quasi-rent stream.[17]

5. Actual evidence

In this section, we consider whether the leading pharmaceutical companies actually support anything like the degree of parallelism in R&D suggested as profit-maximizing by the analysis above. For this purpose, we reviewed the portfolios of Phase II and Phase III clinical trials that were ongoing during 2009 and 2010 for five leading U.S. pharmaceutical firms.[18] The trials were classified by narrowly defined disease areas such as, for example, colorectal

cancers, prostate cancer, depression, or epilepsy. Modifications and combinations of approved molecules along with vaccines were included. Parallelism was recorded when a company had more than one molecule in trial for the same narrowly defined disease.

The results are summarized in Table 2. Altogether, 12 of the 83 Phase II trials, or 14.5 percent, were characterized by some degree of parallelism at the company level. Given a historical probability of roughly 0.3 that a molecule carried into human testing would transition from Phase II to Phase III trials, one might expect from Fig. 1 parallelism of from 2 to 14 molecules per company per disease. Fifteen of the 79 Phase III trials, or 19 percent, exhibited some parallelism at the company level. Although the odds of success are much higher at this stage, the degree of parallelism is again surprisingly modest. In both Phase II and Phase III trials, the Eli Lilly Company had the highest degrees of parallelism, 43 percent and 54

Table 2
Parallelism in five leading U.S. companies' 2009–2010 clinical trials.

	Number of trials	Same condition
Phase II		
Pfizer	15	2
Merck	31	3
Johnson & Johnson	14	0
Lilly	7	4
Bristol-Myers Squibb	16	3
Total	83	12
Percent parallel		14%
Phase III		
Pfizer	12	2
Merck	25	2
Johnson & Johnson	21	2
Lilly	13	7
Bristol-Myers Squibb	8	2
Total	79	15
Percent parallel		19%

Source: ClinicalTrials.gov.

---

[15] To reflect the unusually low capital costs prevailing in the 2008–2012 period because of "quantitative easing," it has been adjusted downward by two to three points relative to the rates reported in earlier empirical studies.
[16] Note the truncated payoff curve, reflecting the fact that with such a low success probability, prospects yielding annual quasi-rents of less than $1.15 billion have negative expected profits.
[17] With a quasi-rent stream depth of $75 million per year, a single path is barely profitable.
[18] The data source is http://www.clinicaltrials.gov.

percent respectively.[19] From Table 1, one can see that Lilly had no significant recorded mergers between 1989 and 2011.

Clearly, the leading U.S. "Big Pharma" companies are not pursuing anything like the degree of parallelism suggested by our earlier analysis. It is of course possible that they are following more sophisticated parallel-plus-series strategies, although that seems too fragile a reed to explain the large disparity between theory and practice. We reach that conclusion because simulations with assumptions similar to those made in Fig. 1 suggest a high optimal degree of parallelism even when series variants are added.[20] Higher cost or much lower benefit expectations from those assumed in Fig. 1 could also alter companies' behavior.[21] It is also possible that company therapeutic candidate "libraries" contained too few promising molecules to warrant the degree of parallelism implied in Fig. 1.

However, an alternative behavioral hypothesis cannot be ruled out: that companies fail to appreciate the full merits of parallel paths and/or view parallelism as a form of wasteful "duplication." That such a misperception of strategic options existed in the U.S. Department of Defense was asserted in an early and influential analysis that was a forerunner to the formal modeling of parallel paths strategies by economists. Hitch and McKean (1960, p. 249) argued that, given the technical and strategic uncertainties pervasive in military weapons R&D, one of the most important "pitfalls" in defense programs was "too little duplication" or parallelism of R&D approaches, with "duplication" put in quotation marks because duplicative programs were often criticized by members of Congress and others as wasteful. For managers to shun "duplication" when it is in fact an optimal strategy under uncertainty would therefore not be surprising.

The portfolio-pruning and cost-cutting practices that often follow a merger could be one reason why parallelism in pharmaceutical companies' clinical testing programs is so low. When a merger occurs, it is common for managers to analyze the R&D portfolios of the combined companies and eliminate those they see as "duplicative."[22] Following its merger with Wyeth, Pfizer closed one laboratory, downsized at least one other, and reduced its 2011 R&D spending by nearly 20 percent relative to the two firms' aggregate 2008 levels, with further cuts anticipated.[23] Merck, on the other hand, held its total spending roughly constant in the wake of its Schering-Plough acquisition.

That mergers do not yield more new drug approvals and may well reduce them is argued by a staff economist at Eli Lilly & Co., shown in Table 1 to be relatively merger-averse and in Table 2 to be one of the most aggressive parallel paths users. See Munos (2009). On Lilly's stated reluctance to rely on mergers for new products, see the message of its CEO, Sidney Taurel, in the company's 2002 annual report (p. 2).[24] Through regression analysis, Munos

(2009) demonstrates that individual firms' cumulative new drug approvals rose more or less linearly over time, whether or not firm size had been enhanced by mergers. In a more focused analysis, he found that for larger companies, new drug approvals did not increase and may actually have declined slightly following substantial mergers. For smaller companies, on the other hand, there was a modest increase in the average number of new molecules approved following a merger.

6. Industry-level analysis

The rationale of Fig. 1 applies not only at the level of individual firms optimizing their R&D decisions but also at the level of the entire pharmaceutical industry. If there were a conscious "invisible hand" guiding the industry's investments, that decision-maker would implement enough parallelism of aggregate R&D approaches in any given therapeutic area to maximize the discounted surplus of benefits over R&D costs. For a planner concerned with society's well-being, however, the benefits included in this maximization process would be those accruing to all participants in the economy, and not simply the profits of individual firms.

It is universally accepted that the society-wide benefits from research and development tend to exceed private benefits realized by the R&D-performer alone.[25] For pharmaceuticals in particular, Lichtenberg (2003) has estimated from a study of longevity effects that the social rate of return on pharmaceutical R&D approximates 68 percent per annum, assuming the value of a life-year saved to be $25,000. This value is roughly six times the private return (i.e., the return realized by specific drug-developing firms) estimated by Grabowski et al. (2002). Recognizing that his life-year value assumption might be considered too high, Lichtenberg argues that an omitted assumption on the opposite side – that new drugs improve the quality of life and individuals' productivity – makes his social return estimate if anything conservative. To the extent that social returns exceed private returns, all else equal, the amount of parallelism sustained at the industry wide level should from the logic of Fig. 1 be even greater than the individual company profit-maximizing level – that is, the optimum shifts to the right on any given success probability curve.

That pharmaceutical companies are indeed pursuing research paths that are parallel to those of their rivals is suggested by the findings of DiMasi and Paquette (2004). They reported that 72 first-in-class drugs approved in the United States between 1960 and 1998 were followed by at least 235 drugs in the same narrow therapeutic categories by the year 2003, many emerging too soon to be influenced by the first-in-class molecules' success.

On the other hand, a further analysis of the data summarized in Table 2 reveals only modest pursuit of parallel paths toward a single disease in the combined efforts of our five subject companies. For Phase II, 55 narrowly defined disease targets were identified. Ten were being pursued by two of the five subject companies; and two (Type II diabetes and rheumatoid arthritis) by three of the five. For Phase III, 52 targets were counted. Six entailed tests from two companies among our five; one (Type II diabetes) from four companies. Dividing the total number of multi-company investigations (not counting within-company parallelism) by the number of targets, one obtains a parallelism measure across the five companies of 1.25 for Phase II and 1.19 for Phase III. Although additional parallelism was undoubtedly underway among the many companies for

---

[19] We were puzzled by the low total number of Lilly Phase II trials relative to its Phase III count. Our research assistant suspected reporting gaps but was unable to find any.

[20] See Scherer (2007).

[21] As we shall stress later, quasi-rent distributions are highly skew after actual market experience is gained, and outcomes on the right-hand-side of Fig. 1 scale are rare. At the other extreme, clinical testing would seldom be pursued for projects with very low quasi-rent expected values. Ex ante, the distribution of quasi-rent expectations is likely to be less skew and centered on the left-hand third of Fig. 1's horizontal axis.

[22] This is explicitly suggested by John L. LaMattina (2011, p. 559), former president of Pfizer Global Research.

[23] From company annual reports. See also Peter Elkind and Jennifer Reingold, "Inside Pfizer's Palace Coup," *Fortune*, August 15, 2011, pp. 76–91.

[24] In a contemporary televised interview no longer available to us, Mr. Taurel expounded at length on his annual report statement that "all the evidence continues to show that such combinations do not create sustained value for shareholders."

[25] For early cross-industry empirical results, see Mansfield et al. (1977), who found social returns to be approximately twice private returns. See more generally Hall et al. (2010).

which data were not compiled, this again reveals less parallelism than our Fig. 1 theoretical analysis suggests.

Whether the degree of parallelism at the industry-wide level is too much or too little cannot be determined conclusively from the available evidence.[26] What is clear, however, is that when a major merger occurs, the number of independent sources of technological initiative is reduced, perhaps appreciably. And given Munos' evidence (2009) that mergers have not on average increased large companies' new product introductions, that lessening of initiative diversity most likely leads to fewer parallel paths pursued and slower rates of pharmaceutical innovation.

This analysis suggests another important consideration. Since the discovery of gene-splicing techniques by Stanley Cohen and Herbert Boyer in the 1970s, the structure of drug research and development has been revolutionized. Hundreds of new "biotech" companies, most of them small and university-linked, have been established.[27] Although they also work on other applications, their principal emphasis has been the discovery and synthesis of new biological agents, usually called "large molecule" drugs, for possible use against a wide array of diseases. Between 1982 and 2011, 12.5 percent of the 705 new molecular therapeutic entities approved by the U.S. Food and Drug Administration were characterized as biologicals, with a rising trend over time.[28]

But there is a problem. Few biotech companies are large enough and have sufficient experience to carry their discoveries through complex and costly clinical testing and regulatory approval hurdles. Nor do they have the marketing capability needed to bring their approved drugs swiftly into broad medical use.[29] For the most part, they rely on much larger pharmaceutical companies to finance and conduct clinical testing and to market the drugs once they have received regulatory approval. This is achieved sometimes through a license agreement and sometimes through outright acquisition of the biotech pioneer by a larger and better-established drug company.[30] In either case, whether or not to assume responsibility for a new biological substance is a decision fraught with nearly as much uncertainty and financial risk as the decision to conduct clinical trials for its own "small molecule" candidates.[31] When mergers reduce the number of well-established pharmaceutical companies able and willing to provide complementary testing and marketing, they presumably also reduce the probability that some company will say "yes" and accept responsibility. New drugs may be lost.

To be sure, biotech startups might arrange alternative means to finance the substantial expenses associated with clinical testing, and indeed, some have succeeded.[32] A few venture capital firms have chosen also to provide financial help.[33] Although the logic of comparative advantage strongly favors "Big Pharma" companies in managing clinical tests and marketing as well as in finance,

there are independent companies that contract to manage complex clinical testing programs.[34] Thus, the path to market for inventive biotech startups is not unequivocally blocked. But it is also not easy, and it has been made harder as the number of "Big Pharma" companies to whom the startups can turn for support declines in the wake of major mergers.

7. Optimal portfolio scope

Pursuing parallel research paths helps ensure that, when several uncertain R&D prospects are available, at least one will yield a technical success. But there is another dimension to uncertainty. Depending upon the market served and timing, some successes are much more profitable than others. Indeed, the distribution of payoffs, measured as the discounted present value of quasi-rents gained by FDA-approved new drugs, has been shown by Grabowski and Vernon (1990) to be quite skew. In their seminal analysis, the top ten percent of new drugs by number were found to capture 55 percent of total sample discounted quasi-rents. Their focus was approved drugs. We know from parallel studies that only 20–25 percent of the molecules carried into clinical trials emerge as approved drugs. Since drugs that are not approved presumably yield no profit returns, the top ten percent of drugs approved is roughly 2.5 percent of the drugs investigated clinically, and those 2.5 percent yield 55 percent of the ultimate returns.

To explore the logic of optimal portfolio choice under such skew-payoff conditions, a "dartboard" experiment was conducted.[35] The selection of R&D projects was analogized to throwing darts at a dartboard, whose 100 cells represented the diverse payoffs contingent upon research and marketing success. The distribution of cells or outcomes was log normal and hence skew, with the most lucrative 2.5 percent accounting on average for 53 percent of total payoffs – a close approximation to the Grabowski and Vernon results. The exact payoff function was:

$$D(P) = kX^{N(0,1)}, \tag{2}$$

where $N(0,1)$ is a random variable distributed normally with mean of zero and standard deviation of 1, $D(P)$ is the payoff function, k and X are scaling parameters, and X was set at 10 and k at 1000 (e.g., dollars, multiplied by whatever further scaling parameter is suited to reflect pharmaceutical market realities).

Choosing R&D projects was analogized to throwing darts at the matrix of potential payoffs, with the location of "hits" randomly and independently distributed across the 100 cells. R&D costs per "throw" were also varied systematically, from zero to $12,000. Under conditions of certainty (e.g., perfect aim), the decision-maker would throw a single dart at each cell for which the payoff exceeds the cost of the throw. With the assumed log normal distribution, the average number of perfect-aim throws varied with R&D cost as follows:

R&D cost ($)	No. of throws
12,000	15
10,000	17
8000	19
6000	22
4000	29
2000	39
0	100

---

[26] See Scherer (2010), pp. 562–569.
[27] See Pisano (2006), especially pp. 100–109.
[28] The data are presented graphically in Scherer (2013).
[29] An example is seen in the history of Amgen, thus far the most profitable of new biotech companies. When it developed its revolutionary red blood cell-enhancing drug Epogen, it was able quickly to build a sales force marketing the drug to the small number of dialysis centers spread throughout the United States, roughly half of them subsidiaries of a single company. But it lacked the sales force needed to present the drug before the much larger number of hospitals and clinics treating cancer patients. As a result, it chose to license Epogen (under the alternative name Procrit) to Johnson & Johnson for use in cancer treatments.
[30] See Comanor (2007).
[31] That success rates on biologicals have at least initially been higher than for small-molecule drugs is shown by DiMasi and Grabowski (2007).
[32] That many new large molecules are accorded "orphan" status by the Food and Drug Administration, permitting less costly testing, also helps here.
[33] On a Boston venture capital company that had raised $800 million to support 25 biotech startups, see Kirsner (2012). But for a skeptical view on venture capital support, see Primack (2011).

---

[34] Indeed, one company, Quintiles, both manages clinical tests under contract and had as of May 2012 provided $2.4 billion in financing for other companies' efforts, http://www.quintiles.com/capital.
[35] See Scherer (2007).

Average Net Payoffs from 40 Dartboard Replications

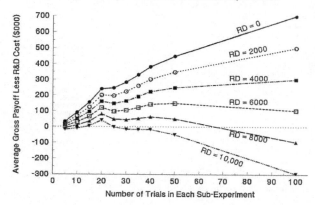

Fig. 2. Average net payoffs from 40 dartboard replications.

When costs are zero, dart-throwing with perfect aim continues until all hundred cells (each with at least a small positive payoff) are covered.

To achieve reasonably general results in the face of widely varying payoffs, 40 full random-aim experiments were carried out.[36] For each experiment, a new set of 100 payoffs distributed according to Eq. (2) was created using a random normal variable generator. As expected under such skew-distributed payoff conditions, right-hand tail values varied widely across experiments. The largest single extreme payoff value was $1,065,124; the minimax (i.e., the lowest maximum across 40 experiments) was $58,010; and the mean among the 40 experiments' maxima was $334,532. At the other extreme, many payoffs were minimal. The average payoff per throw among all payoffs across 40 experiments was $7032.

Fig. 2 summarizes the results for the 40 complete experiments, with the number of trials per sub-experiment incremented by discrete intervals from 5 to 100 (horizontal axis). The values graphed are total payoffs for a given number of trials, averaged across all 40 experiments, less total R&D costs, measured by the assumed cost per trial times the number of trials. Consistent with expectations, the net value-maximizing number of "throws" was higher, the lower the R&D cost per throw, with optima ranging from 20 throws to more than 100 at zero R&D cost per throw.

At low R&D costs – $4000 per trial (throw) or less – average net payoffs are maximized by extending the number of trials to more than 100, which means attempting (given duplicates, unsuccessfully) to hit every cell on the dartboard. With R&D cost of $6000 per trial, two local maxima emerged – one with 20 throws and an average net payoff of $120,650, and a maximum maximorum at 50 throws with an average net payoff of $149,829 after deducting the $300,000 total R&D cost per experiment.[37] With still-higher R&D costs, the 20-trial strategy dominates, so that at R&D costs of $8000 per trial, there are mean net payoffs of $80,650 with 20 trials as compared to $62,979 with 40 trials.

In sum, given the kinds of value uncertainties pharmaceutical developers face, maintaining a substantial portfolio tends to maximize profits. The size of the optimal portfolio falls with increases in R&D costs, all else equal, dropping to as few as 20 trials when inter-firm competition is so vigorous that aggregate industry profits are driven to only a normal rate of return.[38]

To be sure, the optimal number of trials hinges on our assumption that the payoff matrix contains exactly 100 payoff possibilities or cells. In reality, the number of plausible opportunities, both within a given therapeutic target area (i.e., with the pursuit of parallel paths) and across all areas, could be larger or smaller. From the data underlying Table 2, it can be determined that the five large U.S. companies studied were pursuing 52 Phase III disease targets in total, or on average 10.2 targets per company, with four of those targets pursued under parallel paths.

Tapping a much more extensive confidential data set for the years 1960–1990, Cockburn and Henderson (2001) found that their ten pharmaceutical company respondents supported in the average year from 1 to 42 active projects, with a mean of nearly 16. "Project" in this context was defined as a clinical development and testing effort in which at least $1 million was spent. In a multiple regression analysis, they found that the more "projects" a respondent company sustained – i.e., the broader the scope of the company's R&D effort – the higher was the probability that any given project would succeed in receiving marketing approval. No similar significant relationship was found with respect to the total magnitude or scale of the company's R&D spending. However, in their main publication, the authors did not report tests for nonlinear changes in the relationship. In an earlier paper apparently drawing upon the same data set, Henderson (1994) showed that the scope – success relationship was decidedly nonlinear when success is measured by the number of patents received per development program.[39] The peak output of patents per program was achieved at

---

[36] In the Scherer (2007) version, only 10 experiments were conducted.

[37] This duality results from the extreme skewness of outcomes even with replication across 40 experiments. The 20-throw experiments were apparently unusually lucky. Asymptotically, a single optimum would be expected.

[38] On the rationale of such a "rent-seeking" equilibrium, see Scherer (2010, pp. 562–566).

[39] Patents are a better measure of output in pharmaceuticals, where the average number of patents underlying approved new drugs is on the order of three and patents are considered quite valuable, than in fields such as information technology,

W.S. Comanor, F.M. Scherer / Journal of Health Economics 32 (2013) 106–113   113

between six and eight programs, with patents per program declining by roughly half as the number of programs increased from between six and eight to 20. Although the authors do not directly draw the inference, it would appear that too rich a portfolio – i.e., too many pots boiling on the R&D stove – somehow reduced innovativeness. Whether excessive scope resulted from mergers or other managerial causes was not explained. But the results suggest caution in interpreting our dartboard experiment results, if indeed too many "throws" on different kinds of targets – not parallelism per se – reduce R&D productivity and hence the payoff probabilities assumed in the experiment to be given.

8. Conclusions

Our conclusions are suggestive rather than definitive. There are reasons rooted in the logic of uncertainty and parallel paths strategies to believe that large mergers adversely affect R&D investment and the probability that new drugs will be created. There is also some evidence that parallel (read pejoratively, "duplicative") paths are pruned in the wake of mergers. With fewer centers of initiative and decision-making, the chance that new technological prospects will gain large-scale support is probably reduced. Big Pharma mergers also restrict the number of independent decision-making centers able and willing to carry the creative efforts of small biotech companies into the expensive clinical development and marketing stages. To be sure, these conclusions are proposed as possibilities rather than proven phenomena. Our analysis nevertheless provides support for the hypothesis that recent mergers have contributed to the observed decline in the rate of pharmaceutical innovation.

Acknowledgements

We appreciate helpful comments and suggestions from Iain Cockburn, H.E. Frech, Ray Gilmartin, Giorgio Monti and Rudolph Peritz. We are especially grateful for the careful research assistance of Karleen Giannitrapani.

References

Abernathy, W., Rosenbloom, R., 1969. Parallel strategies in development projects. Management Science 18 (June).
Baxter, J.P., 1947. Scientists Against Time (Little-Brown).
Cockburn, I.M., Henderson, R., 2001. Scale and scope in drug development: unpacking the advantages of size in pharmaceutical research. Journal of Health Economics 20, 1033–1057.

Comanor, W.S., 2007. The economics of research and development in the pharmaceutical industry. In: Sloan, F., Hsieh, C.R. (Eds.), Pharmaceutical Innovation. Cambridge University Press, pp. 54–72.
Comanor, W.S., Scherer, F.M., 1969. Patent statistics as a measure of technical change. Journal of Political Economy 77 (May/June), 392–398.
DiMasi, J., Grabowski, H., 2007. The cost of biopharmaceutical R&D: is biotech different? Managerial and Decision Economics 28, 469–479.
DiMasi, J.A., Paquette, C., 2004. The economics of follow-on research and development. Pharmacoeconomics 22, 1–14.
DiMasi, J., Hansen, R., Grabowski, H., 2003. The price of innovation: new estimates of drug development costs. Journal of Health Economics 22, 151–185.
Eli Lilly and Co., 2002. Annual report.
Grabowski, H., Vernon, J., 1990. A new look at the returns and risks to pharmaceutical R&D. Management Science 36 (July), 804–821.
Grabowski, H., Vernon, J., DiMasi, J., 2002. Returns on research and development for 1990s new drug innovations. Pharmacoeconomics 20, 11–29.
Hall, B., Mairesse, J., Mohnen, P., 2010. Measuring the returns to R&D. In: Hall, Rosenberg, N. (Eds.), Handbook of the Economics of Innovation. North-Holland, Amsterdam (Chapter 24).
Henderson, R., 1994. Managing innovation in the information age. Harvard Business Review (January–February), 100–105.
Hitch, C.J., McKean, R., 1960. The Economics of Defense in the Nuclear Age. Harvard University Press, Cambridge, Mass.
Kirsner, S., 2012. Venture firms with a twist. Boston Sunday Globe (June), G1.
LaMattina, J.L., 2011. The impact of mergers on pharmaceutical R&D. Nature Reviews/Drug Discovery 10, 559–560.
Lichtenberg, F., 2003. Pharmaceutical innovation, mortality reduction, and economic growth. In: Murphy, K., Topol, R. (Eds.), Measuring the Gains from Medical Research. University of Chicago Press, Chicago, pp. 74–109.
Mansfield, E., et al., 1977. Social and private rates of return from industrial innovations. Quarterly Journal of Economics 91 (May), 221–240.
Munos, B., 2009. Lessons from 60 years of pharmaceutical innovation. Nature Reviews/Drug Discovery 8 (December), 959–968.
Nelson, R.R., 1961. Uncertainty, learning, and the economics of parallel research and development. Review of Economics and Statistics 43 (November), 351–368.
Peck, M.J., Scherer, F.M., 1962. The Weapons Acquisition Process: An Economic Analysis. Harvard Business School Division of Research, Boston.
Pisano, G., 2006. Science Business: The Promise, the Future, and the Reality of Biotech. Harvard Business School Press, Boston.
Preis, Z.M., 2005. The incentive theory of patents in action. Harvard Law School Doctoral Thesis. September (privately published).
Primack, D., 2011. Why you should blame Wall Street for pharma's startup problem. Fortune (December), 82.
Scherer, F.M., 1966. Time-cost trade-offs in uncertain empirical research projects. Naval Research Logistics Quarterly 13 (March), 71–82, Reprinted in Innovation and Growth: Schumpeterian Perspectives (MIT Press: 1984), Chapter 2.
Scherer, F.M., 1996. Industry Structure, Strategy, and Public Policy. HarperCollins, New York.
Scherer, F.M., 2007, September. Parallel R&D paths revisited. John F. Kennedy School of Government working paper RWP07-049.
Scherer, F.M., 2010. Pharmaceutical innovation. In: Hall, B., Rosenberg, N. (Eds.), Handbook of the Economics of Innovation. North-Holland, Amsterdam (Chapter 12).
Scherer, F.M., 2013. R&D costs and productivity in biopharmaceuticals, John F. Kennedy School of Government working paper RWP11-046. In: Culyer, A. (Ed.), Encyclopedia of Health Economics. Elsevier, Oxford.
Sobel, D., 1995. Longitude. Walker, New York.

---

where a product is often covered by thousands of patents. See Scherer (2010, pp. 552 and 560–56). See also Comanor and Scherer (1969).

PART III

OTHER MONOPOLISTIC PRACTICES

9

Rev Ind Organ (2015) 46:5–23
DOI 10.1007/s11151-014-9425-0

The Federal Trade Commission, Oligopoly, and Shared Monopoly

F. M. Scherer

Published online: 8 July 2014
© Springer Science+Business Media New York 2014

Abstract This paper, written for a centennial commemoration of the Federal Trade Commission's creation, reviews the history of two major cases—the tetracycline case of the 1950s and 1960s and the suit against four (eventually three) ready-to-eat breakfast cereal manufacturers in the 1970s. Those actions addressed one of the most difficult problems in U.S. antitrust jurisprudence: how to deal with the behavior of oligopolistic firms sufficiently few in number that they refrain from active price competition even without entering into explicit price-fixing agreements.

Keywords Antitrust · Federal Trade Commission · Oligopoly · Conscious parallelism

1 Introduction

One of the most important but equally difficult problems faced by antitrust agencies is posed by oligopolistic firms sufficiently few in number that they refrain from active price competition even without entering into explicit price-fixing agreements. Expanding upon a tradition extending back in time at least to Cournot (1838), Chamberlin (1933) crystallized the dilemma (quoting from p. 48 of the 1948 edition):

> If each [seller] seeks his maximum profit rationally and intelligently, he will realize that when there are only two or a few sellers his own move has a considerable effect upon his competitors, and that this makes it idle to suppose that

---

F. M. Scherer: F.T.C. Bureau of Economics director, 1974–1976.

F. M. Scherer (✉)
John F. Kennedy School of Government, Harvard University, Cambridge, MA 02138, USA
e-mail: mike_scherer@hks.harvard.edu

 Springer

they will accept without retaliation the losses he forces upon them. Since the result of a cut by any one is inevitably to decrease his own profits, no one will cut, and, although the sellers are entirely independent, the equilibrium result is the same as though there were a monopolistic agreement among them.

Section 1 of the U.S. Sherman Act (1890) pronounced as illegal "every contract, combination...or conspiracy in restraint of trade or commerce among the several States." Early interpretations by the Supreme Court made it clear that explicit price-fixing agreements among sellers were per se illegal. But what if no evidence of clear-cut agreement could be produced?

Clarification appeared to emerge when the three leading cigarette makers were found to have violated Sherman Act Sec. 1 even without evidence of meetings, messages, or explicit agreements. As the Supreme Court declared:[1]

> No formal agreement is necessary to constitute an unlawful conspiracy. Often crimes are a matter of inference deduced from the acts of the person accused and done in pursuance of a criminal purpose.... The essential combination or conspiracy in violation of the Sherman Act may be found in a course of dealing or other circumstances as well as in an exchange of words. Where the circumstances are such as to warrant a jury in finding that the conspirators had a unity or purpose or a common design and understanding, or a meeting of minds in an unlawful arrangement, the conclusion that a conspiracy is established is justified.

This decision established the basis of a "conscious parallelism" doctrine allowing illegal price-fixing to be inferred circumstantially from the conduct of the relevant oligopolists without direct evidence of formal agreements.

Subsequent judicial pronouncements, including one to be reviewed in more detail here, injected new precedential uncertainty, rejecting without clear delineation some claims of illegality associated with merely parallel and seemingly oligopolistic behavior while sustaining others.[2] It would not be excessive to say that the U.S. competition policy communities found themselves in intellectual crisis. In an influential book, for example, Kaysen and Turner (1959, p. 110) concluded that:

> The principal defect of present antitrust law is its inability to cope with market power created by jointly acting oligopolists.... [W]e believe it is safe to say that a considerable number of industrial markets exist in which oligopolists, acting jointly, possess substantial degrees of market power, which they exercise without engaging in conduct violating the Sherman Act.

Perceiving the inability of competition policy to deal with tacitly cooperative oligopoly behavior, some—e.g., Kaysen and Turner, a 1968 White House task force on antitrust policy, and legislation (S. 1167) offered by Senator Philip Hart in 1972—

---

[1]   American Tobacco Co. et al. v. U.S., 328 U.S. 781, 809 (1946).

[2]   There are many reviews of the cases. For my own, see Scherer and Ross (1990, pp. 339–346).

 Springer

[3]proposed the targeted breakup of tightly oligopolistic industries. These proposals proved to be too ambitious for an era marked by increasing economic conservatism. Still others, such as Posner (1976, pp. 71, 76), advocated invigorated antitrust action against inferentially collusive price-raising in oligopoly markets without requiring "evidence… that the collusion was explicit rather than tacit", contrasting his preferred approach to the "cops and robbers" approach implied in requiring proof of explicit collusion, successful or unsuccessful.[4]

Most of the "great cases" dealing with tacit collusion or conscious parallelism were filed by the Department of Justice, enabled with potentially criminal sanctions, or by aggrieved private parties. The Federal Trade Commission (F.T.C.), however, also has a history of grappling with the problem.

In this paper I analyze two such cases, an early one involving the antibiotic tetracycline, and a "shared monopoly" case in the 1970s against the four leading ready-to-eat breakfast cereal producers. In both cases I played a bit part—in the tetracycline case, as assistant to an economist for the Pfizer Company; in breakfast cereals, as Bureau of Economics director and then witness for the F.T.C. I ignore other F.T.C. cases entailing so-called "facilitating practices"—e.g., its successful challenge to steel and cement industry basing point pricing systems in the 1940s[5] and its thwarted effort concerning the pricing of tetraethyl lead in the early 1980s.[6]

2 The Tetracycline Case

Tetracycline was the most important early member of the broad spectrum antibiotic family, called "broad" because they are effective against both gram-negative and gram-positive bacterial infections. (The terminology is based upon a nineteenth century staining test.) Its earlier (narrow-spectrum) predecessors included Salvarsan, used beginning in 1908 to combat syphilis; the sulfa drugs, effective beginning in the mid-1930s against a limited array of infections; and streptomycin, also effective against some infections. Those were supplemented with the emergence of the antibiotic penicillin, mass-produced by at least 16 different companies in the United States during World War II for military use and then introduced commercially following the war. Recognition of penicillin's molecular structure and efficacy led soon thereafter to the discovery of broad-spectrum antibiotics, among which tetracycline proved to have the best combination of therapeutic efficacy and tolerable side effects.

The large number of companies producing penicillin gave rise to greatly improved productivity and fierce price competition, which drove prices down with astonishing rapidity and led to the exit of many producers. In addition to a wider span of therapeutic

---

[3] For texts of the White House (Neal Report) and Hart proposals, see Goldschmid et al. (1974, pp. 444–456). That volume brings together the principal dissenting schools of thought on industrial concentration and its economic consequences.

[4] That Judge Posner continues to hold this view is implied in the decision he wrote in *High Fructose Corn Syrup Antitrust Litigation*, 295 F. 3rd 651 (2002).

[5] *F.T.C. v. Cement Institute et al.*, 333 U.S. 683 (1948); and *Triangle Conduit and Cable Co. et al. v. F.T.C.*, 168 F. 2d 175 (1948).

[6] *E. I. du Pont de Nemours and Co. et al. v. F.T.C.*, 729 F. 2d 128 (1984).

🕲 Springer

effects, the new broad spectrum "wonder drugs" were patented, which limited entry and hence price competition. Their high and seemingly rigid prices led to an investigation by the Federal Trade Commission, precipitating the publication in June 1958 of a report, *Economic Report on Antibiotics Manufacture*. It can fairly be characterized as a jewel in the F.T.C.'s "sunlight" function crown,[7] ranking with earlier reports on the petroleum industry, the steel industry, and the American Tobacco Company as classics, using historical and statistical analysis to illuminate how important industries function and malfunction.

The *Antibiotics* report documented a number of important phenomena. For one, it showed that the production of post-penicillin antibiotics had become quite concentrated, with half of total antibiotics production eventually attributable to only two companies, Pfizer and American Cyanamid. Second, it traced a history of patent interferences, threatened Patent Office denials, and negotiated inter-company settlements on a key patent protecting tetracycline, which was awarded eventually to Pfizer. Third, after substantial early price reductions were quickly matched by the major producers, list prices to retailers and hospitals for the several main broad-spectrum antibiotics stabilized at $5.10 for bottles of sixteen 250-mg. capsules in September 1951 and remained at that level at least until 1958, when the report was sent to the printers.

Fourth, it showed that the gross profit ratio—i.e., sales revenues less direct manufacturing costs as a percentage of sales—for broad-spectrum antibiotics remained in the neighborhood of 75 percent from 1950 through 1956, when the discovered data terminated. For two antibiotics producers whose identities were not revealed, net profits before taxes were more than 50 percent of assets in 1956. Left in the shadows of the *Antibiotics* report's sunlight were the behavioral phenomena through which entry-excluding patent settlements, rigid prices, and high profits had been achieved. On July 28, 1958—i.e., in the month following the *Antibiotics* report's publication—a complaint alleging antitrust law violations was filed by the Federal Trade Commission. Further discovery and a trial compiling a record of 11,000 testimony pages followed.

2.1 The F.T.C. Proceedings

Five companies were charged in the F.T.C. complaint—Pfizer, ultimate recipient of the basic tetracycline patent; American Cyanamid and Bristol-Myers, early claimants to the invention of tetracycline and ultimately licensed to produce it; and Upjohn and Olin-Mathiesson (later merged with Squibb), who contracted with Bristol-Myers to buy bulk tetracycline and hence sold it to hospitals and retailers. The F.T.C. complaint alleged inter alia that respondent companies had colluded to ensure that an entry-limiting patent would be issued on tetracycline, that they had agreed to restrict licenses on the resulting patent to the five named firms, and that they had colluded tacitly or expressly to fix the prices of tetracycline and related broad-spectrum antibiotics.

To understand the crucial implications of the patent charges, some organic chemistry—perhaps unprecedented in an economics journal—is needed. Figure 1 reproduces, from p. 249 of the F.T.C.'s *Antibiotics* report, chemical structure dia-

---

[7] On the F.T.C.'s "sunlight" function, characterized in a 1914 tract by Louis Brandeis, see Scherer (1990).

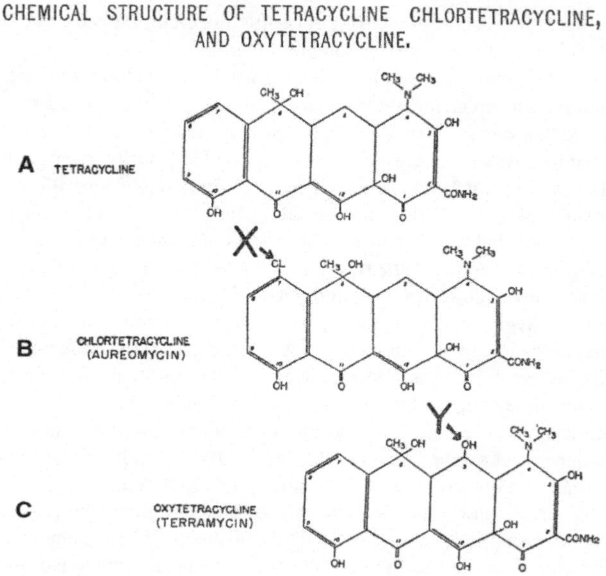

CHEMICAL STRUCTURE OF TETRACYCLINE CHLORTETRACYCLINE, AND OXYTETRACYCLINE.

Fig. 1 Chemical structure of tetracycline, chlortetracycline, and oxytetracycline. *Source*: Henry F. Dowling, Tetracycline, Medical Encyclopedia, Inc., New York, 1955, p. 14

grams for the three leading broad-spectrum antibiotics sold during the 1950s. Each of the three is a quadruple benzene ring, i.e., with each ring containing six interlinked carbon atoms, to which were attached at the vertices diverse additional atoms or combinations of atoms.[8]

The first broad-spectrum antibiotic introduced commercially (in 1948) was American Cyanamid's chlortetracycline (brand name Aureomycin), marked B in the diagram. Pfizer followed in 1950 with oxytetracycline (brand name Terramycin), marked C in the diagram. It differed from the original American Cyanamid B molecule with the addition of an OH (hydrogen–oxygen) radical at the top vertex of the third ring (marked Y in the diagram) and deletion of a chlorine atom at the top of the first ring (marked X in diagram B). Working with a Harvard University professor, a Pfizer chemist, Dr. Lloyd Conover, inferred that superior efficacy and safety might be achieved by simply removing the chlorine ion marked X from chlortetracycline without adding the OH radical marked Y. Conover et al. applied for a patent in 1952. But in short order three other firms—American Cyanamid, Heyden Chemical (promptly acquired by American Cyanamid), and (for a salt of tetracycline) Bristol-Myers—filed patents claiming

---

[8] Another early drug with therapeutic effects extending beyond penicillin was streptomycin. It had a rather different structure comprising six full and one partial benzene rings. I ignore here still another early broad-spectrum drug—Parke Davis' chloramphenicol, which had only one closed benzene ring plus two open ones. It was marketed independently but at prices similar to the drugs featured here.

⌬ Springer

rights to tetracycline. A complex series of conflicting claim procedures (called "inter-ferences") were initiated within the Patent Office.

There were two main allegations of conspiracy in connection with the patent dis-putes. Documents revealed that the companies entangled in the interferences were anx-ious to ensure that *one of them*—which one was of secondary importance—obtained patent protection. American Cyanamid soon conceded priority to Pfizer in exchange for a full license; Bristol Myers followed suit, agreeing to a license allowing inter alia royalty-bearing sales to its bulk customers Olin-Mathiesson (later Squibb) and Upjohn. The F.T.C. alleged that in these negotiations the companies had explicitly agreed to limit the allocation of tetracycline rights to those five, but company executives denied under oath that any such restrictive agreement had been reached.

The second allegation was that the companies participating in the Patent Office's interference procedures had withheld relevant information from the patent examiner. In particular, tetracycline was first produced by "deschlorinating" chlortetracycline, although later, direct fermentation processes eliminating this step were developed. But if chemists could remove the chlorine ion from chlortetracycline, so also might nature. Evidence was produced before the Patent Office examiner that trace quantities of tetracycline were in fact found without further manipulation in the chlortetracycline produced by American Cyanamid. Their magnitude and the feasibility of extracting them for commercial purposes were heatedly disputed. If in fact medically useable tetracycline was co-produced in and recoverable from the previously manufactured chlortetracycline, that fact could serve as proof of prior (i.e., pre-tetracycline patent filing) discovery and commercial availability, which could prevent issuance of a tetra-cycline patent.

When the contending companies agreed to settle their disputes and accede to the grant of a patent to Pfizer, the interference procedure was ended without further explo-ration of the co-production controversy. The Federal Trade Commission alleged that in settling the priority question without resolving the co-production question, the com-panies withheld crucial information from the Patent Office and hence allowed a patent to be issued fraudulently.

The main non-patent facet of the F.T.C.'s complaint alleged conspiracy in setting and rigidly maintaining prices so far above costs that an inference of competitive price-setting appeared implausible. Company executives again insisted under oath that they had not joined collusively to set and maintain common prices. Expert witnesses for the companies adduced a variety of explanations as to why the oligopolistic market conditions fostered high and identical pricing without illegal collusion.

Pfizer retained M. J. (Joe) Peck as its principal economic consultant. Joe in turn hired me, fresh from an MBA program and without graduate-level training in price theory or industrial organization, as his assistant.[9] My principal job was to analyze detailed data on the prices quoted to city-county-state (CCS) hospitals.

I no longer retain any paper records from that analysis, but I have a distinct memory of what I found. Prices were in fact mostly uniform, marred on occasion in deviations initiated by wholesalers for the major tetracycline producers. When significant price

---

[9] My work on that case and my collaboration with Peck on a 1962 book led me to switch from a doctoral program in business administration to Ph.D. studies in economics at Harvard University.

level adjustments did occur, it seemed clear that there was a pattern of price leadership and close followership, although I had not read at all in the economic literature on price leadership. I performed a more perfunctory analysis of transactions involving the Armed Services Medical Procurement Agency, showing much less complete concord among sellers on how those unusually large and profitable transactions should be priced.

Roughly 3 years after this experience I participated in a graduate course taught by Thomas Schelling and read his famous book (Schelling 1960). His discussion on focal point coordination of behavior combined with what I learned in analyzing tetracycline pricing to induce my own theory of focal point pricing, which, I asserted in Scherer (1967), helped explain what actually occurred in tetracycline pricing.

Joe Peck was viewed by Pfizer's lawyers as too young to present as a witness in the F.T.C. proceedings, so he and I briefed a prominent Yale University economist, John Perry Miller, to offer the actual testimony. I no longer remember what he testified. I do recall attending a pre-trial meeting of economists representing each of the five companies accused by the F.T.C. It was disconcerting to realize that each of the economists had a different theory as to how the companies set their prices.[10] It was even more disconcerting, given that all of the economists planned to testify to the absence of explicit collusion, that some of the attendees referred to the five companies as "the club."

In December 1959, Senator Estes Kefauver shifted his attention in a series of *Administered Prices* hearings from steel, autos and the like to pharmaceuticals; see U.S. Senate (June 1961). He was undoubtedly influenced in this choice by the F.T.C. *Antibiotics* report's evidence on high prices and profits. Joe and I discussed Pfizer's request for a briefing on how Pfizer should structure its testimony before the Kefauver committee. We advised Pfizer, "When Kefauver says profits, you respond R&D."

For decades thereafter my conscience was troubled over the realization that I might have contributed in a small way to misleading the Senate and hence the American public. I struggled professionally with several facets of the problem on numerous occasions before reaching what I consider a definitive resolution in Scherer (2010, pp. 562–569).

The trial proceeded, and at the end, the hearing examiner concluded that the Commission staff had not proved conspiracy either to limit competition through the handling of co-production claims before the Patent Office or to fix uncompetitive prices.[11] The F.T.C. enforcement staff appealed this decision to the five-member Commission, and in August 1963, the Commission overturned the examiner's decision and concluded that the respondents had in fact violated antitrust law.[12]

The full Commission agreed that conspiracy to withhold from the Patent Office essential information on co-production was not proven. But Pfizer and American Cyanamid, the Commission ruled, had fraudulently *enforced* the resulting tetracycline

---

[10] As I view the case in retrospect, I wonder whether the divergence of theories may have confused the administrative law judge into accepting an inference of price competition subsequently reversed by the full Commission.

[11] The examiner's 1961 decision does not appear to have been published in the *F.T.C. Reports*.

[12] *In the matter of American Cyanamid Co. et al.*, 63 F.T.C. 1747 (1963).

⑩ Springer

patent when they knew, on the basis of co-production information they had withheld, it should not have been issued. The Commission rejected the hearing examiner's inference that the Conover tetracycline patent was not a vital deterrent to entry because entry could have been blocked anyway by enforcement of American Cyanamid's chlortetracycline patent.

On the pricing charges, the hearing examiner accepted the respondents' claims that they were competing too fiercely for both patent rights and subsequent sales to sustain a plausible price-fixing agreement. The Commission accepted that there was no evidence of an express or formal agreement. But invoking prior conscious parallelism precedents, the commissioners ruled that violation of the law could be found in the parallelism of prices and among other things in the exchange of price lists, documented complaints from one company to others that price uniformity was being violated, and other circumstantial evidence.

The Commission expressly rejected the hearing examiner's finding that the companies' distribution to purchasers of "free" tetracycline supplies was a less visible form of price competition belying the uniformity of prices actually charged. It inferred instead that the award of "free goods" was used as a means for *preventing* general price reductions and therefore (p. 1873) as circumstantial evidence of agreement to stabilize prices.[13] Finding more generally that the five respondents had violated the antitrust laws through their conduct, the Commission (with one Commissioner dissenting on Squibb and Upjohn) ordered them to set new and independent prices for their antibiotics and to license both the tetracycline patent and two chlortetracycline patents to any domestic applicant at a 2.5 percent ad valorem royalty.

Unsurprisingly, the companies appealed to higher authority. A focal point of their appeal was the claim that Paul Rand Dixon, chairman of the Commission at the time of the 1963 decision, was prejudiced because he had served previously as chief of staff in the Kefauver Committee investigation of pharmaceutical prices and profits. The Commission's decision was vacated by an appellate court,[14] and the case was remanded for de novo rehearing without the participation of Commissioner Dixon.

In 1966 the full Commission, with Paul Rand Dixon recused, ordered a partial retrial by a new hearing examiner. The ALJ was ordered to confine testimony to the question of fraud upon the Patent Office concerning possible co-production of tetracycline in the manufacture of chlortetracycline.

The Patent Office examiner who had processed the tetracycline patent was called, along with a Pfizer chemist. The patent examiner's memory of events some 15 years earlier was unsurprisingly indistinct. He testified nevertheless that he was not aware that American Cyanamid's chlortetracycline actually contained tetracycline. And characterizing the law on such co-production, he stated unequivocally that if there was proof that the chlortetracycline broth actually contained tetracycline, the Conover tetracycline patent could not have been issued. The new F.T.C. hearing examiner therefore concluded that the Conover patent could not have been obtained and enforced without

---

[13] I suggest in Scherer (1967, p. 501) that there was focal point coordination of the percentages of order quantities filled through free goods provision as well as in formally quoted pricing.

[14] *American Cyanamid Co. et al. v. F.T.C.*, 363 F. 2nd 757 (1966).

anticompetitive withholding of relevant information by the tetracycline producers and hence that the Commission's earlier order on patent licensing should be reinstated.[15]

The Commission in turn, with Mr. Dixon recused, ordered that its prior decision requiring compulsory licensing of the tetracycline and chlortetracycline patents be enforced.[16] Commissioner Mary Gardiner Jones dissented in part, arguing that, since no valid tetracycline patent would have been issued had the parties provided full information on co-production, the patents should be licensed at zero royalty rates rather than the 2.5 percent rate approved by the Commission majority.[17]

The Commission's final opinion observed inter alia that new firms had already entered the production of tetracycline without a license from Pfizer or American Cyanamid. This was probably attributable to the uncertain validity of the Conover tetracycline patent as a result of the Commission's revelations and an assumption by would-be tetracycline producers that attempts by Pfizer or Cyanamid to sue for infringement would revive the validity question to the patent holders' disadvantage.

On the price collusion aspects of the F.T.C. intervention (not considered afresh by the new hearing examiner), the Commission decided that ordering simultaneous and independent reissuance of price lists was unnecessary. Given evidence of substantial price declines following the original hearing, it observed further that:

> Mindful that the goal of its order is to remove unlawful restraints and foster future competitive conditions rather than punish for past conduct, two of the four participating members ... believe that the public interest will be adequately served by compulsory licensing and by continued close scrutiny of Pfizer's and Cyanamid's readiness to license others to make and sell tetracycline. In the view of these members, it is now unnecessary to decide whether the uniformity of prices in the 1950's was the result of a price-fixing conspiracy as contended by the complaint counsel or the product of conscious parallelism as respondents seem to suggest.

With two commissioners holding this view and no majority to overturn it, the portion of the original complaint charging price fixing was dismissed.

2.2 The Department of Justice Case

Resolution of the F.T.C.'s tetracycline case was not, however, the end of the story. In 1961, while the F.T.C.'s action was proceeding, the Department of Justice filed its own complaint charging the tetracycline producers with illegal price collusion. Since technically the F.T.C. must allege violations of the 1914 F.T.C. Act prohibiting "unfair methods of competition" while the Department of Justice can directly allege criminal violations of Sherman Act Sec. 1, the two agencies are in principle permitted to pursue the same lead more or less concurrently. What followed was another chain of events

---

[15] *In the matter of American Cyanamid Co. et al.*, 72 F.T.C. 623 (1972).

[16] 72 F.T.C. 623, 657 (1967).

[17] 72 F.T.C. 623, 691–692.

🖄 Springer

showing how difficult it is successfully to sustain cooperative oligopolistic pricing charges in the absence of proof that outright agreements have occurred.

The charges were similar to those thrashed out in the F.T.C. case: collusive pursuit and licensing of the basic tetracycline patent, plus collusion in setting and maintaining identical and noncompetitive prices.[18] As in the F.T.C.'s case, company executives denied explicit collusion in either their patent quest or in pricing; the evidence was largely circumstantial. Government attorneys emphasized among other things the uniformly high prices of tetracycline—e.g., $19.1884 to the U.S. Veterans Administration and $30.60 per bottle of 100 capsules to druggists despite new production cost estimates of between $1.99 and $2.59 per bottle.

A 9-week jury trial was held during 1967 in New York City.[19] Judge Marvin Frankel cautioned the jury that they could not find for conviction if the companies' pricing decisions were taken "independently as a matter of individual business judgment, without any agreement or arrangement or understanding among the parties." Especially in their summation to the jury, prosecution lawyers made much of high prices and implicit profits. Judge Frankel cautioned the jury not to decide simply on the basis of the prices' reasonableness, but:

> I think you will find it helpful to translate the word "unreasonable" to mean "unusual" or "artificial" or "extra-ordinary." By these suggested definitions I am trying to convey the thought that the idea of unreasonableness in the present context is meaningful only if it is understood to refer to kinds of price behavior or price levels which appear to be divorced from variations and differences in available supply or demand or cost or other economic factors that may normally be expected to cause variations or changes in the prices charged in a competitive market. To put the thought in another and slightly shorter way, the charge of unreasonableness in this case is material only insofar as it poses the issue of whether the prices involved exhibited qualities or peculiarities of a type that could be deemed evidence that such prices resulted from agreement rather than competition....[20]

The jury found the defendants guilty on all counts, and maximum fines were imposed.

On appeal, however, the conviction was reversed in a 2-1 split of the reviewing judges, and a new trial was ordered. The appeals court majority stated that in devoting substantial attention to such "inflammatory issues" as patents, profits, and pricing, Judge Frankel had failed to focus the jury's attention on the key issue of what agreements if any were reached at company executives' meetings with one another.[21] A 2-1 majority of other Second Circuit appellate judges denied a petition for rehearing

---

[18] This account is abbreviated from my discussion of the Justice Department case in the 1980 and 1990 versions of my textbook.

[19] Apparently, commencement of the formal trial was delayed until it appeared that the F.T.C. case was bogged down.

[20] *U.S. v. Charles Pfizer & Co. et al.*, from pp. 6270–6271 of the trial record. The principal published opinion by Judge Frankel was his rejection of defendants' motion to dismiss at the conclusion of the jury trial. *U.S. v. Charles Pfizer & Co. Inc. et al.*, 281 F. Supp. 837 (1968).

[21] *Charles Pfizer and Co. et al. v. U.S.*, 426 F. 2nd 32, 39–43 (1970).

en banc, and on further appeal, the reversal was implicitly upheld when the Supreme Court divided 3-3 on granting certiorari.[22]

A new trial was then held. Nearly 6 years after the first Justice Department trial and the F.T.C.'s final tetracycline case resolution order, a different district court judge ruled in favor of the defendants.[23] In a brief opinion, Judge Canella found that the Justice Department had not conclusively shown that Pfizer's limits on the number of tetracycline licenses and the several producers' parallel pricing had resulted from conspiracy, since they might alternatively have stemmed from Pfizer's independent business judgment and a natural tendency toward uniform pricing in the highly concentrated, prescription-oriented market for antibiotics. On such reefs can conscious parallelism allegations founder.

3 The Breakfast Cereal Case

During the 1960s the Federal Trade Commission refrained from pursuing "great" cases, focusing instead on less complex antitrust issues such as mergers and price discrimination, the latter often involving relatively small firms.[24] Its tendency to devote its antitrust resources mainly to unimportant matters was criticized by an American Bar Association panel (1969) and by Ralph Nader's "Raiders" in 1972.[25]

On taking office as President in 1969, Richard M. Nixon appointed a new chairman with a mandate to invigorate the Commission's performance. His first chair, Caspar Weinberger, left after nine months to head the Office of Management and Budget. He was replaced by Miles Kirkpatrick, who had previously led the critical American Bar Association report. The third Nixon reform chairman, Lewis Engman, took office in March of 1973.

A widely held belief at the time was that the antitrust agencies should become more vigorous in dealing with monopolistic and tightly oligopolistic industries that maintained high prices and profits without evident overt collusion—i.e., with the conscious parallelism problem. Several major F.T.C. cases were initiated, involving inter alia Xerox Corporation,[26] the eight leading petroleum companies, Continental Baking (producer of Wonder Bread), automobile "crash" parts, tetraethyl lead, and (never carried to the stage of an actual complaint) the broader auto industry. The "shared monopoly" case that hewed most closely to a pure conscious parallelism paradigm challenged the breakfast cereal oligopoly, led by Kellogg, General Mills, and General Foods (i.e., Post).[27]

---

[22] 404 U.S. 548 (1972).

[23] 367 F. Supp. 91 (1973).

[24] On the F.T.C.'s response to House of Representatives Small Business Committee criticism for laxity in its price discrimination enforcement, see my testimony, reproduced in Scherer (2000, Chapter 12).

[25] On the latter, see Green et al. (1972).

[26] For my analysis of the Xerox case, see Scherer (2008, pp. 1054–1057).

[27] The Department of Justice launched its own shared monopoly case against the leading automobile tire producers.

The original case complaint was filed in February 1972—during the chairmanship of Miles Kirkpatrick and when H. Michael Mann, on leave from Boston College, was director of the Bureau of Economics. Elements of the case reflected Mann's past emphasis on advertising as a contributor to monopoly profits in oligopolistic industries. Among other things, the complaint alleged that by proliferating brands and promoting trademarks inter alia through intensive advertising, high barriers to entry had been created.[28] An unusually tough remedy was sought—divestiture of independent companies from the leading cereal makers plus compulsory licensing of some brand formulas and trademarks (up to three percent of industry sales for each new rival) to allow the newly independent entities to compete on roughly equal terms.[29]

In most other respects the case was squarely in the "conscious parallelism" tradition, relabeled "shared monopoly." The four leading ready-to-eat cereal oligopolists controlled roughly 90 percent of industry sales, and profits were high. Numerous competitors had been acquired in the past by the Big Four, and the surviving industry leaders refrained among other things from offering lower-priced private label cereals despite requests from grocery retailers, sometimes closing down the private-label operations of acquired entities. High prices and profits, the complaint alleged, were maintained through "forbearance" in price setting and the handling of such quasi-price competitive tools as discounts to retailers, newspaper "cents off" coupons, and in-pack premiums (e.g., plastic toys). As the ultimate Administrative Law Judge observed, "The words 'conspire', 'contract', or 'agree'... are nowhere to be found in the complaint."[30] Indeed, in an initial clarifying memorandum, attorneys for the F.T.C. stated squarely that "Although conspiracy is not alleged in this matter, the common course of action and the interdependent acts of respondents create a common bond that provides the nexus for joinder."

3.1 Theory and Evidence

As the F.T.C. staff prepared its detailed presentation, it was recognized that traditional economic theories did not provide sufficient support for the proposition that heavy advertising significantly discouraged entry. Rescue was found in the work of Schmalensee (1978), who postulated a theoretical model showing that the proliferation of product variants—in cereals, to approximately 150 brands in 1970 from half that number in 1960—could so fill "product characteristics space" that there is insufficient room for outsiders to enter and come anywhere near realizing necessary economies of scale. I for one was taken by the model.[31] I should perhaps have become wary

---

[28]   The original complaint is reproduced in *In re Kellogg Company, et al.*, 99 F.T.C. Reports 8–16 (1982).

[29]   Divestiture plus compulsory (patent) licensing were previously sought in complaints against General Electric and AT&T, but only compulsory licensing was ordered in the relevant cases.

[30]   99 F.T.C. 8, 18.

[31]   It led inter alia to my analyzing additional economic welfare implications in Scherer (1979).

when my home-town newspaper published a syndicated op-ed column reading in part:[32]

> The Federal Trade Commission, which too often of late has seemed to be completely out to lunch, has now apparently decided to be out to breakfast too. How else can one explain the zany action of the FTC in launching legal battle against the leading U.S. cereal manufacturers on the ground that—-I swear, I'm not making this up—the manufacturer is giving the American housewife too wide a choice?

Or I might have been warned when I explained the case to my favorite cousin, an executive on the Kellogg account for the Leo Burnett advertising agency, and he replied, "Good lord! You're attacking Middle America."

There was no appreciable disagreement among the parties as to whether ready-to-eat breakfast cereals comprised a relevant market and that it was highly concentrated. Opinions varied sharply, however, on the allegation of high profits. Subpoenaed data showed after-tax profit returns on assets for five leading cereal makers over the years 1958–1970 to have averaged 19.8 percent—more than twice the average for all manufacturing industry.[33]

The cereal companies also spent unusually high fractions of their sales on advertising—e.g., approximately 10 percent over the years 1974–1977.[34] The F.T.C. staff recognized that this posed a problem for the interpretation of profitability data, since to the extent that advertising is an investment in future sales, it might more appropriately be capitalized and then depreciated in computing returns on assets. Independent research had shown that when certain advertising level and growth relationships prevailed, capitalization instead of expensing could significantly reduce calculated percentage profit returns. The staff therefore retained Thomas Stauffer, author of the leading theoretical analysis (Stauffer 1971), to recalculate rates of return under a range of alternative assumptions and present the evidence at hearings. For the advertising effect decay rates believed to be most plausible (i.e., in the range of 35–80 percent per annum), Stauffer's calculations showed cereal makers' returns to be well above all-industry averages.

On decay rates, however, economists for the F.T.C. encountered an evidentiary dilemma. The most thorough available econometric study revealed a high annual decay rate on the order of 80 percent. Although it was known informally that the study

---

[32] Louis Rukeyser, "FTC Eating Spiked Cornflakes?" Ottawa, Illinois, *Daily Times*, April 6, 1978. The column appeared only a few days after the *Washington Post* named the F.T.C. as "the national nanny" for announcing an effort to declare as an unfair method of competition the intensive advertising of heavily sweetened and otherwise questionably nutritious products on child-oriented television programs. See also Pertschuk (1982, Chapter 3); and for a new version of the space-packing argument, "Corporate Sardines," *The Economist*, May 3, 2014, p. 68.

[33] Prosecution exhibit CX-701A. F.T.C. Line of Business program data available only later showed breakfast cereal makers' pre-tax operating income over the years 1974–1977 to have averaged 39 percent relative to assets—ranking among the top four among 259 manufacturing industries over those years and first in 1977.

[34] From the Federal Trade Commission's *Line of Business* surveys for 1974–1977, which shows cereal advertising/sales ratios to be consistently among the top eight among 259 manufacturing industries. Similar but less comparable figures were submitted in evidence.

🍂 Springer

focused on cereal brands, the authors were required to keep the identity of the industry confidential, writing only (Bass and Parsons 1969, p. 105) that the products studied were sold in supermarkets and that:

> A handful of firms dominate the industry. Each firm closely follows the actions of competitors and reacts quickly to any significant change in advertising, price, or quality.

Thus, no proof of direct relevance could be offered.[35] Economists representing the cereal companies argued that the effects of advertising were much longer-lived, especially for continuing baseline as compared to incremental advertising, with decay rates as low as 10 percent and correspondingly lower adjusted profit ratios.

A central issue in the conscious parallelism allegation was how the cereal makers set and maintained prices that yielded above-average profits. I was primarily responsible for that part of the analysis. It was clear that a system of price leadership existed, with Kellogg serving most (but not all) of the time as price leader. Documents discovered in the case revealed that Kellogg was proud of its leadership role. For example, in a 1966 talk, a top Kellogg executive quoted an experienced advertising executive as telling him:[36]

> He said this: "In my judgment there is no area in the food business today in which the true qualities of industry leadership are more aptly displayed than in the cereal industry, where Kellogg provides strong and consistent leadership in building and expanding the profitable climate of true growth, virtually free from destructive pricing and promotional practices that—in many similar product categories—have undermined the vitality that is so necessary in their industry's continued progress."

The speech was delivered at a meeting of Kellogg sales managers, but it would not be unreasonable to infer that similar views were expressed at the periodic meetings of the Cereal Institute trade association, encompassing the leading rivals. The same speaker continued:

> Kellogg has a long history of consistently *resisting* price cutting and gimmicks and withstanding competitive pressure in these arenas with notable restraint—up to the point where it was necessary to participate—overwhelmingly—in order to put an end to destructive practices.

The record shows that indeed Kellogg did launch occasional, narrowly targeted, price wars against private label cereal makers (notably, firms other than those charged in the F.T.C. proceeding) and that the usual outcome was a return to higher prices.

Interpretation of the price leadership evidence was complicated by the fact that the main cereal producers offered many different brands at varying prices. My analysis of the data suggested that price leadership was exercised in "rounds," with each round encompassing numerous but not all varieties. Out of 15 unambiguous price increase

---

[35] But see the hint disclosed by the ALJ at 99 F.T.C. 8, 222.

[36] Speech of C. A. Tornebene in December 1966. Exhibit CX-K-549P.

 Springer

rounds between 1965 and 1970 with fairly complete documentation, Kellogg led in 12 and on only one occasion was not followed by its leading rivals, General Mills and General Foods. I presented inter alia a regression analysis relating incremental revenue raised in the rounds to company market shares. The regressions were computed for me by F.T.C. staff economists, but turned out in hindsight to be flawed, since the staff had inadvertently reversed some of the left- and right-hand side variables.[37]

My price leadership testimony was furiously challenged by economic witnesses for the cereal companies. The most telling blow came from Jesse Markham, expert witness for Kellogg. Markham had been the teacher in my first graduate industrial organization course, my colleague and mentor for 3 years at Princeton University, and continued to be a close friend. In both my testimony and the first (1970) edition of my textbook, I referred to Markham's (1951) pioneering analysis of price leadership, distinguishing among other things leadership that was relatively ineffective from leadership "in lieu of overt collusion."

In both cases, however, I differentiated my own analysis of the conditions necessary for price leadership to yield cooperative oligopoly price levels from those articulated by Markham. In particular, I disagreed with Markham's assertion that it was necessary for rivals' products to be "extremely close substitutes" for price leadership to be effective as a coordinating mechanism. In his rebuttal testimony, Markham adopted an attitude of rueful disappointment and said in effect:[38]

> Yes, Dr. Scherer was my student. But I'm afraid he didn't learn his lessons well enough. He overlooks the crucial third condition in my article for the success of price leadership—the requirement that products be extremely close substitutes.

In truth, I did not overlook it but rejected it, largely as a result of my own research on successful price leadership in many industries, including the automobile industry, which Markham singled out in his testimony as one in which products were so heterogeneous as to make price leadership "meaningless."[39]

There was parallelism too in the refusal of leading cereal companies to supply private-label cereal (with Ralston as an exception), in the limitation of special "trade" discounts to retailers, and in the use of "in-pack" premiums. The inclusion of "in-pack" toys and the like was extensive in the 1940s and 1950s. But in the summer of 1957, it fell from as high as 22 percent to 1 percent of boxes sold and remained there

---

[37] I didn't know about the flaw when I testified, because under F.T.C. rules, once a witness begins testifying, he is unable to discuss the substance of his testimony with the staff. My normal procedure in such matters is to "do it myself," but at the time, personal computers with useable regression packages did not exist.

[38] The precis here is my reconstruction from memory, not necessarily true to the original. Markham pursued on multiple occasions a similar routine toward my heretical deviations from his teachings.

[39] Quoted by the administrative law judge in 99 F.T.C. 8, 83. My knowledge of the auto industry was based in part upon the extant industrial organization literature but also on a detailed case study done within Ford Motor Company by Joe Peck and me in 1959. In my May 1976 memorandum urging the Federal Trade Commission to undertake an investigation of the automobile industry, I wrote that "General Motors has traditionally been the price leader, and it sets prices to achieve a target rate of return, no doubt taking into account in recent years the threat of increased imports. The other makers tend to fall into line or even back off when their own price announcements preceded and prove to be inconsistent with GM's."

🖄 Springer

for at least a decade. On my hunch, the F.T.C. staff found an article in a leading trade journal published several months before the decline was observable that:[40]

> The great tide of premiums offered by cereal manufacturers may be stemmed shortly. Several trade sources said last week that the major cereal suppliers are formulating an agreement to drop package inserts. The reason given was excessive package breakage.

A decade later, an internal General Foods staff analysis confronted a rumor that rivals might break "the industry guideline" and observed that:

> To date, the three major manufacturers ... have been respecting an "unwritten rule" stemming from fierce and unprofitable competition in the early and middle '50s, that they have retail exposure with only one pack-in premium in one brand at a given time.

This was the closest the F.T.C.'s evidence came to showing an actual agreement rather than follow-the-leader behavior. But from it an inference might at least be drawn that the cereal makers were consciously working together toward common goals.

3.2 Political and Legal Difficulties

As the Federal Trade Commission wound up its case in chief, it was widely believed that it had presented very strong arguments. At that point, Kellogg realized that its blue-stocking New York law firm was floundering. It fired them and brought in a new team, headed by Frederick Furth with his smaller San Francisco-based firm. Furth recognized that the case might be won not only in the courtroom but also in the halls of Congress and public opinion. A substantial lobbying and public relations campaign was mounted. And among other things, Furth brought into the case the American Federation of Grain Millers' union, persuaded inter alia by a consultants' study (almost surely fallaciously) that divestiture of cereal company plants would cause sizeable employment losses for union members.

Compounding the public relations problem was the fact that the F.T.C.'s new chairman, Michael Pertschuk, contemplated a major rule-making (i.e., consumer protection mandate) that would attack the extensive advertising of breakfast cereals and related products on child-oriented television programs. I remember vividly a meeting of key cereal case staff in 1978 whose thrust was, "Pertschuk is going public on kid vid next week. If he does, our case is lost. What can we do?" The answer was, nothing, because under F.T.C. rules, the enforcement staff are not allowed to communicate with Commission members about ongoing cases. So Chairman Pertschuk went public, the Federal Trade Commission became the "national nanny," and turmoil broke out on Capitol Hill.[41] Among other things, bills were filed (but not passed) that would have ended the case or removed the Commission's authority to impose a divestiture remedy. The F.T.C.'s appropriation was held in limbo for 2 years, with occasional man-

---

[40] "Cereal Makers' Agreement May Stem Premium Tide," *Supermarket News*, March 11, 1957, p. 4.

[41] For Pertschuk's own reflection, see Pertschuk (1982, ch. 3).

 Springer

dated work stoppages. And in the final week of the 1979 presidential campaign, both major candidates—Jimmy Carter and Ronald Reagan—gave speeches in Michigan disavowing continuation of the cereal proceedings.

Another serious problem emerged closer to home. After almost all of the testimonial record (eventually totaling 20,000 pages with exhibits) was completed, excepting only a few remaining witnesses from the cereal companies, presiding administrative law judge Hinkes faced a difficult personal dilemma. His wife was grievously ill and needed constant care, which she could best obtain by moving in with her daughter in California. Judge Hinkes wanted to join her, but felt obliged to see the case through to completion before taking full retirement. He therefore retired formally from the Commission but was retained under a temporary employment contract to complete the case. Cereal company lawyers stormed Capitol Hill, claiming that because Mr. Hinkes' civil service tenure was ended and he could be released from employment on short notice (which he wanted anyway!), he could not be impartial, and therefore he had to be replaced. Pressure from Capitol Hill forced the Commission to discharge Hinkes and appoint a different ALJ, Alvin Berman, to hear the final witnesses, read the record, and render a decision.

After presiding over the remaining testimony (including Jesse Markham's), the new administrative law judge issued his decision, comprising 253 finely printed pages. He agreed that the industry as defined was highly concentrated. On most other points, he rejected the Commission staff's charges. For example, on the profits debate, he opted (p. 221) for the lowest decay rate (10 percent) propounded by cereal company witnesses, asserting that "'because of the admitted imprecision of the Koyck model...I am compelled to accept the lowest rate (the one most favorable to respondents' position) which appears to be possibly correct." This led to adjusted profit returns no higher than those for manufacturing industry benchmarks. That in turn led to a conclusion (p. 260) that "complaint counsel's factual assertion basic to its shared monopoly theory, that respondents and others in the RTE industry realized supracompetitive profits, fails for lack of proof." From this followed a conclusion that the cereal companies could not be held responsible for the lack of competitive entry.

My testimony on price leadership was rejected largely on the basis of Professor Markham's criticism, and so (p. 266) "there has been a total failure to demonstrate pricing coordination among respondents." Other suggestions of tacit or explicit collusion were rejected for lack of conclusive proof, because the cereal companies were found to have been competing vigorously in their new product and advertising efforts, and because the F.T.C. staff's initial assertion that no evidence of explicit collusion would be offered precluded attaching weight to later evidence supporting that hypothesis.[42] Thus, Judge Berman ordered that the case be dismissed.

What happened next was even more unprecedented. It is not uncommon for the losing party to appeal an administrative law judge's decision to the full Commission. Asserting that the ALJ decision was "riddled throughout with major procedural orders," the case staff asked that an appeal be lodged. But division chiefs appointedby

---

[42] For his treatment of the in-pack premium evidence, among other things totally ignoring the lead time requisites emphasized in my testimony, see 99 F.T.C. 8, 121–127.

 Springer

the new Reagan Administration chairman refused to forward their appeal to the Commission. The staff therefore bypassed their superiors and appealed directly to the Commission. Faced with this staff mutiny, the four sitting commissioners (with one chair vacant) weighed the merits of fully reviewing the case findings and (with a dissent from former chairman and still commissioner Pertschuk) chose not to do so. Commissioner Patricia Bailey articulated her own view (pp. 288–289) of the majority's decision to vacate the Administrative Law Judge's decision "with no precedential or even persuasive authority for any proposition whatsoever":

> [W]e should not undertake to restructure an industry under Section 5 of the FTC Act without a clear supportive signal from Congress. In this case, the signals are, for the present, quite to the contrary—as they were not so apparently in 1972 when this complaint was issued.... The paradox we are left with is that while there may be a legitimate concern about the anticompetitive effects of the exercise of oligopoly power, it is rarely true that these concerns will mandate an administrative agency decision to restructure an industry short of a legislative warrant to that effect.

And so ended the Federal Trade Commission's other great conscious parallelism case.

Its consequences, however, did not end. Over 11 years following the case's termination in January 1982, the retail price index for ready-to-eat cereals rose at twice the rate of increase for "food-at-home" and also for all urban consumer goods purchases. See Cotterill et al. (1994, Figure 2). Comparable statistics for earlier periods are not available. However, data from the U.S. Census of Manufactures show that price-cost margins[43] in the consistently defined four-digit S.I.C. industry "cereal breakfast foods" rose from approximately 47.5 percent between 1972 and 1977—i.e., while the case was actively pending—to an average of 61.7 percent over the 10 years 1982 through 1991—among the five highest such margins evident for 459 four-digit manufacturing industries. Multiplying the post-closure price-cost margin differential relative to 1972–1977 averages by sales in the ten post-closure years, one finds that the additional prices paid by retailers for breakfast cereals amounted to approximately $10 billion.

If we assume (not implausibly) that cereal producers no longer found it prudent to restrain their prices and margins once the antitrust threat had ended, this was a high cost indeed for American consumers.

References

American Bar Association. (1969). Report of the ABA Commission to study the Federal Trade Commission.

Bass, F. M., & Parsons, L. J. (1969). Simultaneous-equation regression analysis of sales and advertising. *Applied Economics, 1,* 103–124.

Chamberlin, E. H. (1933). *The theory of monopolistic competition.* Cambridge: Harvard University Press.

Cotterill, R. W., Franklin, A. W., & Haller, L. E. (1994). *Harvesting and tacit collusion in the breakfast cereal industry.* University of Connecticut Food Marketing Policy Center Issue Paper No. 6.

Cournot, A. A. (1838). Recherches sur les principes mathematiques de la theorie des richesses.

Federal Trade Commission. (1958). *Economic report on antibiotics manufacture.* Washington, DC.

---

[43] I.e., the ratio of (value added minus payrolls) divided by value of shipments.

 Springer

Goldschmid, H. J., Mann, H. M., & Weston, J. F. (Eds.). (1974). *Industrial concentration: The new learning*. Boston: Little, Brown.

Green, M. J., et al. (1972). *The closed enterprise system*. New York: Grossman.

Kaysen, C., & Turner, D. F. (1959). *Antitrust policy: An economic and legal analysis*. Cambridge: Harvard University Press.

Markham, J. W. (1951). The nature and significance of price leadership. *American Economic Review, 41*, 891–905.

Pertschuk, M. (1982). *Revolt against regulation: The rise and pause of the consumer movement*. Berkeley: University of California Press.

Posner, R. J. (1976). *Antitrust policy: An economic and legal analysis*. Chicago: University of Chicago Press.

Schelling, T. C. (1960). *The strategy of conflict*. Cambridge: Harvard University Press.

Scherer, F. M. (1967). Focal point pricing and conscious parallelism. *Antitrust Bulletin, 12*, 495–503.

Scherer, F. M. (1970). *Industrial market structure and economic performance*. Chicago: RandMcNally.

Scherer, F. M. (1979). The welfare economics of product variety: an application to the ready-to-eat cereals industry. *Journal of Industrial Economics, 28*, 113–134.

Scherer, F. M. (1990). Sunlight and sunset at the Federal Trade Commission. *Administrative Law Review, 42*, 461–488.

Scherer, F. M. (2000). *Competition policy, domestic and international* (pp. 178–187). Cheltenham: Edward Elgar.

Scherer, F. M. (2008). Technological innovation and monopolization. In W. D. Collins, et al. (Eds.), *Issues in competition law and policy* (pp. 1033–1068). Chicago: American Bar Association.

Scherer, F. M. (2010). Pharmaceutical innovation. In B. Hall & N. Rosenberg (Eds.), *Handbook in economics of innovation* (pp. 539–574). Amsterdam: North-Holland.

Scherer, F. M., & Ross, D. (1990). *Industrial market structure and economic performance* (3rd ed.). Boston: Houghton-Mifflin.

Schmalensee, R. (1978). Entry deterrence in the ready-to-eat breakfast cereal industry. *Bell Journal of Economics, 9*, 305–327.

Stauffer, T. R. (1971). The measurement of corporate rates of return: A generalized formulation. *Bell Journal of Economics and Management Science, 2*, 434–469.

U.S. Senate, Committee on the Judiciary. (1961). *Report, administered prices: Drugs*. Washington: USGPO.

The Antitrust Bulletin/Winter 2004   841

Vertical relations in antitrust: some intellectual history

BY F. M. SCHERER*

All politics is local. And all monopoly strategy is vertical in the sense that it affects the welfare, and perhaps the behavior, of agents located at different vertical stages in the chain of production and distribution. Thus, in asking me to write on the intellectual history of vertical relationships in antitrust, Bert Foer handed me a tabula rasa. It is a small tabula, however, and so I am forced to be selective. Recognizing that my comparative advantage lies in my antiquity, I will place disproportionate emphasis on historical developments from the time when antitrust was still in its infancy, before it became a mass-production industry with thousands of participants stirring the intellectual broth.

In particular, I will focus on three main areas of interest: the ability of powerful enterprises to exert monopsony power, that is, constraining the prices of suppliers located "upstream" in the production and distribution chain; how the pricing of monopoly power reiterated at successive stages in the chain affects market outcomes (the so-called pyramided monopoly problem); and what are now called vertical restraints, that is, when a firm operating at one stage in the chain negotiates or requires restraints of an output-restricting or price-enhancing nature on firms at another stage. Since the activities covered within the third of these categories were the most recent to attract competition policy attention, and also because I

---

*   Professor Emeritus, John F. Kennedy School of Government, Harvard University, and Lecturer, Princeton University.

842 : *The antitrust bulletin*

have said just about everything useful I have to say on the subject in the third edition of my industrial organization textbook,[1] less emphasis will be placed on such vertical restraint issues.

I.   The Steiner dual-stage model

Because the collection of articles here honors the contributions of Robert Steiner, an immediate deviation from this plan is in order. In my opinion, Bob Steiner's most original contribution has been his so-called dual-stage model focusing on the power relationships between manufac-turers and the retailers who distribute their products to consumers. It is an important contribution indeed. To the best of my knowledge, however, it has not yet had much impact on U.S. antitrust policy. There are two probable reasons. First, it is relatively new, crystallized only in the early 1970s.[2] But second, to spread a doctrine, one needs to build a school, and schools are normally propagated by teaching in a well-known uni-versity and/or turning out lots of graduate students. Bob comes from a real-world environment that seldom opens up such school-building opportunities. Today's session creates an alternative venue to provide Steiner's dual-stage model the attention and influence it deserves.

The only "close call" application of the Steiner dual stage model occurred in the FTC's ill-fated breakfast cereal case.[3] Before the case was vacated, a Michigan State University scholar published a book arguing *inter alia* that creating more generic competition at the cereal manufacturing stage, as the FTC staff sought, might reduce advertis-ing and supermarket shelf turnover, leading to an increase in retailer margins and hence higher retail cereal prices.[4] Because I no longer retain the relevant case documents, I do not know whether the book's

---

[1]   F. M. SCHERER & DAVID ROSS, INDUSTRIAL MARKET STRUCTURE AND ECONOMIC PERFORMANCE ch. 15 (3d ed. 1990).

[2]   Robert L. Steiner, *Does Advertising Lower Consumer Prices?*, 36 J. MARKETING 5 (1973).

[3]   *In re* Kellogg Company et al., Federal Trade Commission Docket No. 8883, *vacated at* 99 F.T.C. 289 (1982).

[4]   BRIAN F. HARRIS, SHARED MONOPOLY AND THE CEREAL INDUSTRY chs. 4–7 (1979).

argument was presented by witnesses for the cereal companies and emphasized in respondent briefs. Certainly, the case was decided on other, essentially political grounds, so the role of Bob Steiner's work must be viewed as a possible near miss as well as a misapplication. To the best of my knowledge, Steiner has never argued that simply because generic brands have slower shelf turnover and higher margins than heavily advertised brands, generic prices are necessarily *higher* than those of advertised brands.

II. Monopsony power in antitrust

Monopsony power emerges when a buyer, or a coordinated group of buyers, purchases a sufficiently large share of upstream producers' output that the buyer's influence on upstream prices is recognized and taken into account, typically by restraining the volume of purchases.

A. *The pure theory*

The pure theory is illustrated in the figure. The supply (horizontally summed marginal cost) function of the upstream industry is indicated by the solid line marked *Supply*. If the buying firm sells competitively in its downstream industry, its demand curve for the upstream industry's input is indicated by *VMP* (value of its marginal product).[5] Under competitive conditions on both sides of the market, *VMP* will be equated with the supply schedule at point *A*, leading to the transfer of 53 units of the intermediate product at a price (horizontal dotted line) of $12 per unit. If however the buyer has monopsony power, it will reckon how its increased purchases drive up the supply price by computing the *marginal supply cost* function (dashed line) *MSC*. It then equates *MSC* with *VMP* at point *B*, reducing the quantity of intermediate product purchased to 39 units and the upstream suppliers' price to $10.60 per unit. If, instead of selling its output competitively, the downstream firm is a monopolist, it will take into account the influence of its own output on the end product price, operating along the (dashed) *marginal revenue product* function *MRP*. Buying

---

⁵   The VMP function's equation is assumed to be VMP = 20 − .15 Q; the supply function's equation P = 8 + .05 Q + .005 Q².

Figure
Pricing Under Monopsony

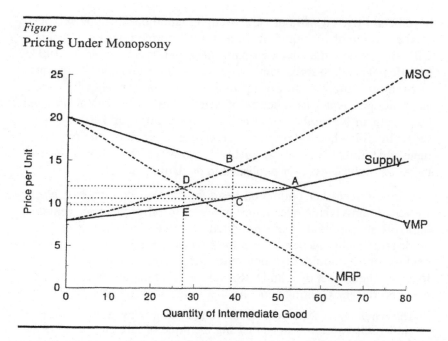

as a monopsonist and selling as a monopolist, it will equate *MRP* with *MSC* at point *D*, reducing the equilibrium exchange of intermediate product further to 27 units and the price paid per unit to \$9.80.

Monopoly on the upstream supply side along with monopsony on the downstream demand side complicates matters further, creating *bilateral monopoly* conditions. Economic theory provides no reliable guidance as to the equilibrium in this case. Output is likely to be restricted. The price per unit could be as high as \$14 or even lower than \$10, depending upon the bargaining power and tactics of the seller and buyer.

B. *Monopsony power and antitrust:* Standard Oil

It is well known that U.S. antitrust concerns itself with monopsony power relatively infrequently. But there are powerful early precedents.

The mother of all monopoly power antitrust case precedents is *U.S. v. Standard Oil*, 221 U.S. 1 (1911). Given the small size of the Justice Department's antitrust staff at the time, the case could scarcely have been litigated without the thorough factual background provided by the Bureau of Corporations in its three-volume report on Standard Oil's operations, the first two parts of which were issued in 1907.[6] President Theodore Roosevelt's request that the Bureau assign priority to Standard Oil was surely influenced by Ida Tarbell's historical account, published as a series of articles in *McClure's Magazine* beginning in November 1902 and then as a book in 1904.[7] Energy sector historian Daniel Yergin observes, perhaps with some overstatement, that Tarbell's book "Arguably . . . was the single most influential book on business ever published in the United States."[8]

Tarbell spent her childhood years in the "oil country" of northwestern Pennsylvania. Her father invested in oil production ventures, built oil storage tanks, and provided hotel services to the early oil wildcatters and producers during the first oil boom of the 1860s. This background undoubtedly motivated her work on the book and its focus on the impact of John D. Rockefeller's strategies on the fortunes of oil producers. Quoting veteran oil producers, Tarbell observes:

> The whole general purpose of the combination is to reap a large margin by depressing crude and raising the price of refined oil. . . . Standard . . . habitually meets the extra-ordinary expenses to which it is put by depressing the price of crude oil—"taking it out of the producer."[9]

Tarbell goes on to assert that: "John D. Rockefeller's one irreconcilable enemy in the oil business has always been the oil producer. And well he might [have seen him as an enemy], for he learned in his first great raid on the industry in 1872 that the producers aroused and united would make a powerful and dangerous foe."[10]

---

[6]   U.S. Bureau of Corporations, Report of the Commissioner of Corporations on the Petroleum Industry, pts. I–III (1907–1909). The third part, on Standard Oil's foreign trade, was suppressed for many decades because it revealed how standard was price discriminating in foreign markets.

[7]   Ida M. Tarbell, The History of the Standard Oil Company (1904).

[8]   Daniel Yergin, The Prize: The Epic Quest for Oil, Money & Power 105 (1991).

[9]   Tarbell, *supra* note 7, at 151, 219.

[10]   2 *Id.* at 156.

However, attempts by the oil producers to restrain Standard through strikes and legal actions brought under state laws were for the most part unsuccessful, in large measure because of their cost and the free-rider problems discouraging individual producers' participation. As a Pennsylvania oil producer wrote in 1879: "[T]he people of the Oil Region have by slow degrees and easy stages been brought into a condition of bondage and serfdom by the monopoly . . . [because] they have not the courage and manhood left to enable them to strike a blow for liberty."[11]

Writing a decade after the University of Chicago was established, Tarbell observes:

> It is a common enough thing to-day, indeed, to hear oil producers in Northwestern Pennsylvania remark facetiously, when a new endowment to the University of Chicago is reported: "Yes, I contributed so much on such a day. Don't you remember how the market slumped without a cause? The university needed the money, and so Mr. Rockefeller called on us to stand and deliver."[12]

The reports of the Bureau of Corporations placed more emphasis on Standard's tactics for gaining control of transportation media, first through eliciting rebates and drawbacks from rail lines and then by controlling crude oil and product pipelines, the least-cost means of transportation. However, they did not neglect the crude oil side:

> It is true that the Standard Oil Company does not control a majority of crude production by actual ownership of wells, but its control of the pipe lines, the only effective means of marketing most of this oil, gives it just as complete a control of crude production as by direct title to the fields, and the result is that the Standard is almost the sole purchaser, and its daily quotations for oil are the "official price" in most of these fields.[13]

When Standard did choose to purchase crude oil sources, e.g., in the second great U.S. discovery around Lima, Ohio, it reduced its acquisition costs through its control of oil prices. Thus, at a time when northwestern Pennsylvania oil was selling at from 66 to 94 cents per barrel:

---

[11]   1 *Id.* at 259.

[12]   *Id.* at 219.

[13]   U.S. BUREAU OF CORPORATIONS, *supra* note 6, part I, at 9.

The price fixed on Lima oil was absurdly low as compared with its true refining value. . . . The maintenance of this price of 15 cents per barrel for three years naturally discouraged producers and owners of oil lands in the Lima field and made it possible for the Standard Oil Company to buy up large territories at low cost.[14]

Standard's reasons for limiting its crude oil field purchases well short of monopoly were said by the Bureau staff to be twofold:[15] because the control of a scarce natural resource was considered "especially obnoxious to most people," likely to stir up "even more bitter public hostility than has existed against the Standard Oil Company"; and because, due to the peculiarly speculative character of the oil business, "it probably costs the Standard Oil Company less on the whole to buy a large part of its crude oil from others than it would cost to produce the entire supply itself."

The district and Supreme Court decisions in the Standard Oil monopolization case are notably short on either historical or economic analysis, no doubt in part because the Bureau of Corporations had provided such a complete record. To the extent that facts are reviewed, they focus mostly on refined petroleum market structures, Standard's predation against and acquisition of competing refiners, and the allegedly high prices of refined products. However, the Supreme Court's decision by no means ignores Standard's control of crude oil production and prices: "[T]he combination during the period named had obtained a complete mastery over the oil industry . . . and thus was able to fix the prices of *crude and* refined petroleum and to restrain and monopolize interstate commerce in those products."[16]

Rejecting a defense that Standard had no monopoly position because it controlled only a small percentage of the crude oil produced, the Court concluded: "As substantial power over the crude product was the inevitable result of the absolute control which existed over the refined product, the monopolization of the one carried with it the power to control the other. . . ."[17]

---

[14]   *Id.* at 115.

[15]   *Id.* at 119–21.

[16]   Standard Oil Co. v. United States, 221 U.S. 1, 33 (1911) (emphasis added).

[17]   *Id.* at 77.

848 : *The antitrust bulletin*

C. Other monopsony allegations

In the *American Tobacco* case decided almost simultaneously by the Supreme Court, there was much less emphasis on the Tobacco Trust's purchasing power, although the Court observes that prior to several formative mergers, the companies had been "competing in the purchase of the raw product," and dissolution of American Tobacco's purchasing subsidiary was one facet of the remedy.[18] Recurring complaints over the next three decades that the successor companies were cooperating in their raw tobacco purchasing operations came to naught.[19] In its 1945 tobacco decision, however, the Supreme Court found that the oligopolistic cigarette companies had "dominance and control over purchases of raw material" and that they conspired to fix raw material prices.[20] Whether the aim of their collusion was to depress raw tobacco prices or simply to assure that no oligopolist obtained a cost advantage over others was left undecided.[21] Whatever the rationale, the level of tobacco prices soon came under the control of a much more powerful cartel master—the United States Department of Agriculture—where it has remained up to the present.[22]

A more strenuous attack on monopsonistic practices was made in the Federal Trade Commission's report on the meat packing industry, completed as World War I drew to a close.[23] Summarizing the findings of its study, the Commission staff stated:

> Foremost of packer practices in evil results is the manipulation of the live-stock market, manifested primarily in violent and unreasonable fluctuations in live-stock prices from day to day. . . . [Live-stock pro-

---

[18]   U.S. v. American Tobacco Co., 221 U.S. 106 (1911).

[19]   *See* 2 SIMON N. WHITNEY, ANTITRUST POLICIES; AMERICAN EXPERIENCE IN TWENTY INDUSTRIES 28–30 (1958).

[20]   American Tobacco Co. et al. v. United States, 328 U.S. 781, 792, 798, 800 (1945).

[21]   *Id.* at 802.

[22]   *See*, e.g., BRUCE L. GARDNER, THE GOVERNING OF AGRICULTURE 69–70 (1981).

[23]   FEDERAL TRADE COMMISSION, FOOD INVESTIGATION: REPORT ON THE MEAT INDUSTRY (1919).

ducers] see in the violent fluctuations of the market—and our investigation confirms their suspicions—manipulations by the big packers in order to secure their raw materials cheaply.[24]

According to the Commission staff, the dominant packers agreed on market locations and purchasing procedures to ensure that each paid a common price, "and in a market where there is an agreed division, the natural law of the market is turned topsy-turvy, and the common price inevitably becomes that offered by the low bidder." Documenting these inferences with a remarkable trove of documents allegedly retrieved *inter alia* from packers' office waste containers, the Federal Trade Commission nevertheless overplayed its hand by leaping to the unwarranted conclusion that the packers were attempting to monopolize the entire U.S. food supply.[25] As a result, jurisdiction over the meat-packing industry was transferred by Congress to a friendlier Department of Agriculture, and threats to transfer the whole FTC to a more benign Department of Commerce during the 1920s were thwarted only through the intervention of populist midwestern senators.

The issue has hardly died, however. Analogous price-suppression allegations by a new set of meat packers were at the core of a jury's finding of guilt and a proposed $1.28 billion damages award in the *Pickett v. Tyson* case.[26] The verdict was voided by the presiding judge, and appeals will undoubtedly continue.

The Federal Trade Commission (FTC) returned to the question of buyer power in its chain store investigation.[27] That ambitious study was motivated by the spread of chain stores, of which A&P was the paramount example, the fear that such chains were securing price discounts that contributed to the demise of "mom and pop" stores, and

---

[24]   1 *Id.*, at 69–71.

[25]   For a critical analysis, *see* Robert M. Aduddell & Louis P. Cain, *Public Policy Toward "The Greatest Trust in the World,"* 55 Bus. Hist. Rev. 217–42 (1981).

[26]   Pickett v. Tyson, U.S. Federal District Court for Alabama; jury verdict February 17, 2004; voided by the trying judge April 23, 2004.

[27]   Federal Trade Commission, Final Report on the Chain Store Investigation (1934).

general depression psychosis. Although the FTC staff found that an estimated 85% of the chains' price advantage over smaller retailers was attributable to operating cost and procurement efficiencies, the FTC's conclusion that some price discrimination favored larger buyers provided support for passage of the Robinson-Patman antiprice discrimination act in 1936.

In this brief retrospective, there is no time to review systematically the turbulent history of Robinson-Patman Act enforcement. Hundreds of discount givers and receivers were challenged by the Federal Trade Commission during the ensuing three decades.[28] A&P's turn came in the mid-1970s. A&P was charged by the FTC with violating the Act by *inducing* milk price discounts from the Borden Company in the Chicago area.[29] Eventually, the FTC's finding of illegal discrimination was overturned when the Supreme Court found that Borden was merely responding to competitive threats of uncertain magnitude.[30] An irony of the case was the fact that the net price at which A&P ultimately bought its milk from Borden was inappreciably lower than the unit cost at which Jewel, the leading Chicago area food retailer, obtained milk from its own vertically integrated dairy.

A&P was also the respondent during the 1940s in a Sherman Act suit alleging that it elicited at wholesale and implemented at retail discriminatory price discounts, using the cost advantages derived thereby to drive other retailers out of business. Its conviction led to a relatively modest fine and the divestiture of one A&P purchasing subsidiary.[31] The case drew scathing criticism from M. A. Adelman, who emphasized the efficiencies achieved by A&P's purchasing methods and the unsystematic character of its loss-inducing price reductions in local markets:

---

[28]   For my own review of the record from the perspective of an FTC official, see my 1975 testimony before the House Small Business Committee, reproduced in F. M. SCHERER, COMPETITION POLICY: DOMESTIC AND INTERNATIONAL 178–87 (2000).

[29]   In the matter of the Great Atlantic & Pacific Tea Co. et al., 87 F.T.C. 962 (1976).

[30]   *Id.*, 440 U.S. 69 (1979).

[31]   U.S. v. The New York Great Atlantic & Pacific Tea Co., 67 F. Supp. 626 (1946), *affirmed at* 173 F. 2d 79 (1949).

It is clear that the prosecution "facts" embodied an attack on price competition per se, and on vertical and horizontal integration when they economized resources and hence were a "competitive advantage." But we cannot say how much of this was sheer economic ignorance and incompetence [on the part of government prosecutors] and how much was policy. Plainly, both elements were there.[32]

Since then, I believe, government antitrust enforcement agencies have developed sufficient competence in economic matters to avoid most, if not all, errors of the sort chastised by Adelman. Nevertheless, there would appear to be ample precedent for cases targeted at the genuinely abusive exercise of monopsony power.

III. Pyramided monopolies

Pyramided monopoly, also called the repeated marginalization problem, occurs when a firm that monopolizes one stage in the chain of distribution sells to a monopolist at the next vertical stage in the chain of distribution. The pricing behavior that results can lead to output restrictions and inefficiencies like those seen at point *D* in the figure (*supra*), where a downstream firm is both monopolist in its selling activities and monopsonist in its role as purchaser.

In all three editions of my industrial organization textbook, I credited a 1950 article by Joseph Spengler of Duke University with the first definitive analysis of the basic problem and the emergence of a "Chicago" position on vertical integration.[33] I was wrong. A fully worked-out intuitive and mathematical treatment was achieved more than a century earlier by Charles Ellet Jr.[34] Ellet was a bridge and railroad engineer. His analysis revealed why both profitability and service to the public were likely to be enhanced when end-to-end railroads

---

[32]   *See* M. A. ADELMAN, A&P: A STUDY IN PRICE-COST BEHAVIOR AND PUBLIC POLICY 418 (1959). *Compare* the more favorable view of Joel Dirlam & Alfred Kahn in *Antitrust Law and the Big Buyer: Another Look at the A&P Case*, 60 J. POL. ECON. 118 (1952).

[33]   *See, e.g.*, SCHERER & ROSS, *supra* note 1, at 522.

[34]   CHARLES ELLET JR., AN ESSAY ON THE LAWS OF TRADE IN REFERENCE TO WORKS OF INTERNAL IMPROVEMENT IN THE UNITED STATES 77–82 (1839; reprinted 1966).

were vertically integrated, rather than engaging in independent monopoly profit maximization over their individual lines.

Actually, recognition of the problem had an earlier genesis, although not in the mathematical form currently required to capture economists' attention. Two-plus centuries ago, those romantic "castles on the Rhine" that illuminate German travel posters played a much more sinister role. Each served as a river toll collection point, ready to fire 12-pounders at Rhine-traversing ships failing to stop and pay their toll to the reigning prince or duke. Over the 53-mile stretch of the Rhine from Mainz to Koblenz in 1780, there were nine such *Raubritter* (robber baron) emplacements, and from Koblenz to the Dutch border, there were 16 more.[35] Similar conditions prevailed on the Main and Elbe rivers. Each such toll station attempted to maximize profits over the short river segment it monopolized. The resulting pyramiding of tolls choked off nearly all of the traffic that otherwise would have used those waterways—in principle, much more advantageous than the primitive roads existing at the time.[36] Not until 1831 were the monopolists expropriated under a treaty among the nations and states abutting the Rhine. Free passage along the Rhine (combined with steam power) was a significant contributor to Germany's rapid industrialization in the ensuing decades.

Vertical integration or expropriation (e.g., through structural measures that eliminate monopoly power) are standard solutions to the pyramided vertical monopoly problem. They may also help solve a related problem, e.g., when monopoly at an upstream stage raises the price of one input, inducing the technologically inefficient substitution of an alternative competitively-priced input downstream. However, vertical integration can also enhance monopoly power, especially when market structures are oligopolistic but functioning reasonably well without some vertical relationship change that tips behavior in restrictive directions. The problem is quite complex mathematically, and it is difficult to extract simple rules of thumb. A rela-

---

[35] *See* THAYER'S LIFE OF BEETHOVEN 38 (Elliot Forbes, ed., rev. ed. 1967).

[36] *See* F. M. SCHERER, QUARTER NOTES AND BANK NOTES: THE ECONOMICS OF MUSIC COMPOSITION IN THE 18TH AND 19TH CENTURIES 143–45 (2004).

tively tough stance against vertical mergers that foreclosed significant sales opportunities to upstream sellers was taken in the Supreme Court's *du Pont-General Motors* decision of 1957.[37] The enforcement agencies' position has been relaxed since then, but vertical mergers likely to raise barriers to entry into concentrated industries can still draw antitrust condemnation.

My knowledge of whether these insights have been incorporated in more than a pro forma way into antitrust decisions is limited. I know of only one attempted application. In an amici curiae brief following Judge Thomas Penfield Jackson's finding of liability in the *Microsoft* case, Litan et al. warned *inter alia* about the vertical divestiture remedy advanced by the Clinton administration:

> Economic theory suggests a further difficulty with the functional divestiture approach. WinCo would continue to have a monopolistic position in the sale of operating systems while AppCo would have substantial monopoly power in some important "downstream" applications programs (such as Office). When one monopoly sells a product located "upstream" to the product of another monopoly, each may maximize its own profits and set prices higher than would be the case in a competitive market, with correspondingly lower combined profits, than would be the case with an integrated monopoly (such as the present Microsoft).[38]

The possibility that significant output restrictions might result led us to favor a further divestiture of WinCo into three segments, each with full rights to the operating system software. Needless to say, our caveat had little or no influence on the Department of Justice position at the time or following a change of administration.

IV. Classic vertical restraints

Everything I have discussed thus far has involved some kind of monopoly power exercise with ramifications for vertically related stages in the chain of distribution. However, the standard literature has tended to identify as classic "vertical restraints" such competition-

---

[37]   U.S. v. E. I. du Pont de Nemours Co. et al., 353 U.S. 586 (1957).

[38]   ROBERT LITAN, ROGER NOLL, WILLIAM NORDHAUS & F. M. SCHERER, REMEDIES BRIEF OF AMICI CURIAE 49 (April 2000).

reducing extensions from one stage to the next as manufacturer-mandated resale price maintenance (RPM), agreements by a distributor not to deal in rival manufacturers' products (exclusive dealing agreements), exclusive territorial allocations for distributors, and the tying of a customer's purchase of one product to the purchase of another. This may have been what Bert Foer wanted me to emphasize. I dispatch my obligation with fewer than all cylinders firing in part because I dislike repeating what I have said in previous publications and partly because the problem is so formidably complex.

Vertical restraints became a subject of first-line antitrust concern with the passage of the Clayton Act, and in particular section 3, in 1914. One of the most knowledgeable contemporary observers, Eliot Jones, states that section 3 was made imperative by failures of existing antitrust law to deal effectively with the tying and exclusive dealing requirements imposed by the United Shoe Machinery Company and the A.B. Dick Company on their customers.[39] I undertake no effort here to review systematically the turbulent history in both litigated decisions and (with respect to RPM) legislation since then.

The most interesting issue from an economist's perspective is the existence of a seeming paradox. On one hand, the simple theory of two- or multiple-stage monopoly suggests that extending through restrictive covenants monopoly power from one stage to an adjacent stage can lead to repeated marginalization, output restrictions, and inefficiency. On the other hand, it is argued that under some circumstances, the imposition of seemingly monopolistic restraints by, say, a manufacturer selling a differentiated product to what would otherwise be a competitively functioning retailing sector can enhance economic welfare. Resolution begins with the recognition that marketing efforts matter—a verity that Bob Steiner has been emphasizing throughout his highly productive career. In particular, it is possible that relieving some of the competitive pressure under which retailers labor widens retail price-cost margins, permitting and even (under some variant of the Dorfman-Steiner theorem[40]) motivating the retailers to provide

---

[39] ELIOT JONES, THE TRUST PROBLEM IN THE UNITED STATES 361 (1921).

[40] Robert Dorfman & Peter Steiner, *Optimal Advertising and Optimal Quality*, 44 AM. ECON. REV. 826 (1954).

marketing services that better inform consumers' purchasing decisions, leading to greater consumer satisfaction and increased output of
the relevant products. On this complex issue, I offer only three
insights.

First, let us assume that widening retailers' margins through resale
price maintenance or the assignment of exclusive territories does in
fact induce intensified marketing effort, which in turn shifts consumer
demand curves for the product in question to the right, perhaps
enough to leave an equilibrium in which the output of the product is
greater than it would have been without the margin-widening retail
price increase. Thanks to a pioneering contribution by Robert Bork,[41]
it has become an article of faith, accepted uncritically in some circles,
that the expansion of output proves that economic welfare has been
increased. This may be true, but it is not true in all generality. The
counterexample was proposed simultaneously and independently by
William S. Comanor and myself.[42] The difference, it turns out,
depends upon the *way demand curves shift* as a consequence of the
enhanced marketing effort. The proof is intricate. Rather than spelling
it out in detail here, I simply refer to figures 15.2 and 15.3 from the
1990 version of my textbook and describe the key difference
verbally.[43] In the first case, a welfare-enhancing demand shift is
shown; in figure 15.3, the shift is welfare-reducing. The difference
between the two cases lies in the fact that in figure 15.2, the demand
curve following a vertical restraint's inducement of additional promotional effort shifts to the right in parallel, whereas in figure 15.3, the
new demand curve pivots about the point at which the prerestraint
curve intersects the vertical (price) axis. In the latter (welfare-reducing)
case, consumers with high willingness to pay, and hence receiving substantial consumers' surplus from the product in any event, strive to

---

[41]   Bork, *The Rule of Reason and the Per Se Concept: Price Fixing
and Market Division*, 75 Yale L.J. 402–403 & 424 (1966).

[42]   William S. Comanor, *Vertical Price Fixing and Market Restrictions and the New Antitrust Policy*, 98 Harv. L. Rev. 990 (1985); and
F. M. Scherer, *The Economics of Vertical Restraints*, 52 Antitrust
L.J. 687 (1983). Comanor and I discovered at a breakfast in Philadelphia
that we had each proved the same theorem.

[43]   Scherer & Ross, *supra* note 1, at 545 & 547.

inform themselves without special marketing activities by the retailer, and hence experience relatively little expansion of demand due to the retailer's efforts. Only the consumers with relatively low reservation prices and hence relatively low consumers' surplus from consuming the product benefit significantly from the retailer's marketing efforts. And those differing conditions, a fairly intricate geometric analysis shows, means that the increased marketing effort does not lead to an increase in total consumers' surplus.

Second, if resale price maintenance is widely adopted, it can frustrate price competition in specific product lines or, more seriously yet, inhibit the spread of innovative lower-margin retailing forms, with consumers as the losers. In the United States, the suppression of retailing innovations was only mild, but in some European nations it was serious and protracted.[44]

Third, the "Chicago" explanation of why manufacturers must implement vertical restraints to widen retailer margins and thereby induce enhanced marketing effort is that, absent such restraints, retailers who choose not to increase their marketing costs and hence are in a position to undercut the high-effort retailers' prices will free ride on the marketing efforts of those who do, undermining the incentives of the latter to provide the demand-expanding marketing services. Bob Steiner and I have long been skeptical of how widely the free-rider story applies in real life, among other things suggesting myriad ways desired services can be sustained without being undermined by free riding.[45]

The most direct confrontation of the contending theories known to me came in the *Toys "R" Us (TRU)* case. TRU claimed that it was justified in attempting to induce toy manufacturers to withhold first-line toys from low-price warehouse clubs because the clubs were free riding on the early stocking, full-line display, and advertising services provided by TRU. In its decision rejecting the free-rider defense, the Federal Trade Commission systematically analyzed each of TRU's

---

[44] *See* F. M. Scherer, *Retail Distribution Channel Barriers to International Trade*, 67 ANTITRUST L. J. 79 (1999).

[45] *See* SCHERER & ROSS, *supra* note 1, at 551–55 for an explanation and five references to the Steiner works.

free-rider claims, concluding that TRU was compensated monetarily by toy manufacturers for most of the presale services it provided, that toys differed from the complex, expensive durable goods on which the free riding of demonstration and similar presale services was most likely, that TRU did not ask the toy makers to curb alleged free riding by low-price outlets such as Wal-Mart, that less restrictive means of assuring the provision of presale services were available, and that TRU documents had not even mentioned free riding as a problem until it was threatened with litigation.[46] Sustaining the Commission, the Seventh Circuit Court of Appeals, to which TRU had presumably appealed expecting that in Chicago the free-riding defense would receive a sympathetic hearing, observed *inter alia*:

> Here, the evidence shows that the free-riding story is inverted. The manufacturers wanted a business strategy under which they distributed their toys to as many different kinds of outlets as would accept them: exclusive toy shops, TRU, discount department stores, and warehouse clubs. . . . What TRU wanted or did not want is neither here nor there for purposes of the free rider argument. . . . Furthermore, we note that the Commission made a plausible argument for the proposition that there was little or no opportunity to "free" ride on anything here in any event. The consumer is not taking a free ride if the cost of the service can be captured in the price of the item. . . . [T]he manufacturers were paying for the services TRU furnished, such as advertising, full-line product stocking, and extensive inventories.[47]

One can assume that in the future free-rider defenses will again be accorded the detailed critical scrutiny they deserve.

V. Conclusion

The extension of monopoly power to other vertical stages in the chain of distribution is a phenomenon that matters. Powerful buyers can turn what would be a competitive outcome into one with restricted output and depressed supplier incomes. When a powerful

---

[46]   Opinion of the Federal Trade Commission In the matter of Toys "R" Us et al., Docket No. 9278, public record slip op., section 4, at 75–81 (1998).

[47]   Toys "R" Us, Inc. v. Federal Trade Commission, slip op., section II.C. (August 1, 2000) (Court of Appeals for the Seventh Circuit).

buyer confronts powerful sellers, e.g., with bilateral monopoly, inefficiencies may be lessened or aggravated, depending upon intricate
details of the buyer-seller relationships. Vertical integration often
helps solve vertical restraint problems, but it can also create problems
where none existed previously. The extension of power through resale
price maintenance, exclusive territorial assignments, or exclusive
dealing arrangements also has complex effects. Sorting out the good
from the bad is hard work. It can be done, but a good deal of economic and marketing sophistication is needed to do the job properly.
In the *Toys "R" Us* case, the requisite sophistication was clearly present in the Federal Trade Commission and an appellate court whose
presiding judge was well-trained in economics. It would be naive to
expect that so much competence is always brought to bear in vertical
market power cases. For important cases in which judges recognize
that they lack the necessary economics and marketing background,
the rule of reason might be applied more successfully if the presiding
judge retains the advice of an impartial expert, who among other
things would prod the litigating parties to substitute relevant facts and
focused logic for vacuous theory. This has been done in a few cases,
but it deserves wider consideration.

[11]

No. 06-480

In the

Supreme Court of the United States

LEEGIN CREATIVE LEATHER PRODUCTS, INC.,

Petitioner,

v.

PSKS, INC.,

Respondent.

On Writ of Certiorari to the
United States Court of Appeals for the Fifth Circuit

BRIEF FOR WILLIAM S. COMANOR AND FREDERIC M. SCHERER AS *AMICI CURIAE* SUPPORTING NEITHER PARTY

Eugene Crew
  Counsel of Record
Nancy L. Tompkins
Townsend and Townsend and
Crew LLP
  Two Embarcadero Center
  Eighth Floor
  San Francisco, CA 94111
  (415) 576-0200

Attorneys for Amici Curiae

COUNSEL PRESS
(800) 274-3321 • (800) 359-6859

i

TABLE OF CONTENTS

ii

TABLE OF CITED AUTHORITIES

Page

Cases

Other Authorities

iii

Cited Authorities

1

STATEMENT OF INTEREST OF *AMICI CURIAE*[1]

Amici are two economists who have been writing and teaching in the field of industrial organization since the mid-1960s. Both served as Directors of the Bureau of Economics at the Federal Trade Commission and both are former presidents of the Industrial Organization Society. Both have written extensively about the economics of resale price maintenance (RPM) and vertical restraints more generally.

William S. Comanor is Professor of Economics at the University of California, Santa Barbara, and Professor of Health Services at the University of California, Los Angeles. He also served as Special Assistant to the U.S. Assistant Attorney General for Antitrust in 1967 and 1968. Frederic M. Scherer is Aetna Professor of Public Policy Emeritus at the John F. Kennedy School of Government, Harvard University. Neither *amicus* has had any employment or consulting relationship with the parties to this litigation, although work by *amicus* Scherer was cited in briefs to the Court by counsel for both petitioner Leegin and respondent PSKS.

Amici submit this brief in part to set the record straight on Scherer's views, but also to provide insights on the economic literature concerning resale price maintenance (RPM) and to suggest a tractable approach for implementing antitrust standards on RPM.

---

[1] Counsel for both parties have consented to the filing of this brief, and their consents have been filed with the Clerk of this Court. No counsel for either party had any role in authoring this brief, and no person other than the named *amici* and their counsel has made any monetary contribution to the preparation and submission of this brief.

2

SUMMARY OF ARGUMENT

The assertion that output-expanding resale price maintenance enhances consumer welfare, often cited as a defense of RPM, should be recognized as a special case not applicable under plausible conditions. The free-rider justification for RPM is also not universally applicable and should be subjected to critical scrutiny, as the Federal Trade Commission did in *In the Matter of Toys "R" Us*, 126 F.T.C. 415, 567-607 (1998). To the extent that the economic literature provides support for resale price maintenance as welfare-enhancing, the support is limited to cases of manufacturer-induced RPM, not retailer-induced RPM. The distinction should be recognized in adjudicating RPM complaints. Retailer-induced RPM should give rise to a rebuttable *per se* approach, whereas manufacturer-induced RPM should be subjected to a rule of reason when it is widespread within a product line or effected in concentrated oligopolistic markets.

ARGUMENT

A. The Conflicting Citations

In its *certiorari* brief filed before the Court on November 6, 2006 at page 16, respondent PSKS cites work by *amicus* Scherer to support the position that "the elimination of resale price maintenance has led to significant savings for consumers." In its reply brief filed on November 20, 2006 at pages 6-7, petitioner Leegin quotes a statement by *amicus* Scherer from the cited work that "[m]y own view has long been that vertical restraints are benign or efficiency enhancing more often than not, leading me to recommend that a rule of reason be applied." It goes on to observe that *amicus* Scherer

3

was among the 25 economists submitting an *amicus curiae* brief urging that the *per se* rule against resale price maintenance be overturned.

There is no necessary conflict here. It is entirely possible for resale price maintenance arrangements to be efficiency enhancing in some circumstances but injurious to consumer welfare in others. And given this diversity of effects, one could reasonably take the position that a *rule of reason* rather than a *per se* approach is warranted. What does need clarification, however, is that *amicus* Scherer agreed to sign the 25 economists' brief only on the condition that the cited article by Scherer summarizing research on the consumer harm from RPM, along with one by *amicus* Comanor, be referenced in the section acknowledging that there is "disagreement within the economics literature, and among *amici*, regarding the frequency with which minimum RPM has pro-competitive or anticompetitive effects." [Section I.C.4 of the 25 economists' brief.]

The 25 economists' *certiorari* brief urges that the long-standing *per se* rule against resale price maintenance be replaced by a *rule of reason*, but offers no suggestion how the rule of reason would be implemented. If the Court accepts that plea, it is essential that the Court articulate guidelines for implementation by the lower courts. A primary purpose of this brief is to suggest such guidelines. *Amici* believe strongly that a rule allowing all RPM, good and bad, to proliferate would impose significant burdens on the U.S. economy. That lesson was clearly recognized when Congress repealed the Miller-Tydings Act in 1975. It should not be forgotten.

4

B. Theoretical Foundations

Before making policy suggestions, we need to clarify certain points that are both theoretical and empirical. It is uniformly acknowledged that RPM and other vertical restraints lead to higher consumer prices.[2] And studies have suggested that these higher prices can be substantial.[3] According to an argument originally advanced by Robert Bork, however, the higher RPM-induced retailer margins lead to increased pre-sale services by retailers, which in turn causes output to expand. As a result, the higher margins promote enhanced consumer welfare and efficiency.[4]

Although Bork's point is sometimes correct, it is not always so. *Amici* Comanor and Scherer have both shown that consumer welfare can decline even though output is increased.[5] The net welfare consequence depends critically

---

[2] As long ago as 1984, Judge Frank Easterbrook wrote: "Every argument about restricted dealing implies that the restrictions influence price. There is no such thing as a free lunch; the manufacturer can't get the dealer to do more without increasing the dealer's margin." Frank H. Easterbrook, *Vertical Arrangements and the Rule of Reason*, 53 Antitrust L.J. 156 (1984).

[3] F.M. Scherer and David Ross, *Industrial Market Structure and Economic Performance*, 3rd ed. (1990) at pp. 555-556.

[4] Robert H. Bork, *The Antitrust Paradox* (1978), p. 290; and *Resale Price Maintenance and Consumer Welfare*, 77 Yale L.J. 950 (1968).

[5] The most transparent synthesis of two earlier proofs is found in Scherer and Ross, *supra* note 2 at pp. 541-548. It extends and simplifies F.M. Scherer, *The Economics of Vertical Restraints*, 52 Antitrust L.J. 687 (1983); and William S. Comanor, *Vertical Price Fixing and Market Restrictions and the New Antitrust Policy*, 98 Harv. L. Rev. 990 (1985).

5

upon the nature of the demand shift induced by the provision of pre-sale services as well as the magnitude of the shift (*i.e.*, the elasticity of demand with respect to the volume of pre-sale services).

The intuition for this result follows from the likelihood that consumers who derive substantial consumer surplus from a product are likely to be informed of the product's merits without any special help from retailers. These infra-marginal consumers are harmed by the higher prices resulting from RPM. On the other hand, it is the less informed, marginal consumers who derive most of the benefits from the services and whose purchases increase. This is a plausible situation, as it is recognized that the consumers most likely to be influenced by additional pre-sale services are those "who are indifferent between purchasing or not."[6] Furthermore, to the best of *amici*'s knowledge, no one has rebutted their proof that the Bork result is a special case not applicable under many circumstances. The Bork argument should not be accepted by the Court as a general principle.

A second point concerns the most popular defense for supplier-mandated RPM, which is the so-called free-rider argument.[7] It asserts that unless all distributors are required to charge the same high price, a high-price retailer may provide pre-sale services, after which a customer who has received those services without charge will purchase the item from a "free-riding" distributor who provides no such

---

[6] James Cooper, Luke Froeb, Daniel O'Brien, and Michael Vita, *Vertical Restrictions and Antitrust Policy: What About the Evidence?* 1 Competition Pol'y Int'l 45, 49, 51 (2005).

[7] This argument was made originally by Lester Telser, *Why Should Manufacturers Want Fair Trade?*, 3 J.L. & Econ. 86 (1960).

6

services but sets a lower price. RPM is needed to prevent free-riding and ensure that desired services are supplied.

Although this result is possible, there is skepticism in the economic literature about how often it actually occurs.[8] In the most thoroughly litigated antitrust case known to *amici*, Toys "R" Us argued that a different type of vertical restraint — a boycott of warehouse clubs TRU coerced from toy manufacturers — was justified because the warehouse clubs free-rode on TRU's inventory stocking and advertising activities. The Federal Trade Commission found TRU's free-rider defense to be without merit,[9] and on appeal, the Seventh Circuit agreed:[10]

> Here, the evidence shows that the free-riding story is inverted. The manufacturers wanted a business strategy under which they distributed their toys to as many different kinds of outlets as would accept them: exclusive toy shops, TRU, discount department stores, and warehouse clubs. . . . What TRU wanted or did not want is neither here nor there for purposes of the free rider argument. . . .

---

[8] The literature is reviewed in Scherer and Ross, *supra* n. 4, at pp. 551-555. *See also* William S. Comanor, *The Two Economics of Vertical Restraints,* 5 Rev. Indus. Org. (Summer 1990), and William S. Comanor, F.M. Scherer and Robert L. Steiner, *Vertical Antitrust Policy: Getting the Balance Right,* American Antitrust Institute, September 6, 2005.

[9] *In the Matter of Toys "R" Us,* 126 F.T.C. at 567-607. *Amicus* Scherer was the economic witness for the FTC staff.

[10] *Toys "R" Us v. Federal Trade Commission,* 221 F.3d 928, 938 (2000).

7

> Furthermore, we note that the Commission made a plausible argument for the proposition that there was little or no opportunity to "free" ride on anything here in any event. The consumer is not taking a free ride if the cost of the service can be captured in the price of the item. . . . [T]he manufacturers were paying for the services TRU furnished, such as advertising, full-line product stocking, and extensive inventories.

What this example shows is that arguments supporting RPM and other vertical restraints on free-riding grounds should not be accepted without the most careful analytic and factual scrutiny.

C. The Two Economics of RPM and Other Vertical Restraints

More than fifteen year ago, *amicus* Comanor observed that there are two separate bodies of economic literature dealing with vertical restraints, with distinct welfare and policy implications.[11] Both are relevant for determining appropriate antitrust standards.

In the first, restraints are imposed unilaterally by the seller, normally a manufacturer, to achieve increased sales; while in the second, they are instigated by buyers, normally distributors of the manufacturer's products, in order to protect their high prices. Strikingly, **the efficiency defenses of RPM and other similar restraints arise preponderantly from circumstances where the manufacturer is the moving**

---

[11] Comanor, *The Two Economics of Vertical Restraints, supra*, n. 6.

8

party. To the knowledge of the *amici*, there are no arguments in economic analysis supporting restraints arising from distributor actions or pressures. In such circumstances, RPM and similar restraints lead to higher consumer prices with no demonstrated redeeming values, unless one subscribes to the notion that protecting small retailers is desirable in its own right.

In the past, retailers initiated RPM by threatening to boycott manufacturers' goods unless RPM is imposed, or by bringing other kinds of pressures to bear on local and state governments. An important historical example is that of the retail pharmacists. Their trade association lobbied extensively for state RPM laws and offered draft statutes that were often enacted with little or no amendment by state legislatures.[12] Retail pharmacies were among the last bastions of widespread "fair trading" when the Miller-Tydings Act was repealed in 1975. From the late 1960s to 2003, retail pharmacy margins fell from an average of 40 percent to approximately 20 percent — a saving to consumers and health care insurers of some $40 billion at 2003 sales volumes.[13]

D. Designing Appropriate Standards

The source of the restraint is thus a significant consideration in determining appropriate antitrust standards. For this reason, a "quick look" approach is appropriate.

---

[12] F.M. Scherer, *How U.S. Antitrust Can Go Astray: The Brand Name Prescription Drug Litigation*, 4 Int'l J. Econ. Bus. 239, 244-6 (1997).

[13] F.M. Scherer, *Comment on Cooper et al.'s "Vertical Restrictions and Antitrust Policy,"* 1 Comp. Pol'y Int'l 65-74 (2005).

9

Evidence from a quick look that the restraint was induced by distributors should lead to the presumption of a *per se* violation, rebuttable on the presentation of credible contradictory evidence. On the other hand, preliminary evidence that the restraint was instigated by the manufacturer should trigger a *rule of reason* adjudication.

Where a *rule of reason* approach is appropriate, a test of quantitative substantiality should be applied. The reason is that RPM is most likely to be harmful to consumers when widely applied in a meaningful product line. In such circumstances, consumer choice is restricted to goods bearing high distribution margins in the absence of possible lengthy and energy-guzzling shopping trips. And if under the umbrella of high margins, most retailers engage in substantial pre-sale promotion, their efforts will largely cancel each other out in the aggregate, leading to a high-price, high-margin, high promotional cost equilibrium with relatively little if any expansion of demand.

A rule that takes these considerations into account and strikes a desirable balance between judicial economy and maintaining competition would entail a rebuttable presumption of illegality when the volume of fair-traded sales in a relevant narrowly-defined line of commerce exceeds, say, 50 percent. If this structural criterion is satisfied, antitrust standing would be granted if RPM is *extended* to cover an additional 10 percent of the relevant sales — an increment consistent with the 100 point Herfindahl-Hirschman index change under which anti-merger actions are triggered under the joint Department of Justice - Federal Trade Commission Merger Guidelines.

10

This structural test would be only the first stage in a RPM *rule of reason* proceeding. Respondents could then rebut the presumption of illegality by proving that the relevant market is improperly defined, that consumers' choices have not in fact been significantly limited, and/or that the restraints were necessary to sustain the provision of services valuable to consumers.

Alternatively, the triggering rule could conform even more closely to the approach taken in the Merger Guidelines. The first structural test would inquire whether the relevant line of commerce is oligopolistic, *e.g.*, with a Herfindahl-Hirschman index exceeding 1800. Focusing on oligopolistic sellers' market structure is appropriate because under oligopoly, imitation of one leading seller's marketing strategy by other sellers is more likely than with atomistic market structures. Antitrust action could then be triggered when RPM is implemented by a seller with a relevant market share of 10 percent or more, *i.e.*, with a Herfindahl-Hirschman change of 100 or more. Again, the presumption of illegality could be rebutted under a *rule of reason* defense.

11

CONCLUSION

The issue before the Court is an important one for American consumers. The wrong set of rules could encourage proliferation of RPM contracts, impose substantial losses on consumers, and impair the impressive efficiency of the distribution sector in the United States. Marketing innovation should not be discouraged by the imposition of RPM-type restraints. *Amici* believe that some approximation to the approach suggested here would achieve an appropriate tradeoff between consumer benefit, limited government intervention in the marketplace, and adjudicative feasibility.

Respectfully submitted,

EUGENE CREW
Counsel of Record
NANCY L. TOMPKINS
TOWNSEND AND TOWNSEND AND
CREW LLP
Two Embarcadero Center
Eighth Floor
San Francisco, CA 94111
(415) 576-0200

Attorneys for Amici Curiae

12

CASE 16

Retailer-Instigated Restraints on Suppliers' Sales: Toys "R" Us (2000)

F. M. Scherer*

INTRODUCTION

During the early 1990s Toys "R" Us[1] (hereafter, TRU), by a considerable stretch the largest retailer of toys in the United States, persuaded leading toy manufacturers to restrict the range of products they sold to warehouse clubs—a newly emerging form of consumer goods retailing. The restrictions were challenged under the antitrust laws by the Federal Trade Commission (FTC) in May 1996.[2] The extensive litigation that followed clarified in important ways the kinds of "vertical restraints" a retailer could impose upon its suppliers and the role of efficiency defenses, and especially claims of free-riding on services provided by the retailer, in justifying such restraints.

INNOVATION IN RETAILING

The tensions that arose among TRU, warehouse clubs, and toy manufacturers during the 1990s were a natural sequitur from the several revolutions that occurred in retailing during the prior century and one-half (Chandler 1977, chs. 1 and 7; Adelman 1959; and Scherer 1999).

As the United States emerged from its great Civil War, most consumer goods were provided at retail by general stores or "mom and pop" stores.

---

*The author was testifying expert economist on behalf of the Federal Trade Commission in this matter.

[1] The company's logo prints the "R" backward, which is not easily accomplished in type-set publications. We use quotation marks to note that our usage is not strictly accurate.

[2] *In the matter of Toys "R" Us, Inc.,* docket no. 9278.

These outlets were challenged competitively at first in the larger cities by department stores and then by mail-order houses such as Sears, Roebuck. During the twentieth century new retailing approaches appeared successively in the form of the chain stores (such as A&P and Walgreen's), supermarkets, hypermarket chains (such as Kmart and Wal-Mart), and specialized "category killer" chains (such as Home Depot for hardware and garden supplies and Staples for office supplies). These innovations in retailing were often accompanied by reductions in the percentage margin between prices and wholesale merchandise acquisition costs (hereafter, percentage retail margin, or PRM), and hence reductions in the prices that consumers paid, to the competitive disadvantage of more traditional retailing forms.

The traditional retailers fought back in part by seeking governmental protection—for example, in unsuccessful attempts during the 1880s and 1890s to secure state legislation curbing department stores' lower prices, through delays in the spread of free rural mail delivery aimed at inhibiting the growth of Sears, Roebuck, and in the passage of tougher antiprice discrimination laws (the Robinson-Patman Act) and laws enabling mandatory minimum resale price maintenance (so-called fair trade laws) during the 1930s. Gradually, these barriers proved ineffective or were repealed, and the retailing innovations took root and spread, with consumers as principal beneficiaries.

Toys "R" Us made important contributions to this innovative process. Founded by Charles Lazarus in 1948, with expansion to a Washington, D.C., branch first bearing the Toys "R" Us logo in 1954, it was one of the first category killer discount chains. It offered an unprecedentedly broad line of toys, encompassing some sixteen thousand different items (stock-keeping units, or SKUs) by the 1990s (reduced to roughly eleven thousand in 1996), and priced its products to realize margins between selling price and acquisition cost well below the 40 to 50 percent values that were the norm in more traditional toy outlets. It reached the fifty-store threshold in 1974 and continued its expansion to operate 497 retail toy outlets in the United States during 1992, along with 126 stores in other nations, to which it had introduced the previously unfamiliar concept of systematically discounted toy prices.

The Rise of Warehouse Clubs

The warehouse clubs, among which the most important examples were Costco, the Price Club, Sam's (affiliated with Wal-Mart), Pace (affiliated with Kmart), and BJ's, made further additions to retailing innovation history. At first, beginning in 1976, they sold merchandise mainly to small business customers. But in the late 1980s they began accepting individual retail customers who paid an annual membership fee of roughly $30, or approximately 2 percent of the average member's annual purchases. They purchased selected nationally branded food, appliance, electronic,

Case 16:   Toys "R" Us (2000)

automotive, and other consumer products in large quantities, transported them to austere warehouse-like buildings at low-rent locations, and moved them onto the selling floor still heaped upon the pallets with which they had been transported from the manufacturer to the store. Customers served themselves from the pallets and packed their purchases into oversize shopping carts after bringing them through a streamlined checkout counter. Despite selling a wide array of consumer products, the typical warehouse club outlet carried only some three thousand individual SKUs, with the product mix varying over the year to reflect both seasonal demands and the opportunistic purchases made by the clubs' buyers. Because the product mix varied so widely, shopping at the clubs was viewed by many consumer members as a kind of treasure hunt—one never knew what specials one might encounter.

Because of their extraordinarily low overhead, the large volumes in which members typically bought, and the annual admission fee, the clubs were able to offer their goods at uniformly low percentage retail margins— on the order of 9 to 12 percent. By 1992, there were 576 warehouse club stores in the United States. Their appeal was spreading rapidly, and marketing researchers projected in 1992 that the number of club outlets would double during the following decade.

The low PRMs taken by the clubs on the 100 to 250 toy items they stocked, depending upon availability and season, were perceived as a serious threat by the management of TRU. Although its principal draw to consumers was the huge array of products TRU stocked, it also emphasized its role as a low-price, if not *the* low-price, outlet, leading consumers to sample that array. To be sure, it faced price competition from other toy retailers— increasingly, from hypermarkets led by Wal-Mart, which was expanding rapidly from its Arkansas base during the 1980s and 1990s, and which carried as many as three thousand toy items at seasonal peaks, sold at PRMs averaging 22 percent but considerably lower for "hit" items.[3]

TRU responded to this competition by varying its prices inversely with the popularity of the item, and hence with the extent to which consumers might make price comparisons at alternative outlets. The best-selling hundred or so TRU toys were sold at substantially discounted PRMs; margins then ascended into the 32–38 percent range for products ranked 1000 to 10,000 in sales volume. Especially after competition from Wal-Mart intensified, TRU recognized that it could not always be the lowest-price outlet, but it tried to keep prices of the most popular items close to those of the toughest rivals. Customers were drawn to TRU through the advertising of a few hundred low-margin, popular items (along with disposable diapers and baby formula, priced at razor-thin margins, and shelved near the back of the stores); TRU's profits were then enhanced substantially as the typical customer made several impulse purchases of higher-margin products.

---

[3]Compare Steiner (1973, 1985).

THE ANTITRUST REVOLUTION

With their uniform low-margin policies, the clubs added a new quantitative dimension to this marketing equation. The prices they asked on popular items were seen by TRU executives as a serious threat to TRU's reputation as a low-price vendor, and hence to TRU's ability to draw customers in for additional higher-margin purchases. To be sure, this adverse "image" effect could be minimized by reducing TRU's prices on the relatively few popular products stocked by the clubs. TRU's initial reaction to the clubs' rapid ascent in the early 1990s was to make selective downward price adjustments, with a maximum negative impact on its retail margins estimated at roughly $55 million per year. But it sought a better solution.

Following preliminary discussions with many of the leading toy manufacturers, TRU made the club problem the main theme of its meetings with toy manufacturers at the New York Toy Fair in February 1992—the annual meeting at which retailers join manufacturers to scrutinize the newest toy designs and book orders for the forthcoming pre-Christmas peak season. Through these meetings, TRU articulated to toy makers what its policy would be toward manufacturer sales to warehouse clubs:[4]

- Toy makers should sell to the clubs no new or advertised products unless the clubs purchased the manufacturer's entire product line.

- All special products, exclusives, and close-out clearance items offered to the clubs should be shown to TRU first to see whether TRU wished to preempt the clubs and stock them itself.

- Old and basic products should be sold in special combination packages, for example, with a bridesmaid doll added to a basic Barbie Bride doll package.

- There was to be no discussion between TRU and the toy makers as to the prices at which these special, typically more complex and costly, products were sold to the clubs.

The penalty for violation was that TRU would not purchase offending products.

Subsequent fine-tuning discussions clarified the basic theme: that the manufacturers would not sell to the clubs products that were identical to those stocked by TRU, rendering it difficult for consumers to make straightforward comparisons between club and TRU prices. Since TRU tended to order all products expected to become best-sellers or receive television advertising support, this meant that the clubs would be able to obtain only by happenstance the most popular "hit" merchandise. (Predicting what new toys will catch consumers' fancy is an extremely uncertain game; even the most experienced retailer executives err.)

---

[4]Opinion of the Federal Trade Commission, 126 FTC 415, 539–540 (1998).

Most of the leading manufacturers accepted TRU's new policy with minor variations, and the supply of best-sellers to clubs atrophied. Despite the continuing growth of club merchandise sales more generally and an increase in the number of club outlets to 695 in 1995, warehouse clubs' toy sales peaked at 1.9 percent of total U.S. toy sales in 1992 and then declined to 1.4 percent in 1995. By 1993, TRU no longer found it necessary to adjust "high profile" products' prices downward to deal with club competition.[5]

THE ANTITRUST CHALLENGE

The clubs responded to these changes in part by threatening legal action against TRU and the manufacturers, but they also informed the FTC of what had happened. Following an investigation, the FTC, pursuing more activist policies after twelve years of relative inactivity during the Reagan and Bush administrations, issued in May 1996 a formal complaint charging TRU with diverse antitrust violations.

Critics of U.S. antitrust policy often assert that in responding to information provided by aggrieved rivals (e.g., the clubs, as rivals of TRU), the federal antitrust agencies are protecting "competitors" rather than the processes of competition and hence consumer interests, as should properly be their mandate. There are two responses to this criticism. First, antitrust agency staff are acutely aware of the criticism and try hard to limit their cases to those that serve the broad public interest. Whether they succeeded in the TRU case is for the reader to judge. Second, agency staff have only limited insight into what is happening in the vast world of business enterprise. Consumers, too, and especially consumers at retail, lack the information needed to defend themselves against abuses. Without information from aggrieved market participants and other affected parties, the antitrust enforcement agencies would overlook many genuine violations of the antitrust laws.[6]

The complaint against TRU was the subject of a bitterly contested trial before an FTC administrative law judge, who found in September 1997 that the antitrust laws had in fact been violated.[7] As is customary, the judge's decision was appealed by the losing party, in this instance TRU, to the FTC as a whole. In a meticulously reasoned decision that was plainly intended to make a definitive pronouncement on the extent to which retailers could initiate restraints limiting the purchasing opportunities of their rivals, the four Commission members (one of the five commissioner slots was vacant at the time) affirmed that TRU had violated the antitrust laws.[8]

---

[5]Opinion of the Commission, 126 FTC 415, 597 and note 15 of the Commission's opinion.

[6]See Scherer (1990).

[7]*In the Matter of Toys "R" Us,* initial decision, September 25, 1997, 126 FTC 415, 418.

[8]Opinion of the Commission, 126 FTC 415 (1998).

THE ANTITRUST REVOLUTION

The Vertical Restraints

TRU was charged with, and found responsible for, two rather different violations of the antitrust laws. For one, the agreements it elicited from individual toy manufacturers not to sell popular items to the warehouse clubs fell under the rubric of *vertical restraints*—that is, where a firm (i.e., a retailer) located at one tier in the chain from production to consumption imposes restraints upon the distribution practices of firms (in this case, manufacturers) located at a different tier in the chain. But in addition, TRU was accused of orchestrating a set of horizontal agreements among manufacturers to deny popular products to—that is, to boycott—the warehouse clubs.

Antitrust law makes a distinction between unilateral vertical restraints—for example, TRU announces, "If you sell product X to the clubs, we will not stock it, end of discussion, full stop"—and restraints between vertically stacked parties in the distribution chain that comprise a meeting of minds and hence mutual agreement between the parties. The relevant case precedents show greater willingness to accept vertical restraints imposed unilaterally, as compared with those achieved by agreement, without a detailed investigation of the pros and cons.[9]

Although TRU claimed that in announcing to toy manufacturers its intent not to stock products they sold to the warehouse clubs it imposed only unilateral restraints, the facts clearly established that what occurred was much closer to a bilateral meeting of minds. TRU executives met repeatedly with each major toy manufacturer to present their list of demands. There was give-and-take in the discussions to modify the policies and adapt them to special circumstances. TRU sought, and from at least ten leading manufacturers received, assurances that the manufacturers would conform to the negotiated restrictions on supply to clubs. TRU executives inspected in advance the special products toy makers proposed to sell to the clubs and in some instances requested, and obtained, modifications that differentiated them more clearly from products stocked by TRU. There was continuing feedback as TRU monitored the availability of manufacturers' products on the shelves of warehouse clubs and reported apparent policy violations to the manufacturers, threatened and in some cases removed offending products from TRU shelves (actions that standing alone would be unilateral), and through subsequent negotiations achieved policy convergence.

Considering this record, the Commission found that a series of anticompetitive vertical agreements was reached that prima facie violated Sherman Act Section 1, but whose legality depended upon the analysis of additional considerations, to be addressed here shortly.

---

[9]The precedents are discussed at length in the Opinion of the Commission, 126 FTC 415, 569–615.

Case 16: Toys "R" Us (2000)

The Horizontal Boycott

Three of the four FTC commissioners, with one dissenting, concluded that TRU also acted as the "hub" in a horizontal "hub and spoke" agreement among toy manufacturers to deny top-line and advertised products to the warehouse clubs. Such horizontal agreements are treated harshly under the antitrust laws as illegal per se, with consideration of extenuating circumstances only when the agreements yield plausible efficiency gains that cannot be achieved through alternative policies restricting competition less—conditions that are difficult to satisfy.

What gave rise to a horizontal agreement problem was the fact that most leading toy manufacturers viewed the clubs as an attractive and rapidly growing outlet for their products, sales to which would among other things lessen their growing dependence upon TRU as their largest and most powerful customer. To placate TRU and prevent it from taking product placement actions detrimental to their interests, the toy makers were willing to go along with TRU's proposed restraints—but only if they could be assured that they were not, in so doing, sacrificing sales to rival manufacturers.

Toys are highly differentiated products; as a rule, one toy maker does not consider itself to be competing head-to-head with all other toy makers, but rather with only a handful of firms that offer products (especially advertised products) similar in function and design to its own products. The manufacturers expressed concerns to TRU that if they complied with the proposed TRU policies, specifically named rivals might not, causing them to sacrifice significant sales in the clubs. As a top TRU executive testified, "They would always tell us, 'I'm only there because my competitor is there.' And we would say, 'Well, he keeps saying he's only there because you're there.'"[10] To deal with the problem, he testified, "We communicated to our vendors that we were communicating with all our key suppliers. . . . We made a point to tell each of the vendors that we spoke to that we would be talking to other key suppliers."[11]

TRU executives repeatedly informed toy manufacturers that a "level playing field" was being maintained and that their rivals had agreed to pursue the TRU-suggested policies. They received manufacturer complaints about rival noncompliance and communicated back to the originators reassurances that perceived deviations had been eliminated. And this, three of the four FTC commissioners concluded, was a classic "hub and spoke" horizontal agreement.[12] The dissenting commissioner questioned the strength of the factual evidence supporting a horizontal agreement inference and argued that "TRU's very indispensability gave each toy manufacturer every

---

[10]Testimony of Roger Goddu, quoted in Opinion of the Commission, 126 FTC 415, 554.

[11]Ibid. at p. 55, from CX 1658 p. 278.

[12]Among the precedents cited was *Interstate Circuit Inc. v. U.S.*, 306 U.S. 208 (1939).

447

THE ANTITRUST REVOLUTION

incentive—every *unilateral* incentive—to knuckle under to TRU's demands regarding the clubs," rendering horizontal agreements among the manufacturers unnecessary.[13]

A limitation of both the horizontal and vertical agreement allegations is that the agreements were not pervasive among toy manufacturers. The vertical agreements were found to have been implemented only by ten named producers, the horizontal agreements by seven—to be sure, those who originated most of the nationally advertised toy products.[14] Electronic game maker Nintendo in particular rejected TRU's overtures, in part because it sold its products through electronic specialty stores and was therefore less dependent upon TRU. Nintendo's noncompliance in turn posed problems for rival Sega, which adhered only intermittently to TRU's proposed policy. And at times Little Tikes, a manufacturer of large blow-molded toys, opted out because compliance might jeopardize more voluminous sales to warehouse clubs by its parent, the Rubbermaid Corporation. But there are strong antitrust law precedents holding that substantial but less than complete compliance with restrictive agreements does not reverse the illegality of such agreements if the impact on consumers is substantial.

The Role of Market Power

An appreciable fraction of the testimony by economists in the TRU case addressed the question of whether TRU possessed "market power" in the sense defined by prior antitrust precedents. As events ensued, this emphasis was misdirected, since proof of market power is normally unnecessary to infer illegality when horizontal agreements are shown. But for the vertical aspects of the case, the existence of market power would strengthen an inference of illegality, since an actor at one stage in the vertical chain of distribution was more likely to implement restraints with a meaningful impact on consumers if the initiator at another stage had a powerful position, and significant anticompetitive effects would ensue if the restraints applied to substantial shares of the affected markets.

The concept of "market power," said by a reviewing appellate court to imply a degree of market dominance less than "monopoly" in the sense normally used by economists,[15] is not well defined. There are at least three ways of showing that it exists or does not exist—structure-oriented measurement of market shares in relevant markets, statistical analyses of the relationship between prices and market shares, and analysis of the effects of restrictive actions on market outcomes. All three avenues were pursued in the Toys "R" Us case.

---

[13]Opinion of Commissioner Orson Swindle dissenting in part and concurring in part, 126 FTC 415, 620 (emphasis in original).

[14]Opinion of the Commission, 126 FTC 415, 575.

[15]*Toys "R" Us, Inc.* v. *Federal Trade Commission,* 221 F. 3d 928 (2000).

Case 16:   Toys "R" Us (2000)

Although there are hundreds of toy manufacturers and thousands of firms retailing toys in the United States, both markets exhibit what at face value would be called intermediate concentration levels. At the manufacturing stage, the top four U.S. suppliers during the early 1990s originated from 34 to 45 percent of total toy supplies (many imported from southeast Asia), varying with whether only traditional or also video game toys are counted and to some extent with the data source used. However, the focus of TRU's clubs policy was on nationally advertised toys, and for those, roughly two-thirds of the national television advertising was done by only eight toy makers, three of them divisions of Mattel, the source inter alia of Barbie dolls. By accepted antitrust standards, toy manufacturing was sufficiently highly concentrated that an inference of "market power" could be supported.

At the retailing level, Toys "R" Us accounted for approximately 20 percent of all retail toy sales in the United States. However, all parties acknowledged that the relevant retail markets for toys were localized. TRU maintained stores principally in the larger metropolitan areas. Its marketing research revealed that in population areas within a thirty-minute drive from a TRU store, its average share of the total toy market was approximately 32 percent—again, a structural position sufficient to imply the existence of "market power" under the received vertical restraints precedents.

TRU maintained rich internal data on the competitive structure of the localized retail markets surrounding its U.S. sales outlets. Tapping these data and information on individual store percentage retail margins, economists representing TRU computed regression equations relating store PRMs to the number of significant rivals (mainly, hypermarkets such as Wal-Mart and Target as well as, briefly during the early 1990s, warehouse clubs) within a local market. They showed that TRU realized somewhat lower PRMs in markets with one or two major rivals than in markets where no major retailing rival existed, and that the presence of additional rivals beyond two made no significant difference. The PRM differences with and without major competition were said to be sufficiently small as to be *de minimus*. However, TRU adjusted prices to deal with local market conditions for only about 250 items, typically those that were nationally advertised and/or "hot," out of the nearly sixteen thousand items it stocked at the time. For the majority of SKUs, prices were uniform nationally. A witness for the FTC testified that, given the modest share of total TRU sales associated with the items whose prices were geared to local competitive conditions, the implied price differences on those competition-sensitive items could be as much as 6 to 7 percent—a not negligible magnitude.

Economists representing TRU argued, using regression and qualitative evidence, that TRU's ability to raise prices in any given retail market was severely constrained by the presence of vigorous low-price competitors such as Wal-Mart, Kmart, and Target, and therefore that TRU lacked the "market power" required to find its vertical restraints inconsistent with antitrust law. It is undoubtedly true that TRU's ability to raise prices was

449

THE ANTITRUST REVOLUTION

constrained by strong competitors. However, the argument skirted a fundamental point. The purpose of TRU's warehouse clubs policy was directed not toward raising prices in local retail markets whose structure reflected the encroachment of hypermarkets, but toward curbing additional and rising competition from warehouse clubs that could otherwise force *reductions* in retail prices. To the extent that TRU's warehouse club policies were successful in suppressing the clubs' competitive threat, downward price changes were avoided—a clear manifestation of market power. As the FTC concluded, rejecting the constrained price increase argument, "there is little question that the boycott of the warehouse clubs that TRU organized *could* and *did* lower output by avoiding a decrease in toy prices by TRU and TRU's non-club competitors."[16]

The "Free-Riding" Efficiency Defense

The U.S. courts have accepted as a defense to some vertical restraints the argument that such restraints help solve problems that would otherwise render the distribution of goods or services less efficient. The basic theoretical premise was formulated by Telser (1960). Telser observed that retailers often provide presale services that help consumers make well-informed product choices and, by enhancing the demand for the products, are valuable to manufacturers. Although other presale services might fall within the scope of Telser's argument, the standard example is a retailer that maintains display models in its showroom, explains to consumers (or allows them to experiment and learn) how the product functions, and hence enlightens their choices. Providing these services usually entails costs for the retailer. However, consumers might visit the high-service retailer's showroom, utilize the presale services, and then travel down the street to a low-service outlet and buy the product at discounted prices. In this case, the discount retailer is said to "free-ride" on services provided by the high-service retailer, and if such free-riding occurs with sufficient frequency, the high-service retailer will lose its incentive to provide desirable services and the market will implode to a low-service equilibrium. Restricting the availability of products to low-service retailers and/or preventing them from quoting steeply discounted prices restores the incentive for retailers to provide the desired presale services.

How important such free-riding market failures are in the real world, their implications for consumer welfare, and whether there exist alternative, less restrictive ways of solving the free-riding problem are questions on which unusually intense disagreement exists among professional economists, with those advocating vertical restraints identified more or less closely with the so-called Chicago School of thought.[17]

---

[16]Opinion of the Commission, 126 FTC 415, 597 (emphasis in original).

[17]For sharply differing textbook views on the problem, compare Carlton and Perloff (2000, ch. 12); and Scherer and Ross (1990, ch. 15).

Case 16:   Toys "R" Us (2000)

There was little dispute over the fact that TRU provided valuable presale services. With its large selection of products, it acted as a kind of "showroom" for toy industry manufacturers, ensuring that most of their products, and not just the best-sellers, were available to consumers. It tended to order products for the Christmas rush a few weeks earlier than did other toy retailers and to take delivery of the products slightly earlier, helping the manufacturers economize by spreading their production over a longer time period. It claimed also that its early stocking decisions signaled to other retailers what products were likely to be in strong demand, but this was contradicted by evidence showing that other retailers, and especially the warehouse clubs, made purchasing decisions on the basis of their own independent market assessments, taking into account manufacturers' announced advertising plans. Perhaps most importantly, several times a year TRU placed in leading metropolitan area newspapers catalogue inserts with full-color illustrations of several hundred products featured on its shelves, informing consumers of what was available and at what prices.

There were, however, several logical and factual problems with the TRU free-riding argument. For one, TRU's large product selection was unlikely to have provided presale information on which consumers then free-rode to make purchases at warehouse clubs. TRU merely put its products on its shelves, without providing the kind of demonstrative services emphasized in the original free-rider theories. The average price of items advertised in TRU's newspaper insert catalogues in the spring of 1997 was $45.41, the median price $29.99. With such low ticket prices, few consumers inspect the product in a TRU showroom and then make a special trip to buy the item at a lower-price (e.g., warehouse) outlet. The FTC found no evidence that consumers "sought demonstration or explanation of a toy at TRU and then purchased the product at a club."[18] In addition, TRU derived direct competitive advantage in consumers' eyes from having the largest selection of toys, and thus its large stock conferred consumer image benefits upon itself and was not something on which rivals plausibly free-rode.

Second, the costs that TRU incurred to take early delivery of seasonal products and to inform consumers about available toys and their prices through its widely distributed catalogues and newspaper inserts turned out not to be very high. It was compensated for its early stocking practices by the deferral of invoice payment requirements—for example, from June, when delivery was taken, to December, when sales were at peak levels. When products taken into inventory turned out to be "duds" in consumers' eyes, manufacturers compensated TRU for the ensuing closeout discounts by granting substantial retroactive wholesale price discounts. Indeed, manufacturers testified that no other retailer received deferred payment terms and closeout discounts as favorable as those accorded TRU. They also paid

---

[18]Opinion of the Commission, 126 FTC 415, 603–604.

THE ANTITRUST REVOLUTION

TRU advertising allowances to compensate for the cost of distributing cat-alogues to consumers. The case evidence revealed that more than 90 per-cent of TRU's advertising outlays during the mid-1990s were reimbursed by manufacturers.[19] If TRU bore little of the cost of providing presale advertising and early product stocking, it was implausible to infer that free-riding by others on those services could lead it to eliminate them, as the standard theory of free-riding assumes.

TRU's principal economic witness attempted to demonstrate through a series of regression analyses that other retailers nevertheless experienced sales increases as a result of TRU's catalogue advertising, and hence free-rode on that advertising. What ensued was a war of alternative regression equation specifications. The first TRU analysis revealed that for items featured in TRU's April 2, 1995, catalogue, TRU achieved substantial sales gains relative to nonadvertised items. But in addition, other toy retailers experienced smaller but still appreciable sales gains on those items relative to nonadvertised items. The FTC's economic expert questioned whether there might have been something special about the items selected for the April 1995 catalogue that induced high subsequent sales growth independ-ent of the advertising effect—an example of what econometricians call "omitted variables" bias. Re-estimating the original TRU regression equa-tion with variables added to measure the pre-April growth momentum achieved by advertised as compared to nonadvertised products, the FTC analysis showed that catalogue inclusion indeed augmented TRU's sales, but had a *negative* impact on rival retailers' sales of the advertised products. Another round of competing regression equation specifications yielded similar inference reversals, prompting the administrative law judge to call a halt to the war and view the statistical inferences as not proven.

Finally, in rejecting TRU's free-rider defense, the FTC observed that before February 1992, when the warehouse club policy was announced at a Toy Fair, "no toy company document . . . even hints that 'free-riding' by one toy retailer on the efforts of another could be a problem in the indus-try."[20] Rather, TRU's concern was the damage that low warehouse club prices could do to its reputation as a low-price merchandiser and the neces-sity of reducing popular toys' prices to warehouse club levels to avert that adverse reputation effect. The first recorded mention of free-riding in the voluminous case record occurred later in 1992, when the clubs threatened to sue TRU and its suppliers for discriminatory sales policies. The record is silent as to whether the notion originated spontaneously or whether it was suggested by outside consultants hired to evaluate the legal threats. Whatever the origin, the Commission concluded that TRU's concerns about

---

[19]National television advertising was sponsored almost exclusively by the manufacturers, not TRU. Toy advertising outlays on television in 1995 amounted to roughly five times TRU's outlays for (mostly) local catalogue advertising.

[20]Opinion of the Commission, 126 FTC 415, 567. See also pp. 579–580 of the opinion.

Case 16:   Toys "R" Us (2000)

free-riding as a justification for its restrictive policies were a "pretext" and not a valid basis for the policies' implementation.[21]

THE OUTCOME

Rejecting the free-rider defense and concluding that TRU had orchestrated both a horizontal boycott and restrictive vertical agreements, the FTC ruled that TRU had violated the antitrust laws. It ordered TRU to cease entering into vertical agreements with its toy suppliers that limited the supply of toys to discounters, to cease facilitating horizontal agreements among its suppliers concerning the sale of toys to other retailers, and to refrain from requesting information from manufacturers about their sales to toy discounters.

Throughout the proceedings, counsel for TRU openly expressed doubts that they could obtain a fair trial at the FTC, combining as it does in a carefully compartmentalized way the functions of prosecutor and judge. TRU therefore sought, as many losing parties do, reversal from an independent federal appellate court. Operating in all parts of the United States, it could as the appealing party choose the jurisdiction in which to file its appeal. It selected the Seventh Circuit Court of Appeals, situated in Chicago, with three members of the University of Chicago law faculty as sitting judges. It presumably believed that its chances were best in the environment where the theory of free-riding had originated. If so, then it was mistaken.

A panel of three appellate judges headed by a University of Chicago law faculty member unanimously ratified the FTC's decision.[22] It found that the horizontal boycott, to which the contested market power issues were less relevant, clearly violated Section 1 of the Sherman Act. Observing that, given this conclusion, it did not have to rule formally on the case's vertical issues, it nevertheless opined that TRU's pleadings "fundamentally misunderstood the theory of free riding." This was so, the court said, because in the absence of TRU threats, most leading manufacturers wanted to sell to the clubs without restrictions and since, with manufacturers paying for most of TRU's presale services, there was little opportunity for meaningful free-riding.

THE AFTERMATH

The Federal Trade Commission's October 1998 decision finding TRU in violation of the antitrust laws precipitated a flurry of additional class action

---

[21]Opinion of the Commission, 126 FTC 415, 607.

[22]*Toys "R" Us, Inc.* v. *Federal Trade Commission,* 221 F.3d 928 (2000).

antitrust suits against TRU and leading toy manufacturers, some by private parties seeking compensation for damages sustained and one by the attorneys general of forty-four U.S. states plus Puerto Rico and the District of Columbia. "To avoid the cost and uncertainty of protracted litigation," TRU along with three toy manufacturers negotiated in 1998 and 1999 settlements valued at a total of $56 million, some paid in cash and most in the form of toys to be distributed to needy children.[23]

In addition to the rejection of its policies toward warehouse clubs, whose overall sales growth slowed during the late 1990s, TRU experienced increasing competition from hypermarkets, and especially from a Wal-Mart that was continuing its "march to the sea." Wal-Mart's toy sales share exceeded TRU's beginning in 1999 and continued rising to nearly 30 percent of national toy sales by 2006.[24] TRU's share declined to an estimated 15 percent in 2006, when TRU was overtaken also by Target. TRU's profits ebbed and turned negative in some years, despite strenuous efforts to modernize many stores, close others, secure exclusive deals on toys that were predicted to become hits, and induce its staff members to devote more of their time helping shoppers.[25]

With its stock price stalled at only 60 percent of its all-time peak value, TRU agree in 2005 to "go private" in a $6.6 billion transaction. Two other toy retailing chains, KB Toys and F.A.O. Schwartz, filed for bankruptcy.

Meanwhile, the warehouse clubs continued to pursue their selective strategy, stocking a limited array of toys mainly during the Christmas season. A warehouse club executive reported to this author that, following the FTC order, his firm had no special difficulty securing the toys that it wanted. The largest warehouse club chain, Costco, expanded its number of stores from 374 in 2002 to 474 at the end of 2006. However, its principal independent rival, BJ's, experienced disappointing sales in 2006 and a resignation by its CEO, accompanied by rumors of a possible takeover. The rise of Wal-Mart, in particular, had created a new competitive environment for both specialist and general retailers.

REFERENCES

Adelman, Morris A. *A&P: A Study in Price-Cost Behavior and Public Policy.* Cambridge, Mass.: Harvard University Press, 1959.

Barbaro, Michael. "No Playtime on Recovery Road." *New York Times*, November 19, 2006, sec. 3, pp. 1, 8, 9.

---

[23]Annual Report, Toys "R" Us, 2000, "Other Matters" (www.shareholder.com/toy/toysrus00 .t2000ar36); Canedy (1998); and Gargiulo (1999).

[24]See Barbaro (2006).

[25]See Hays (2001) and Barbaro (2006).

Case 16:   Toys "R" Us (2000)

Canedy, Dana. "Hasbro to End Suit with $6 Million Donation." *New York Times,* December 11, 1998, p. C-20.

Carlton, Dennis W. "Market Power and Vertical Restraints in Retailing: An Analysis of *FTC* v. *Toys 'R' Us.*" In *The Role of the Academic Economist in Litigation Support,* edited by Daniel J. Slottje, 67–96. Amsterdam: Elsevier, 1999.

Carlton, Dennis W., and Jeffrey M. Perloff. *Modern Industrial Organization,* 3d edn. Reading, Mass.: Addison-Wesley Longman, 2000.

Chandler, Alfred D. *The Visible Hand: The Managerial Revolution in American Business.* Cambridge, Mass.: Harvard University Press, 1977.

Gargiulo, Linda. "Putting Children First in a Toy Settlement." *New York Times,* May 30, 1999, p. III-4.

Hays, Constance L. "Toys 'R' Us Plans to Lay Off 1,900 and Close 64 Stores." *New York Times,* December 29, 2001, p. C-1.

Scherer, F. M. "Sunlight and Sunset at the Federal Trade Commission." *Administrative Law Review* 42 (Fall 1990): 461–487.

Scherer, F. M. "Retail Distribution Channel Barriers to International Trade." *Antitrust Law Journal* 67(1) (1999): 77–112.

Scherer, F. M., and David Ross. *Industrial Market Structure and Economic Performance.* Boston: Houghton-Mifflin, 1990.

Steiner, Robert L. "Does Advertising Lower Consumer Prices?" *Journal of Marketing* 37 (October 1973): 19–26.

Steiner, Robert L. "The Nature of Vertical Restraints." *Antitrust Bulletin* 30 (Spring 1985): 346–359.

Telser, Lester G. "Why Should Manufacturers Want Fair Trade?" *Journal of Law & Economics* 3 (October 1960): 86–105.

13

3. Class actions in the U.S. experience: an economist's perception

Frederic M. Scherer

My role in this book, addressing important changes being considered actively in Europe, is akin to what Augustine of Hippo did: confessing and distilling lessons from the sins of my youth. Specifically, how do class action suits work from the perspective of an economist who has participated as an expert witness in several? My focus has been mainly on antitrust suits, but I will recognize the relevance of other types.

1. THE RATIONALE OF CLASS ACTION LITIGATION

There are two main reasons for laws permitting class action litigation:

(1)   To do justice, that is, to compensate a nation's citizens for harm that is done to them by powerful (usually industrial or medical) actors – e.g., through price fixing, selling defective and dangerous products or services, polluting the environment, polluting the information environment with false and misleading statements, and engaging in unwarranted discrimination – price or otherwise.
(2)   To deter actions that might be illegal, but that might either escape the attention of law enforcement authorities, or be committed because the expectation of penalties administered by government agencies is insufficient, or to solve free-rider problems when no individual has a sufficient incentive to take corrective action that will benefit many fellow citizens.

Let us consider first the second of these explanations. Does deterrence from class action litigation actually work? In principle, the prospect of paying treble damages for violations of U.S. antitrust law ought to be a formidable deterrent. Whether it actually deters is questionable, given the plethora of large-scale price-fixing conspiracies brought to light in recent years, in both the United States and Europe. Examples include vitamins, carbon electrodes, airline fares, auction house fees, lysine, citric acid, dynamic random access memory chips, and most recently (January 2007, from a European Commission action), in electric power switchgear. (It was a 1950s case in electrical equipment, including switchgear, that precipitated some of the largest early damages awards under the U.S. antitrust laws.[1]) Similarly, much litigation against the U.S. cigarette manufacturers by private parties and state attorneys general has led to fines and punitive damages awards measured in the hundreds of millions of dollars, which, given inelastic demand for cigarettes, have been passed on to consumers in the form of greatly elevated prices. Despite the past history of litigation and damages, recent research has suggested that the cigarette makers have knowingly increased average nicotine levels by 10 to 11 per cent since 1998, presumably in the expectation of enhancing addiction effects for new smokers.[2]

Why does deterrence appear to be ineffective? There are two plausible reasons: a perceived low probability of being caught and assessed damages; and/or the insufficiency of the damages actually awarded when violation of the law is proven.[3] I find the latter explanation hard to believe, given the fact that class action plaintiffs under the U.S. antitrust laws can claim three times the actual amount of damages proven. Clearly, further analysis of what is happening is needed.

2. IS JUSTICE SERVED?

Closely related to the question of the sufficiency of damages is the question: is justice served? Are consumers in fact made whole as a result of class action suits? According to the preamble of the Class Action Fairness Act, which was passed by the U.S. Congress in 2005, justice is being served inadequately:[4]

(3) Class members often receive little or no benefit from class actions, and are sometimes harmed, such as where:
 (A) Counsel are awarded large fees, while leaving class members with coupons or other awards of little value;

---

[1] See Smith (1961a,1961b).
[2] See Gladwell (2007).
[3] See White (1988), for conference proceedings that thoroughly explore both the theory and evidence on class action suits under the U.S. antitrust laws.
[4] Public Law 109–2, 119 Stat. 4 (February 2005). See also the roundtable discussion, Anonymous (2005, pp. 18–21).

(B)   Unjustified awards are made to certain plaintiffs at the expense of other class members; and

(C)   Confusing notices are published that prevent class members from being able to fully understand and effectively exercise their rights.

The coupon remedy is indeed a problem. What they often do is allow a discount on the purchase of another iteration of the same unsatisfactory product. And if I were a clever business manager forced to issue such coupons, I would try to offer a special product priced with such a high margin that I would profit even though I must grant what is purported to be a discount. My own experience is that I have been offered several such coupons and found it troublesome to obtain them and take advantage of them. Only once did I receive monetary damages from a class action settlement, and in that case, the amount was tiny.

The new Class Action Fairness Act attempts to create a process under which the adequacy of damages and the legitimacy of compensation to counsel are carefully considered by the federal courts, at least, in those nationwide cases where the federal courts assume jurisdiction from decentralized state courts.

3.   BLACKMAIL?

Complementary to the problem of low damages actually accruing to the persons who have suffered from actionable conduct is the incentive for blackmail by entrepreneurial law firms. There are many such firms in the United States whose specialty is bringing class action suits in the expectation that the defendants will settle and pay substantial negotiated fees rather than incurring the costs and risks of protracted litigation. Steven Salop and Lawrence J. White found in an analysis of 1,959 U.S. class action antitrust suits that 88 per cent settled without a trial.[5] Only 106 cases, or 5.4 per cent of the sample, actually went to trial. For those that went into trial, the average trial length was 11.4 days. For cases that settled without a trial on which information was available, the attorneys initiating the actions realized on average 20.3 per cent of the total damages settlements as attorneys' fees.[6] However, the distribution of fees was highly skew. The *median* attorney's fee in cases ending through settlement was 110 per cent of

---

[5]   White (1988, pp. 10–11).
[6]   Ibid. p. 14.

the damages recovered by those named as plaintiffs (by the initiating attorneys) and hence those who were in principle injured.

Acknowledging that I have also participated in class action suits that I considered well-justified, let me illustrate this point with details on three actions that were either poorly based in facts or (I am unable to distinguish) brought for purposes of blackmail.

One was a class action alleging a price-fixing conspiracy by Canadian producers of potash, extensively used as fertilizer by farmers in the United States and elsewhere.[7] The Canadian province of Saskatchewan is the OPEC of world potash production, controlling roughly half of the world's minable potash reserves. The industry in Saskatchewan is tightly oligopolistic; six companies originated nearly all of the province's potash output. The suit was based upon evidence of abrupt and substantial price increases, shown in Figure 3.1 as occurring during mid-1987. But there was a simple and obvious non-collusive explanation for the price shock. Competing potash producers in the United States had achieved the initiation of an anti-dumping suit against the Canadians, and in March of 1987 (second dotted vertical line in Figure 3.1), the U.S. International Trade Commission ruled that the Canadian producers were likely to be subjected to substantial anti-dumping tariffs on future shipments. In fact, on August 21 (third vertical dotted line), the U.S. International Trade Administration announced preliminary anti-dumping margins, for which a bond had to be posted, averaging 37 per cent for all of the Canadian potash producers and 52 per cent for the largest seller. Anticipating that decision and hoping to minimize its future tariff liabilities, the leading firm announced a substantial price increase and then, two weeks after the preliminary dumping margin decision, added a further increase of $35 per ton. Other smaller members followed its price lead – not an actionable offense under U.S. law. A protracted and expensive legal process followed. But the Canadian potash producers refused to settle, and eventually, the suit was voided.

On my next example I must tread carefully, since parts of the litigation are still pending. In the so-called Branded Drug Litigation,[8] a group of law firms filed class action complaints against the leading U.S. pharmaceutical manufacturers, alleging that they conspired to deny discounts to drug

---

[7]   Potash Antitrust Litigation, MDL (multi-district litigation) Docket No. 981, U.S. District Court for the District of Minnesota. For more details, see Scherer (2000, pp. 364–7). I was a consultant for Kalium Ltd. and in my preparation visited the world's deepest potash mine.

[8]   MDL–997, Master File no 94 C 897 (U.S. Federal Court for the Northern District of Illinois). The case is described at greater length in Chapter 10 of Scherer (2000). I submitted testimony on behalf of Pfizer Inc.

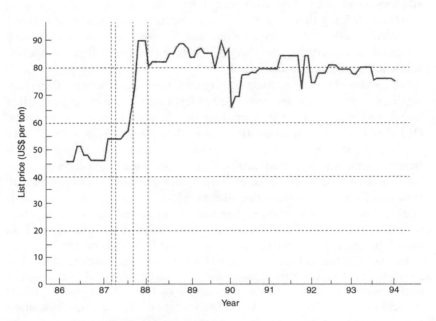

Figure 3.1 Movement of Saskatchewan potash prices, 1986–93

retailers even while they were offering large discounts to hospitals and
health maintenance organizations. There were several flaws in the class
action plaintiffs' claims. For one, they were not able to present direct
evidence that the drug manufacturers actually conspired to orchestrate the
discount structure. The most that could be proved is that the manufacturers
cooperated with drug wholesalers on a computerized rebate system so that
customers who had been granted discounts could be reimbursed promptly.
The discounts themselves varied widely from case to case. Second, the
hospitals and health care maintenance organizations had substantial bargaining power vis-à-vis the manufacturers, since they could deny a manufacturer's patented drug a place on their formulary of useable drugs unless
acceptable discounts were offered. Retailers, on the other hand, had no
such bargaining power. They were by law required to dispense a named
patented compound if the patient arrived with a valid prescription. Thus,
substitution was possible by the health care organizations but not by the
retailers. Third, the drug retailers had a long history of advocating resale
price maintenance (so-called 'fair trade') and shunning price competition
among themselves. It was only when the U.S. laws supporting fair trade

were abolished during the 1970s that retailers' gross margins declined from roughly 40 per cent to the 20 per cent value achieved under pressure from the U.S. government and so-called 'pharmacy benefit managers' bargaining over the margins they would reimburse.

A third such case accused the leading credit card companies of colluding to set the fees they charge for converting into dollars transactions consummated in non-U.S. currencies.[9] The principal alleged evidence of collusion turned on the participation of company attorneys at meetings whose principal subjects were government regulation of fee disclosures and the arbitration of disputes, and in which, the evidence showed, the magnitudes of conversion fees were mentioned only in passing. Persons present at the meetings denied under oath any attempt to agree on fees. Announcements of fee increases (from a 1 per cent base) extended over a period of several years, and by the end of 2004, when the suit was initiated, most Visa card providers were charging 3 per cent, one important Visa provider was charging 1 per cent, and American Express and Diner's Club were charging 2 per cent. The case continues.

4. IMPROVING THE LITIGATION PROCESS

The new U.S. Class Action Fairness Act seeks to correct some of the problems I have identified, but it will have little or no impact on cases such as the three I have described above that would be in federal courts rather than state courts. Even when jurisdiction is with federal courts, it is difficult for judges to sift through mounds of complex evidence and eliminate before a full trial is held the cases that are without merit. And even when a full trial is held – i.e., when the accused parties do not succumb to a settlement – judicial error is possible. One remedy that may place too much trust in the ability of economists is to have the court employ an expert economist as a clerk or expert advisor to the court. The first known instance of an economist serving in that role was not a class action, but a case litigated during the early 1950s by U.S. federal antitrust authorities against the United Shoe Machinery Corporation. In that case, Harvard University economist Carl Kaysen served as advisor to Judge Charles Wyzanski.[10] Since that time economists have served as court-appointed clerks or experts

---

[9]   *Robert Ross et al.* v. *American Express Co. et al.,* Case No. 04 CV 05723 (WHP) (Southern District of New York). The author submitted evidence on behalf of American Express.

[10]   *U.S.* v. *United Shoe Machinery Corporation* 110 F. Supp. 295 (1953). On his experience see Kaysen (1956).

in a handful of class action suits. Such service is no panacea. My own experience in two such cases reveals the difficulties.

For the damages phase of the folding carton litigation, I was retained by Judges Charles Robson and Hubert Will in Chicago to determine the reasonableness of the negotiated damages settlements.[11] (Shortly before, the U.S. Supreme Court had ruled that such consideration was necessary when class action suits were settled by negotiation.) Another economist had been retained by the Court to advise on the liability segment of the litigation. To the best of my knowledge, I received no information on the division of payments between attorneys and the carton users on whose behalf the suit was brought. Damages were computed for individual carton buyers. One thing that struck me was that the Pillsbury Company claimed by far the largest percentage elevation of prices as a result of the remarkably well-documented price-fixing conspiracy. The question was, why? Investigation revealed that Pillsbury, unlike other users of special, preprinted cartons, had required carton makers to bid on *all* of the 50 or so cartons it wanted in one annual competition. At the time there were more than 100 vendors of folding cartons, but only the 10 or 12 largest companies were party to the price-fixing conspiracy. By consolidating its bidding requirements, Pillsbury made it difficult for smaller, more specialized carton makers to bid, thereby rendering itself especially vulnerable to the relatively few large carton producers, who comprised the core of the conspiracy. I asked the judges whether a doctrine of contributory negligence was relevant to the assessment of damages. The answer was, no. But I believe there should be such a consideration when a buyer adopts a bidding system that is unusually well-suited for successful conspiracy by sellers.

Although I retain little documentation, I recall a similar issue in the treble damages suits that followed the 'great' electrical equipment conspiracy of the 1950s. Many of the products on which the conspiracy turned were sold to electric power producing utilities. At the time, those utilities were regulated, and their profits were established on the basis of a 'fair return on fair value' principle – the larger their asset base, the higher the profit they were allowed to retain. If the allowed rate of return on assets was higher than the cost of capital, as was commonly the case, the regulated firms had an incentive to increase their asset bases beyond the bounds of economic efficiency.[12] It was rumored at the time that at least some of the electric power companies knew about the conspiracy, but since it enhanced

---

[11]   MDL-250 (U.S. Federal Court for the Northern District of Illinois).
[12]   On the theory, see Scherer (1970, pp. 523–37).

34   *The law and economics of class actions in Europe*

their net profits under the regulated profit-setting formula, they did nothing to combat it. Again, a doctrine of contributory negligence would be appropriate to deal with such anomalies.

Similar negligence has been alleged in connection with the collapse of the Enron Corporation, harming many investors who had been misled by Enron's wildly optimistic financial reports. The accounting firm, Arthur Andersen, which had audited Enron's books and approved its financial reports, was held liable in part for the losses to Enron shareholders and had ceased operating as a result of the legal actions brought against it after the collapse. However, an article in the *New Yorker* magazine by Malcolm Gladwell revealed that a skilled and diligent analyst could see through Enron's accounting methods and realize that it was concealing substantial losses.[13] The indications of concealed trouble included the fact that Enron paid no U.S. income tax for several years, even though its financial reports claimed substantial profits, and that its cash flow was negative. Careful investors and the Wall Street analysts who advised them should have been wary, but hardly anyone did the necessary homework. Here too one might argue that damages claims should have been mitigated by the failure of prudent analysis.

In 1991 I participated again as advisor to Judge Will, this time in the Glass Bottles treble damages litigation.[14] With the benefit of previous experience, we established what appeared to be an ideal working arrangement. I was to be compensated half by attorneys for the plaintiffs and half by the defendants. At an intermediate stage of the proceedings, I met separately with counsel for plaintiffs and defendants, asking them to sharpen unclear points in their briefs and expert affidavits and suggesting statistical tests to focus the issues. When the actual trial began, I read the daily testimony transcript and prepared analytic summaries for Judge Will. My analysis confirmed testimonial evidence of a price-fixing conspiracy during the 1960s. An analysis of pricing revealed almost no deviation of actual transaction prices from list prices until roughly 1972, but after that time, transaction prices deviated by increasingly large percentages from list prices, suggesting that the conspiracy (of which there was no testimonial evidence for the 1970s) had indeed broken up. An expert economist witness for the defendants placed considerable stress on the transaction-list price deviations during the 1970s, but when asked on cross examination whether there was *ever* any price-fixing conspiracy, he denied its existence. Judge Will had planned to have me testify and be cross-examined by both parties after the testimony by

---

[13]   Gladwell (2007).
[14]   MDL 89C 5251 (U.S. Federal Court for the Northern District of Illinois).

plaintiffs and defendants was concluded. However, the proceedings lasted longer than anticipated, the Christmas recess was approaching, and my testimony would have meant that there would be a substantial interval between the completion of evidentiary proceedings and the time when the jurors would deliberate over their decision. Anxious to complete the case before the Christmas recess, Judge Will decided to forgo my testimony. Had I testified, I would have credibly contracted the defense witness's testimony alleging no conspiracy ever. However, I would have stated that the conspiracy broke up before the statute of limitations tolled, so plaintiffs would not be entitled to damages. Disbelieving the defendants' expert, the jury concluded that the conspiracy had continued into the 1980s, when it was not protected by the statute of limitations. As a result, recognizing that an injustice was being done, Judge Will stepped in and brokered a modest damages settlement. We were both left frustrated. Justice had gone astray because of an economist's refusal to concede his client's damages-free guilt.

5.   THE PASS-ON PROBLEM

In 1977, the U.S. Supreme Court rendered an important decision in the *Illinois Brick* case, stating that only those who had directly purchased goods or services from conspirators to a price-fixing scheme were entitled to recover damages.[15] Awarding damages to 'downstream' purchasers – e.g., consumers who had bought the price-fixed product from a retailer, who in turn bought it from the manufacturer – was ruled out because of the difficulty of determining how much or how little of the conspiracy-induced price increase middlemen had passed on to ultimate consumers and because letting both middlemen and consumers sue for damages would unduly complicate class action litigation. But although the amount of pass-on depends upon the structure of the intermediate market, the degree of product differentiation, and other variables, it is highly probable that most of the burden of a price-fixing conspiracy falls upon ultimate consumers rather than the middlemen who are immediate purchasers from the conspirators.[16] Thus, justice is denied to the consumers. This problem was corrected in part as many states adopted their own antitrust damages laws without an *Illinois Brick* pass-on barrier. The asymmetry between state and federal laws encouraged litigation at the decentralized state level, among other things increasing the costs of damages recovery suits. How this

---

[15]   *Illinois Brick Co.* v. *Illinois*, 431 U.S. 720 (1977). See also *Hanover Shoe Inc.* v. *United Shoe Machinery Corp.*, 392 U.S. 481 (1968).
[16]   For a solidly-based predictive model, see Lynch (2004).

practice will be affected by passage of the federal Class Action Fairness Act, which seeks to reduce the amount of state-level litigation, remains to be seen. The implication for this conference is that if European nations develop their own class action procedures, they would be well advised to avoid the *Illinois Brick* pass-on precedent.

6. CONCLUSION

The U.S. experience with class action litigation reveals many difficulties that impair the working of the wheels of justice. The possibility of bringing class action suits does not appear to have deterred a substantial number of serious law violations, although increasing the damages multiple for serious offenses might have some deterrent effect. Entrepreneurship by specialist class action law firms often leads to opportunistic cases brought more for purposes of settlement blackmail than in the anticipation that a full trial will reveal the truth. Even when a full trial ensues, the decisions are not always in accord with either truth or justice. To be sure, some good is done. But in considering what kinds of class action laws they will enact, our European cousins are well advised to learn from the mistakes of the United States as well as from its positive experience.

BIBLIOGRAPHY

Anonymous, (2005), 'Class Action Fairness Act of 2005', *The National Law Journal*, May 16.

Gladwell, M. (2007), 'The Formula: Enron, Intelligence, and the Perils of Too Much Information', *The New Yorker*, January 8.

Harris, A. (2007), 'Study on Nicotine Levels Stirs Calls for New Controls', *New York Times*, January 19.

Kaysen, C. (1956), *United States v. United Shoe Machinery Corporation*, Cambridge: Harvard University Press.

Lynch, M.P. (2004), 'Why Economists Are Wrong to Neglect Retailing and How Steiner's Theory Provides an Explanation of Important Regularities', *Antitrust Bulletin*, **49**, 911–940.

Scherer, F.M. (1970), *Industrial Market Structure and Economic Performance*, Chicago: Rand McNally.

Scherer, F.M. (2000), *Competition Policy, Domestic and International*, Cheltenham: Edward Elgar.

Smith, R.A. (1961a), 'The Incredible Electrical Conspiracy', Part I, *Fortune*, **63**(4), 132–180.

Smith, R.A. (1961b), 'The Incredible Electrical Conspiracy', Part II, *Fortune*, **63**(5), 158–224.

White, L.J. (ed.) (1988), *Private Antitrust Litigation: New Evidence, New Learning*, Cambridge: MIT Press.

PART IV

POLICY FOR DEVELOPING COUNTRIES

HARVARD Kennedy School
JOHN F. KENNEDY SCHOOL OF GOVERNMENT

Competition Policy and Intellectual Property: Insights from Developed Country Experience
Faculty Research Working Paper Series

F. M. Scherer
Harvard Kennedy School

Jayashree Watal
World Trade Organization

February 2014
RWP14-013

Visit the **HKS Faculty Research Working Paper Series** at:
http://web.hks.harvard.edu/publications

www.hks.harvard.edu

COMPETITION POLICY AND INTELLECTUAL PROPERTY: INSIGHTS FROM
DEVELOPED COUNTRY EXPERIENCE

F. M. Scherer and Jayashree Watal
Feburary 2014 Revision

To encourage technological innovation and the international transfer of
technology on a harmonized basis, the Agreement Establishing the World Trade
Organization (WTO), adopted at Marrakesh in April 1994, included a TRIPS agreement
(i.e., agreement on the trade-related aspects of intellectual property rights). TRIPS
contains rules on how nations should protect, utilize, and enforce intellectual property
rights (IPRs) and articulates measures to prevent the abuse of IPRs. Before TRIPS
was negotiated, some WTO members already had active policies to combat IPR
abuses, among other things, under their patent and competition policy laws. For most
newly developing nations, however, the TRIPS abuse provisions necessitate policy
innovations, including the development of criteria to identify actionable abuses and to
formulate appropriate remedies. As a guide to nations that must evolve their own
policies and practices *de novo*, this paper reviews the history of abuse mitigation
measures implemented by jurisdictions with the most extensive relevant experience and
supplements those insights with an analysis of policies adopted in particularly patent-
sensitive fields of technology.

Background

TRIPS recognized that harmonized and strengthened intellectual property rights -
- e.g., patents, trademarks, copyright, trade secrecy rules, and similar legal provisions --
could be abused as well as performing their economically laudatory functions. It
therefore stipulated in Article 8.2 that appropriate measures, otherwise consistent with
the broader agreement, could be taken to prevent the abuse of IPRs through practices
by rights holders that restrain trade or adversely affect the international transfer of
technology. Our focus here is competition law, although abuses might also occur in
other substantive areas of relevant law.

More specifically,   TRIPS recognized in Article 40.1 that some competition-
restraining IPR licensing practices or conditions might have an adverse effect on trade
or impede the transfer of new technology. TRIPS therefore permits in Article 40.2
participating governments to take measures to prevent or control abuses, provided that
the measures are otherwise consistent with the TRIPS agreement. However, there was
an early difference of opinion among TRIPS negotiators. Developing countries
preferred administratively convenient *per se* rules like the 14 rules recognized in the
defunct UNCTAD draft Code of Conduct for the Transfer of Technology.   Actions
inconsistent with the rules were presumed to constitute abuse. Developed nations
tended to prefer a so-called "rule of reason" approach, where abuse was inferred on a
case-by-case basis following appropriate documentation and analysis of monopolistic

1

effects. In the end, the TRIPS agreement was adopted with ambiguous language, allowing WTO members to specify in their national laws, and take measures to prevent or control, licensing practices or conditions that might in particular cases be deemed an abuse of IPRs with an adverse effect on competition in relevant markets.

Article 31 of the TRIPS agreement permits national authorities to issue mandatory licenses -- also called compulsory licenses -- permitting the domestic use of relevant IPRs by parties other than the original rights holder. Article 31(b) authorizes such licensing, subject to judicial review, for non-commercial governmental uses, in national emergencies, and when bargaining stalemates impede the implementation of economically significant technological advances. In addition, Article 31(k) allows compulsory licensing without satisfaction of those conditions in order to remedy practices determined through judicial or administrative processes to be anti-competitive, i.e., those addressed in Article 40. WTO members are left free to flesh out the details for such licensing, or other abuse remedies, in their national laws and practices.

Again, this paper seeks clues from competition policies adopted by developed countries in the past as to how developing nations might implement the authority granted them in Articles 40 and 31 of TRIPS.

Differing IPR Environments

It must be recognized preliminarily that the conditions under which intellectual property rights are exercised in developing countries often differ from those found in the more developed nations. In particular, one might expect differences in the sources of technical innovations and hence whether the patents or other rights applicable in a particular jurisdiction are of local origin or whether they originated elsewhere. We therefore begin by investigating the mix of resident vs. non-resident patents, and how it varies with the level of economic development and other relevant variables. To explore this question, we compiled a data base on patent applications for the year 2011, drawn from surveys by the World Intellectual Property Organisation.[1] It was linked to data on individual nations' population and gross domestic product per capita, drawn from the Pocket World in Figures 2013 edition published by The Economist newspaper. Links were established for 58 nations, ranging in population from Estonia to China and in GDP per capita from Bangladesh and Kenya (tied) to Singapore. Plainly, not all nations were covered, and the least-developed nations were under-represented. But the sample does cover a wide range of national conditions.

For the 57 nations on which 2011 patent applications were broken down between domestic residents and non-residents, residents filed on average 53.6 percent of total applications. However, there was a wide range, from 2.1 percent for Venezuela to 97.9 percent for Greece. Among the 15 sample nations with the lowest GDP per capita, resident applications averaged 21.6 percent -- significantly lower than the all-nation

---

1   . The source is www.wipo.int/ipstats/en/wipi/figures.html.

mean. Evidently, less-developed nations receive on average a disproportionately a high fraction of their patent applications from abroad -- e.g., from multinational enterprises.

For more insight into patterns, a multiple regression analysis was conducted, with either total patent applications TOTPAT or the percentage of domestic resident patent applications to the total PCTDOM as dependent variables. The explanatory variables were population POP (in millions), GDP per capita GDPCAP,[2] and a dummy variable RES with a value of 1 for nations with a high fraction of exports in the form of natural resources (e.g.., minerals and raw agricultural products) and 0 otherwise. With PCTDOM as dependent variable and t-ratios in subscripted parentheses, the regression is:

(1) PCTDOM = 56.96 + .38 GDPCAP - 11.47 Log POP - 31.6 RES;
     (3.76) (2.60)   (1.64)   (2.82)

$$R^2 = 0.334.$$

Local inventors contribute a significantly higher share of home-jurisdiction patent applications in nations with higher GDP per capita and a smaller share in natural resource-intensive jurisdictions. There is a weak tendency for the locally originated share to be smaller in larger nations -- which are presumably more attractive targets for foreign multi-national corporations. With total patent applications (in logarithms) as the variable to be explained, the regression is:

(2) Log TOTPAT = 0.91 + 1.227 log POP + 0.018 GDPCAP + 0.07 RES;
     (4.05) (11.84)   (8.05)   (0.41)

$$R^2 = 0.738$$

Not surprisingly, total patent applications exhibit a strong positive association with national population. The coefficient 1.227 can be interpreted as an elasticity. Since it is significantly greater than unity, it reveals that patenting rises more than proportionately with population. Nations with higher GDP per capita also draw significantly more patent applications, taking population into account too. The natural resources variable is statistically insignificant.[3]

---

2   . The Pocket World in Figures indexes this variable relative to a U.S.A. value of 1.0.

3   . A parallel analysis focused on the OECD compilation of so-called "triadic" patents, i.e., those issued within three jurisdictions -- the European Union, Japan, and the United States, but originating in 37 diverse nations. See OECD, Compendium of Patent Statistics (2008). These data are of course quite different from those analyzed above, focusing on applications filed within 57 different national jurisdictions. The results in an analysis of the origins of the "triadic" patents were similar to those in text equation (2). The origin nations filed significantly more triadic patents, the larger their home population, the higher their gross domestic product per capita, and the lower their dependence on natural resource exports was. More detailed results are

Presumably, nations will enforce their competition policies mainly with respect to the use or abuse of patents issued within their home jurisdictions. For lower-income (i.e., developing) nations, this implies a possible asymmetry of litigating power (i.e., the ability to hire top-notch legal counsel and technical consultants). To compensate for that differential, developing nations may be well advised to emphasize relatively clear and simple, i.e., *per se*, rules and downplay complex rule of reason proceedings.

Exceptions may of course exist. An example known to the authors was a Taiwan proceeding with respect to Intel's U.S. microprocessor patents.[4] When Intel's rival Advanced Micro Devices (AMD) regained momentum following a delayed transition to 32-bit microprocessors, its initial strength was in processors using less electric power than Intel's offerings. This in turn permitted longer batter life -- an important advantage for laptop computer purchasers. Given this advantage, AMD chips were chosen to drive most of the laptop computers assembled in Taiwan -- at the time, the world's leading laptop computer source. By virtue of an early IBM sourcing decision and then a dispute arbitration, AMD had full licenses to Intel's microprocessor patents. But Intel attempted to block the importation of AMD-driven laptops into the United States by claiming that when the ultimate buyers of AMD chip-driven laptops invoked certain data processing operations, they (i.e., the U.S. purchasers) violated Intel's U.S. patents. The Taiwan Fair Trade Commission intervened in 1994. Although no formal decision record is retained by us, we know that Intel's attempts to block such imports were abandoned. The probable logic of the case was that by attempting to extend its patent rights to control purchasers one or more steps downstream from the first transaction between AMD and Taiwanese computer assemblers, Intel violated the internationally honored exhaustion of rights doctrine.[5] In earlier U.S. cases, domestic attempts by a dominant firm to enforce exhausted patent rights were viewed as an abuse of monopoly power.

Early Precedents: The U.S. Experience

Before the TRIPS agreement was accomplished, by far the most active program of abuse control through competition policy institutions existed in the United States. It is more accurate, however, to characterize U.S. experience in terms of four long cycles in its history as a nation. In the early decades of its existence, the United States strove inter alia to build its manufacturing capabilities, which had been suppressed during British colonial rule.[6] As one component of that strategy, non-residents were not

---

available on request.

4   . Co-author Scherer testified on behalf of AMD before the Taiwan Fair Trade Commission in March 1994. Unfortunately, no documents from that case remain in our possession, nor were we able to find records of the TFTC's actions through an internet search.

5   . See e.g. Jayashree Watal, Intellectual Property Rights in the WTO and Developing Countries (Kluwer: 2001), pp. 294-295. Jayashree, check me on this. I couldn't find anything on exhaustion in the Robert Merges' patent law textbook.

6   . In this, it was implementing policies advocated in Alexander Hamilton's 1791 Report on

allowed to receive U.S. invention patents until 1836, and between 1836 and 1861, they had to pay higher patent registration fees than U.S. residents.[7] There followed a long period in which intellectual property (IP) holders, domestic and foreign, were allowed substantial leeway in the exercise of their government-granted rights as long as they conformed to the relevant U.S. patent laws. Beginning in the late 1930s and continuing into the 1970s, however, U.S. competition policy agencies and the courts adopted a much tougher line toward the permissible boundaries of patent utilization for both domestic and foreign patent holders. A second reversal occurred during the 1980s with shifts toward more conservative Federal government administrations and judicial appointments.

To illustrate the limits of what competition policies have sought to achieve, we focus in this section mainly on enforcement between the 1930s and 1970s, describing in a later section the subsequent reversion but noting the seeds of reversion in earlier cases. The great depression of the 1930s precipitated soul-searching about the relationships between government and business, crystallized in extensive investigations undertaken by the so-called Temporary National Economic Committee (TNEC).[8] Among other things, it was believed that business firms might be retarding emergence from the economic slump through patent-based cartel price-raising activities and the suppression of inventions.

One consequence was the initiation of numerous law suits alleging violation of the U.S. antitrust (i.e., competition policy) laws. New legal precedents were articulated, and more than 100 enforcement actions led between 1941 and January 1959 to the issuance of compulsory patent (and sometimes know-how) licensing decrees.[9] The number of patents licensed under these decrees has been estimated at between 40,000 and 50,000, or approximately 7.5 percent of all patents in force in any given year during that period. To differentiate the U.S. experience from that which smaller, less-developed nations are likely to face, it is important to recognize that among the 107 decrees tabulated in a definitive U.S. Senate report, only six were directed expressly toward foreign, as opposed to U.S.-resident, corporations, with two additional cases (involving foreign corporations' U.S. subsidiaries) counting as ambiguous. Two other

---

the Subject of Manufactures and opposed by Adam Smith. See F. M. Scherer, "General Hamilton and Dr. Smith," John F. Kennedy School of Government working paper no. RWP12-029, Harvard University, 2012.

7   . Foreign residents were not permitted to obtain U.S. copyright (or enforce their home-base copyright in the United States) until 1891.

8   . The work of the "TNEC" is reviewed inter alia in a special supplement to the American Economic Review, "Papers Relating to the Temporary National Economic Committee," vol. 32, June 1942.

9   . U.S. Senate, Committee on the Judiciary, Subcommittee on Patents, Trademarks, and Copyrights, Staff Report, Compulsory Licensing under Antitrust Judgments (Washington: 1960). A muck-raking survey of the substance underlying challenged patent abuses is found in Floyd L. Vaughan, The United States Patent System (University of Oklahoma Press: 1956).

facts must be recognized. For one, most of the compulsory licensing orders were so-called "consent decrees," issued not as the result of fully-litigated adversary proceedings in court, but receiving judicial approval after they were negotiated as a voluntary settlement of pending antitrust disputes without a formal court judgment affirming anti-competitive conduct. Of the 107 decrees described above, only 13 emerged from fully litigated cases. Consent settlement is much less costly for all parties to a litigation and may for accused violators be seen as a means of avoiding harsher penalties. Second, patents were not always the prime initial focus of antitrust cases that led to these settlements. In a substantial number of instances, compulsory patent licensing was seen as the most effective available remedy for more broad-based anti-competitive conduct or market structure.

An important ground for some patent-based antitrust actions was the use of patent licenses and cross-licenses to orchestrate cartels that raised prices, restricted the output of individual producers, and inhibited the entry of imports and new domestic producers. A leading case entailed the activities of the Hartford-Empire Company, at the time a developer of glass bottle-forming machinery, and the market-leading bottle producer, Owens-Illinois.[10] Through internal development, acquisitions, and restrictive licenses, those two companies dominated U.S. bottle-making machinery patent holdings, choosing to license production under them or not so as to reduce the number of machines available when business was slack and hence to maintain prices, even in the face of the worst economic depression in U.S. history. Testifying before the TNEC,[11] Hartford-Empire's president argued that his company's judgment was better than that of a competitive market "to protect the present manufacturers, to make money, and to produce milk bottles cheaper.... Who is better able to say whether we shall have 1,000 licensees or 500 or 50? We know the trade...." Assessing the TNEC record, (later Nobel laureate) George J. Stigler saw the cartelization of the glass container industry by Hartford-Empire as "an eloquent example of an evil demanding correction."[12] Hartford-Empire and Owens-Illinois were required in the resulting judicial decisions to cease their cartelizing activities and to license their extensive patent portfolios at reasonable royalties to all would-be takers.

Other prominent targets of the early patent-based antitrust actions was the General Electric Co. and Westinghouse Electric, the leading manufacturers of electric light bulbs in the United States. Those cases revealed more clearly than others the drastic changes in what was allowed and not allowed with respect to patents and competition policy.[13] General Electric was formed on a foundation of Thomas Edison's electric lamp patents, but solidified its position by acquiring rival firms and their patents

---

10   . U.S. v. Hartford-Empire Co. et al., 323 U.S. 386 and 324 U.S. 570 (1947).

11   . Hearings Before the TNEC, Part 2, pp. 412-413 (1939).

12   . George J. Stigler, "The Extent and Bases of Monopoly," American Economic Review, June 1942 Supplement, p. 14.

13   . See F. M. Scherer, "Technological Innovation and Monopolization," in Issues in Competition Law and Policy (American Bar Association Section of Antitrust Law: 2008), vol. II, pp. 1039-1042.

and entering into highly restrictive licenses with remaining rivals, fixing prices, allocating customers, and issuing market share quotas. Among other things, it negotiated licenses with foreign manufacturers that effectively prevented them from selling in the U.S. market. An early antitrust decision holding that GE and Westinghouse could not set the prices at which their wholesalers and retailers resold lamps was circumvented. Another action allowed the circumvention, but more important for precedential reasons, it confronted squarely the question of whether GE could prescribe licensee Westinghouse's ex-factory prices. It ended in defeat for the government when the U.S. Supreme Court ruled that such restrictive actions were acceptable when they were "normally and reasonably adapted to secure pecuniary reward for the patentee's monopoly."[14] However, with the change in perspectives accompanying the TNEC hearings, new antitrust complaints were lodged, leading to rejection of that early precedent. Assessing the evidence, the judge in the court of first instance ruled that:[15]

> ... [T]here can be no doubt that [General Electric] paced its industrial achievements with efforts to insulate itself from competition. It developed a tremendous patent framework and sought to stretch the monopoly acquired by patents far beyond the intendment of those grants. It constructed a great network of agreements and licenses, national and international in scope, which had the effect of locking the door of the United States to any challenge to its supremacy in the incandescent electric lamp industry ... Its domestic licenses gave fiat to a few licensees whose growth was carefully limited to fixed percentages of its own production and expansion so that over the years its share of the business was not materially diminished and its dominant proportion was never exposed to any hazard...

Most of the 1940-1970 decrees imposing compulsory patent licensing allowed patent holders to receive "reasonable royalties" for the use of their technology. However, finding that General Electric was "mounted upon an arsenal of a huge body of patents that can easily overwhelm and defeat competition by small firms," Judge Forman required that the General Electric patents be available to all would-be licensees royalty-free.[16]

Not all restrictive actions by dominant patent holders led to legal sanctions, however. One of the most prominent setbacks for U.S. government antitrust enforcers came in a case charging du Pont with monopolizing cellophane production in the United States. Du Pont obtained its original cellophane patent licenses from a French company and then expanded its portfolio through internal development. It licensed only one domestic competitor and kept that licensee, Sylvania, in check by elevating the

---

14   . U.S. v. General Electric Co., 272 U.S. 476, 489-490 (1926).

15   . U.S. v. General Electric Co. et al., 82 F. Supp. 753, 905 (1949) (Judge Philip Forman).

16   . There is reason to believe that at the negotiations leading to TRIPS, U.S. representatives observed that if a compulsory license is issued to remedy an anticompetitive practice, royalty-free licensing could be consistent with TRIPS.

royalty rate from 2 percent to 30 percent if Sylvania exceeded the roughly 25 percent market share stipulated by du Pont. Imports were kept out of the market by inducing the U.S. Congress to set tariffs as high as 60 percent. In 1953 a Wilmington, Delaware, judge accepted du Pont's defense that it had been a progressive cellophane producer and also ruled that du Pont was not a monopolist in the sense of competition law because it faced competition from other flexible packaging materials such as waxed paper, polyethylene, and Saran-wrap. The market definition decision, sustained on appeal to the U.S. Supreme Court, was sharply criticized by economists and characterized as "the cellophane fallacy."[17] This defeat for the antitrust enforcers foreshadowed later doctrines holding that to find abuse of monopoly power through patent restrictions, it was necessary that the market for the patented items be meaningfully defined following sound economic principles.

A quite different abuse that led to some compulsory licensing remedies is what is called "tying," although even before competition policy principles were applied to patent cases, it could be a cause of patent revocation or denial of infringement claims under what was called the "misuse" doctrine -- i.e., extending the scope of a patent to place restrictions on the purchase of unpatented items.[18] A typical tying arrangement is one in which a firm holds patents on some machine and then requires purchasers of the machine to buy exclusively from the machine-maker unpatented materials processed in the machine. In 1988 the U.S. Congress amended patent law to allow a finding of illegal tying or misuse only if the patent holder requiring the concomitant purchase of unpatented products was shown to have monopoly power in selling the patented product, i.e., that price-constraining substitutes were either absent or ineffective.[19] An independent producer of ink that functioned effectively with a patented package-labelling machine whose maker had insisted that its own unpatented ink be used was thereupon rebuffed in an important Supreme Court decision.[20] Relying on earlier precedents, the independent ink maker had not presented evidence assessing the patent holder's monopoly power, so the case was remanded to lower courts for possible further consideration.

Long before the intensification of antitrust actions against alleged abuses of patent grants, it was viewed as illegal to extend the control of a patented item's prices or

---

17 . George Stocking and Willard Mueller, "The Cellophane Case and the New Competition," *American Economic Review*, vol. 45 (March 1955), pp. 29-63. In "Technological Innovation and Monopolization," supra note 14, co-author Scherer argues that from a longer-run perspective the no-monopoly inference may have been justified.

18 . See e.g. Herbert Hovencamp, "The Intellectual Property - Antitrust Interface," and Janet McDavid et al., "Patents and Tying Arrangements," in American Bar Association, Issues in Competition Law and Policy, supra note 14, vol. III, pp. 1983-1995 and 2037-2059.

19 . 37 U.S.C. para. 271(d).

20 . Illinois Tool Works vs. Independent Ink, 547 U.S. 28 (2006). We were unsuccessful in attempts to learn from Independent Ink's management whether it followed the Supreme Court's judgment with further actions alleging that Illinois Tool had a monopolistic market position.

other aspects of consumption to any but the first purchaser of the patented item. For example, when General Electric sold light bulbs to retailers, it was found to violate the U.S. Clayton Antitrust Act when it specified the prices the retailers had to charge selling to third-party customers. For many decades such "resale price maintenance" was declared to be illegal per se, that is, without further investigation of broader impacts on the vigor of competition. However, a "rule of reason" approach to evaluating resale price maintenance was adopted at the expense of this per se approach by the U.S. Supreme Court in 2007.[21] Under the new rule, a full consideration of how competition and consumer welfare are affected by restraints must be undertaken -- presumably, at considerably greater litigating cost. Applications to the pricing of patented articles are likely to come.

Strong patent positions can be attained through a company's own research and development efforts, the purchase of other inventors' patents or other intellectual property, or some combination of the two. In an early case, the U.S. Supreme Court observed as a probable obiter dictum that "The mere accumulation of patents, no matter how many, is not in and of itself illegal."[22] When monopolistic market structures have been challenged under the U.S. patent laws, the specific contributions made by diversely acquired patents may have played a subtle role in the courts' decision-making, although no hard and fast rules for separating the causal effect of patent accumulation from other business policies have emerged.

One way patent positions may be strengthened is through mergers and acquisitions. Since 1950, the United States has aggressively challenged mergers that "tend substantially to lessen competition." In a number of cases under which mergers have been found to violate the U.S. anti-merger law, and especially in the pharmaceutical and biological fields, remedial efforts to restore effective competition have sometimes included the compulsory licensing or sale of patents in the relevant overlapping lines of business.[23]

---

21   . Leegin Creative Leather Products vs. PSKS, 551 U.S. 877 (2007). The case did not involve patented items.

22   . Automatic Radio Manufacturing Co. v. Hazeltine Research, 339 U.S. 827, 834 (1950). The Supreme Court recognized that Hazeltine produced no radios, but merely supplied under license the designs and other technology described in its 570 patents. Without patents, therefore, it would have been difficult for Hazeltine to obtain remuneration for its R&D efforts. But the Supreme Court attempted no explicit tradeoff between the special circumstances of Hazeltine's situation and its patent accumulation. The situation of Hartford-Empire in the 1930s was similar, although after it was required to license its bottle-forming machinery patents, it began manufacturing and selling machines of its own design. See the U.S. Senate committee report, supra note 10, at pp. 19-20.

23   . See for example In re Ciba-Geigy Ltd., 123 F.T.C. Reports 842 (1997), under which Ciba-Geigy was required to license at modest royalties its gene therapy patents. In "The Effects of Patent Relief on the Incentive to Invest and the Incentive to Disclose," unpublished S.J.D. dissertation, Harvard Law School (2005), pp. 108-109, Ziv M. Preis lists 21 cases between 1980

The most extensive compulsory licensing order in U.S. antitrust history, involving the dominant national telecommunications provider, AT&T, came in a consent settlement. Toward the end of the 19th Century and the beginning of the 20th Century, AT&T's dominant position was built in part by aggressive patent acquisition, restrictive cross licensing, and tough-minded pursuit of alleged patent infringers. But then AT&T changed its business policies, submitting to governmental price and entry regulation, allowing smaller local rivals to use its inter-city transmission facilities, and advancing telephone technology largely through the efforts of its Bell Telephone Laboratories (correctly said by Fortune magazine in November 1958 to be "the world's greatest industrial laboratory"). Its patent policy in later decades was exemplary. For example, following its breakthrough discovery of the transistor effect, it conducted symposia to explain the product and process technology and licensed all interested applicants to its semiconductor patents at modest royalties.[24] It did however take aggressive advantage of its regulated position in a variety of ways to hold back rival expansion, buy equipment mainly from its own manufacturing affiliate (Western Electric), and adopt or authorize only its own preferred improvements in telecommunications service.[25] A consensus favoring vigorous antitrust action grew in the 1950s. An antitrust complaint sought divestiture and fragmentation of Western Electric. With important components of the U.S. government hierarchy opposing the breakup, a consent settlement was negotiated calling for compulsory licensing, mostly without royalties, of Bell's roughly 9,000 patents and a ban on most Western Electric sales to customers other than the government and AT&T affiliates (which probably changed the way the semiconductor industry evolved).[26]

Quite possibly the last "great" compulsory licensing order under U.S. antitrust occurred with respect to Xerox in 1975.[27] Xerox had for more than a decade sustained a virtual monopoly of plain-paper copying machines, protected mainly by a portfolio eventually including some 900 patents. It chose to grant rivals licenses only to patents covering more expensive coated paper copying processes. Patent acquisition played an early but trivial role in the company's growth. The original patents issued to inventor Chester Carlson were transferred to the Battelle Research Institute which, with no manufacturing capacity, transferred them to a small firm that invested heavily to develop copying technology and enjoyed extraordinary market success from the time of its first general-purpose copier introduction in 1959. By 1975, its monopoly had endured for 16 years and was likely to continue because of Xerox's internally-generated improvement patents. Xerox pursued a variety of policies to derive advantage from its monopoly position, e.g., deploying machines at first only on a leased basis, which supported its

and 1999, eight of them involving pharmaceuticals, in which merger challenges were resolved inter alia by compulsory patent licensing.
24   . See John Tilton, International Diffusion of Technology: The Case of Semiconductors (Brookings Institution: 1971), pp. 73-77.
25   . See Scherer, "Technological Innovation and Monopolization," supra note 14.
26   . CCH Trade Cases Para. 68,246 (1956).
27   . In the matter of Xerox Corporation, 86 F.T.C. 363 (1975).

ability to use profit-maximizing price discrimination, and informally tying the purchase of toner (priced so high it was called "black gold" by company insiders) to the lease of Xerox machines.[28] Had the case been fully litigated, it would have been a close call, perhaps establishing new precedents as to what a dominant patent holder can do. But to minimize ongoing legal costs and risks and those anticipated when other firms tried to enter the market and triggered new patent infringement suits, Xerox chose to negotiate a settlement. A principal provision was the non-discriminatory licensing of Xerox's entire patent portfolio, the first three patents royalty-free for any licensee, the next three at 0.5 percent ad valorem royalty each, and the remainder at zero incremental royalty.

Consequences of U.S. Compulsory Licensing Actions

The widespread compulsory patent licensing ordered under U.S. antitrust decrees evoked fears that incentives for innovation would be jeopardized. Following the 1956 AT&T order and a parallel one covering IBM's large patent portfolio, the Wall Street Journal warned:[29]

> So it may turn out that these are dangerous victories the Government boasts about. The settlements in these cases indicate a belief that everybody's patents should be everybody else's. But this is a philosophy that strikes at incentive; new ideas and new inventions may be lost. Such Government victories may turn out to be far more costly for the nation than for the companies.

The actual impact turned out to be more complex but decidedly less dire. Spurred by the Wall Street Journal editorial quoted here, a group of nine Harvard Business School students fanned out across the nation to ask companies, including those subjected to major compulsory patent licensing decrees, how such licensing, actual or prospective, affected their incentives to invest in research and development. The results were astonishing, at least to the student group. The decrees were found to have very little negative effect on R&D incentives, although companies covered by the decrees did reduce their patenting, especially with respect to process inventions that could be kept secret.[30] More general responses about the role patents played in research and development decision-making were equally surprising. With limited exceptions, R&D investments were little affected by the expectation or lack thereof of patent protection. Much more important in company decision-makers'

---

28   . The best available analysis of Xerox' strategies is Erwin Blackstone, "The Copying Machine Industry: A Case Study," Ph.D. dissertation, University of Michigan, 1968.

29   . "Dangerous Victory," Wall Street Journal, January 22, 1956, p. 6.

30   . F. M. Scherer et al., Patents and the Corporation (Privately published, 1958, 2nd ed. 1959). It is noteworthy too that the extensive compulsory licensing during the 1940s and 1950s did not prevent a substantial "technology gap" from emerging between the United States as technological leader and otherwise comparable but lagging OECD member nations. See Organization for Economic Co-Operation and Development, Gaps in Technology: Comparisons between Member Countries (Paris: 1970).

analyses were the advantages of a head start, the power of established marketing channels to reach consumers, and very importantly, the pressure of actual and potential rivals threatening market positions with their own innovations. A follow-up study found that variably many years after compulsory patent licensing decrees had been imposed, the subject companies on average spent more on R&D relative to their sales than rival companies not operating under such decrees.[31]

These inferences were replicated in diverse later studies using interview and questionnaire methodologies. For a sample of firms in Great Britain, Taylor and Silberston found that companies subjected to hypothesized worldwide compulsory patent licensing at "reasonable" royalties would reduce their R&D expenditures by 8 percent on average.[32] From 100 companies in the United States, Edwin Mansfield and associates found that the impact of having no expected patent protection would be a 14 percent decrease in the number of innovations actually introduced.[33] Pharmaceutical companies were an exception in both studies, with reductions of 64 percent in the United Kingdom and 60 percent in the United States. Several other surveys using different questionnaire methodologies found that the expectation of patent protection was relatively unimportant compared to other means of capturing the benefits from technological innovations.[34]

Several reasons help explain why the expectation of weak or unavailable patent protection does not significantly impede investment in industrial invention and innovation. All fall under the category of "first mover advantages" achieved through first or early innovative entry into markets. For one, it usually takes would-be imitators time to observe the first mover's innovation, to recognize its commercial attractiveness, and to carry out the R&D needed to field a competing innovation. Relatedly, when would-be

---

31 . F.M. Scherer, The Economic Effects of Compulsory Patent Licensing (New York University Graduate School of Business Administration monograph: 1977), p. 73.

32 . C.T. Taylor and Z. A. Silberston, The Economic Impact of the Patent System (Cambridge University Press: 1973).

33 . Edwin Mansfield, "Patents and Innovation: An Empirical Study," Management Science vol. 32 (1986), pp. 173-181.

34 . Richard Levin et al., "Appropriating the Returns from Industrial Research and Development," Brookings Papers on Economic Activity (1987), pp. 783-832; Wesley Cohen et al., "Protecting Their Intellectual Assets: Appropriability Conditions and Why U.S. Manufacturing Firms Patent (or Not)," National Bureau of Economics Research Working Paper no. 7552 (2000); and Stuart J. H. Graham et al., "High Technology Entrepreneurs and the Patent System," Berkeley Technology Law Journal, vol. 24 (2010), pp. 1255-1327. In the third of these studies, patent protection was found to be more important for startup companies, especially in the biotechnology field, than for well-established firms.

On other nations' experience, see Andres Lopez, "Innovation and Appropriability," in the World Intellectual Property Organisation compendium, The Economics of Intellectual Property, www.wipo.int/export/sites/www/freepublications/en/economics/1012/ wipo_pub_1012.podf.

imitators observe the innovation's success, the research and development required to replicate the pioneer's contribution often takes both time and a substantial fraction of the expense the pioneer required.[35] Third, imitation can be delayed, especially for process innovations, when secrecy is feasible. Fourth, and very importantly, the first mover with a product innovation often gains in the minds of consumers an image advantage that allows it for at least a considerable time period to hold prices well above costs while maintaining a substantial market share.[36] In industries amenable to production cost savings through learning-by-doing, the first mover often gains significant (even if temporary) cost advantages over later imitators.   And finally, the fear that rivals will introduce their own innovations at an early date and preempt substantial market shares -- i.e., what is often called following Joseph A. Schumpeter's conception "creative destruction" -- forces firms to undertake their own defensive R&D activities.

The second of these reasons applies poorly in the pharmaceutical industry, suggesting why pharmaceutical innovation has been found to be exceptionally dependent upon patent protection. For one, patents on pharmaceuticals often delineate with particular clarity the molecule that has been invented. But more importantly, under modern systems for regulating entry into pharmaceutical markets, most of the innovator's substantial expense (in the hundreds of millions of dollars) is incurred for clinical testing to prove that a new molecule is both safe and efficacious in human subjects. Once that information is attained, it becomes in effect a pure public good, available (absent regulatory constraints) at minimal cost to would-be generic imitators. When regulations allow, all the generic imitator needs to do is invest a few million dollars in process design and proof of bioequivalence. Thus, in pharmaceuticals, there is an especially great asymmetry between innovation costs and imitation costs, leaving an important role for patents to fill the gap.[37]

The Xerox settlement in 1975 illuminates the role creative destruction can play. The company's officers anticipated that the main new competitors to Xerox would be Eastman Kodak and IBM, but in fact, the compulsory licensing decree was followed by a wave of successful entry into the U.S. market by Japanese firms. Xerox's response to this new competition might be surprising: Xerox intensified its product improvement efforts. In his memoirs, Xerox chief executive officer David Kearns describes how his predecessor saw the company's position in 1977:[38]

[McColough delivered] a blunt appraisal of the marketplace and Xerox's

---

35   . See Levin et al., supra note 34, at p. 809.

36   . For early recognition, see F. M. Scherer, Industrial Market Structure and Economic Performance (2nd ed., Rand McNally: 1980), pp. 378-385 and 446-447; and Richard Schmalensee, "Product Differentiation Advantages of Pioneering Brands," American Economic Review, June 1982, pp. 349-365.

37   . Under current U.S. regulatory rules, agricultural pesticides and herbicides are similar.

38   . David Kearns and David Nadler, Prophets in the Dark: How Xerox Reinvented Itself and Beat Back the Japanese (Harper: 1992), p. 100.

13

position in it. In no uncertain terms, he made it clear that Xerox was being "out-marketed, out-engineered, outwitted in major segments of our market." He underscored the fact that Xerox would never have it the way it did when it was protected by its patents, when it could take its sweet time developing and marketing products and when it made no difference how much it cost to make something because the company could charge almost whatever it wanted.... "We are now faced with the urgent need for change within this company."

Mr. Kearns continues in his own words:[39]

> The real problems that afflicted us ... were that we had lost touch with our customers, had the wrong cost base, and had inadequate products.... The monopoly environment that Xerox thrived in encouraged internal competition, but not external. We would measure the quality of a new Xerox machine according to the specifications of older Xerox copiers. Those specifications didn't mean very much if other companies were producing something altogether better.

A possible implication of these findings is that an ideal patent system should be fine-tuned to differing environmental circumstances -- e.g., by varying the length of time for which patents can inhibit imitation. But it is doubtful whether national patent office staffs and jurists have the information and insight needed to implement such a flexible approach competently. And for individual patents (but not patent families), TRIPS requires that the term be 20 years from the date when the initial application is filed.

The Change in U.S. Policies

The 1970s saw the culmination of tough U.S. antitrust enforcement with respect to patents. Reflecting on what had been accomplished, the second-ranking official in the U.S. Antitrust Division articulated in 1972 what came to be known as the "nine no-nos" in the licensing of patents:[40]

1) It is unlawful to require a licensee to purchase unpatented materials from the licensor [i.e., tying].

2) It is unlawful for a patentee to require a licensee to assign to the patentee any patent which may be issued to the licensee after the licensing arrangement is executed [i.e., an exclusive grantback provision].

3) It is unlawful to attempt to restrict a purchaser of a patented product in the resale of that product.

---

39 . Ibid. pp 68, 123.
40 . Remarks of Bruce B. Wilson before the Michigan State Bar Antitrust Law Section on September 21, 1972, reproduced in the current documents binder of the Trade Regulation Reporter, para. 13,126 (1972).

14

4) A patentee may not restrict his licensee's freedom to deal in products or services not within the scope of the patent.

5) It is unlawful for a patentee to agree with his licensee that he will not, without the licensee's consent, grant further licenses to any other person.

6) Mandatory or coercive package licensing [i.e., of groups of patents] is an unlawful extension of the patent grant.

7) It is unlawful for a patentee to insist, as a condition of the license, that his licensee pay royalties in an amount not reasonably related to the licensee's sales of products covered by the product. (Examples included assessing a royalty on sales of all relevant products, unpatented as well as patented).

8) The law may be overstepped when the owner of a process patent places restrictions on the licensee's sales of products made using the patented process.

9) It is unlawful for a patentee to require a licensee to adhere to any specified or minimum price with respect to the licensee's sale of the licensed products.

These suggested rules have the ring of per se prohibitions, although Deputy Assistant Attorney General Wilson clarified that the conduct of licensors and licensees was to be judged under a rule of reason.

The regulatory framework began to change markedly in the 1980s. In 1982, a new patent-friendly court was created to hear patent case appeals. And more conservative president Ronald Reagan ensured from the time of his inauguration in 1981 that business-friendly officials were appointed to key policy positions. Soon thereafter, a newly-appointed Antitrust Division leader asserted than the nine no-nos "contain more error than accuracy."[41] The federal antitrust agencies prosecuted restrictive patent licensing practices less aggressively, and in 1995, i.e., under William Clinton's Democratic administration, new Antitrust Guidelines for the Licensing of Intellectual Property were published jointly by the Department of Justice and Federal Trade Commission. The guidelines articulated general principles holding inter alia that "intellectual property licensing allows firms to combine complementary factors of production and is generally procompetitive" and that the antitrust agencies would not presume without analysis that intellectual property creates market power (i.e., monopoly pricing power). Rather, meaningful markets had to be defined, as in other antitrust cases.

---

41   . See on this and related themes F. M. Scherer, "The Political Economy of Patent Policy Reform in the United States," Journal of Telecommunications & High Technology Law, Spring 2009, especially pp. 176-179, 186-195, and 199-207.

In effect, a rule of reason framework was embraced, requiring the analysis of how much pricing power patent holdings actually confer and weighing whatever anticompetitive effects license restrictions might have against their benefits in terms of stronger incentives for innovation, wider technology diffusion, and reduced research and production costs. In principle, this approach is eminently sensible. But implementing it depends upon the mental predisposition brought to the task by competition policy enforcers. And on that, doubts emerge -- most notably, because the Guidelines and an interpretive report published by the two agencies in 2007 fail almost entirely to acknowledge the accumulated research showing that in most instances, patent protection is not the principal means by which innovators recoup sufficient profits to reimburse their risky investments in research and development.[42] The difficult task of enforcing laws whose laudable objective is technological progress is likely to be misguided if enforcers embrace faulty premises about the mix of incentives favorable to innovation.

Other Jurisdictions Modify Their Competition Laws

Although other countries were less aggressive than the United States during the 1940s and 1950s in targeting intellectual property abuses, many have evolved their own approaches to the competition policy interaction.

European Community

We begin with the European Community. Its innovative doctrinal approach first gained prominence in copyright rather than patent matters. A leading precedent was the so-called Magill case.[43] In Ireland during the early 1980s, there was no comprehensive weekly publication to guide television viewers in selecting among alternative broadcasts. Three publications, two owned by broadcasters, provided coverage of only subsets of offerings. Magill offered a unified guide, drawing inter alia upon the copyrighted materials in the more selective publications. The latter refused to grant permission, claiming the exclusive right from their copyright. The European Court of Justice ruled in 1995 that Magill could assert competition law to license the three publishers' materials, ruling that they were dominant providers in their own respective program guide domains and that the information they published was an essential input into providing a new product for which there was potential consumer demand. The resulting precedent is widely known as the essential facility doctrine.

It was developed further inter alia in the IMS case.[44] IMS was (and is) the

---

42 . U.S. Department of Justice and Federal Trade Commission, Antitrust Enforcement and Intellectual Property Rights: Promoting Innovation and Competition (April 2007).

43 . Radio Telefis Eireann v. European Commission, joined cases C-241/01 and C-242/91 (1991).

44 . IMS Health Case v. NDC Health, case C-418/01 (2004). A year after the EC decision, NDC was acquired by another firm, Per Se Technologies, which in turn was acquired by

dominant provider of detailed information on the prices and quantities of individual pharmaceutical products sold in narrowly-defined geographic territories. It obtains the information through surveys of a large sample of individual pharmacies. Its data for Germany, sold to pharmaceutical manufacturers (which used them in their marketing) and also distributed free to health insurers, were aggregated into 1,860 geographic areas that it called "bricks." IMS filed for copyright on its brick structure. NDC Health began conducting its own surveys and providing reports by geographic area. Its customers preferred to have the data for areas comparable to those used by IMS. When NDC Health thereupon adopted a brick structure very close to that of IMS, IMS alleged breach of copyright. Supervening a 2002 German judicial decision, the European Commission ruled that the 1860-brick market definition scheme was an "indispensable" input for competition in supplying the desired sales data and that IMS' refusal to enter into a licensing agreement was an abuse of its dominant position under Article 82 of the European Community Treaty. By way of clarification, the European Court of Justice ruled that:[45]

> [R]efusal to grant a license for the use of an intangible asset protected by copyright entails an abuse of a dominant position ... where (a) there are no objective justifications for such refusal; [and] (b) use of the intangible asset is essential for operating on a secondary market with the consequence that ... such refusal would ultimately eliminate all competition on the market.

The judge qualified these conditions, however, to require that the firm seeking a license "intends to produce goods or services of a different nature which, although in competition with those of the owner of right, answer specific consumer requirements not satisfied by existing goods or services."[46] Anticipating issues we shall discuss later, the judge also ruled that the collaboration of pharmaceutical manufacturers in establishing the brick structure led in effect to the establishment of a de facto standard, which in turn warranted licensing. Surprisingly not considered in the European Court's analysis was the likelihood that assembling detailed data on retail sales entailed fixed costs so high that the activity was what economists call a natural monopoly. There was no evident tradeoff between the higher cost of dividing the compilation and sale of such data between two sources and the benefits (e.g., reduction of sampling errors) associated with having two sources.

An important exercise of the dominant firm abuse principle closer to the realm of high technology occurred in the European Commission's 2004 decision and subsequent enforcement actions with respect to Microsoft's dominant Windows operating system.[47]

McKesson Corporation in 2007. The principal remaining competitor to IMS in prescription data gathering, Symphony Health Solutions, was itself the result of a four-way merger.

45   . Opinion of Advocate General Tizzano (October 2, 2003).
46   . Ibid.
47   . European Commission decision in COMP/C-3/37.792 (2004). See also F. M. Scherer, "Abuse of Dominance by High-Technology Enterprises: A Comparison of U.S. and E.C.

Microsoft had diversified from desktop computer operating systems to sell server systems too. It claimed that because of its superior knowledge of ubiquitous desktop computers' software code, its servers "interoperated" with Windows code better than other companies' servers. Following a complaint from Sun Microsystems, the European Commission successfully prosecuted an abuse of dominance complaint. When Commission consultants reported that Microsoft had not disclosed sufficient information (claimed by Microsoft to be unpatented trade secrets) to allow smooth interoperability, as it had been ordered to do, fines escalating by 2 million Euros daily were assessed. Eventually a settlement was reached. For licensing its code information, Microsoft initially demanded a royalty of 5.95 percent on the value of the data-using equipment. As daily fines were mounting, Microsoft settled for a royalty of 0.4 percent.

Actually, the Microsoft case was not the first European Commission intervention into the computer interface information issue. Beginning with the introduction of System 360 in the mid-1960s, IBM offered a computer architecture under which peripheral functions such as add-on memory, printers, and the like plugged into a common central processing unit connection interface. This prompted the rapid emergence of "plug-compatible" peripheral equipment manufacturers (who eroded IBM's substantial profits from leasing its own devices). IBM pursued a variety of actions to thwart such competition. Following an unsuccessful U.S. government suit, the European Commission began its own investigation, leading to a 1984 "undertaking" (in U.S. terms, a consent decree) between the Commission and IBM under which IBM agreed to disclose within 120 days of a new System 370 computer's introduction all interface information required to allow all hardware and software producers to attach their offerings to IBM mainframes. A follow-up survey revealed mixed views on the agreement's efficacy. One important plug-compatible memory device manufacturer reported that the disclosures were "absolutely essential to our ability to compete," whereas another said that interfaces had been sufficiently standardized that the agreement added little vital information.[48]

In 2004 the European Commission adopted formal regulations (amending earlier 1965 and 1996 statements) that clarified what intellectual property licensing and technology transfer practices are deemed consistent with European competition policies.[49] Declaring that technology transfer agreements "usually improve economic efficiency ... as they can reduce duplication of research and development ... and strengthen the incentive for the initial research and development," the regulation provides for them what as a first approximation is a "block exemption" or safe harbor

---

Approaches," Economia e Politica Industriale, vol. 38 (March 2011), pp. 39-62.

48   . F. M. Scherer, "Microsoft and IBM in Europe," Antitrust and Trade Regulation Reporter (January 24, 2003), p. 65.

49   . Commission Regulation No. 772/2004, published in the Official Journal of the European Union, April 27, 2004. The regulation was scheduled to expire in April 2014. Preliminary indications at the time this paper was written suggest that the regulation would be renewed with only marginal changes.

from competition policy prohibitions.[50] However, the regulation then articulates market share thresholds and lists specific license restrictions that could be subjected to what is in effect per se prohibition. For technology transfer agreements between firms with a combined relevant market share less than 20 percent, or including parties with individual shares of distinct markets less than 30 percent each, it is presumed that agreements are pro-competitive. The regulation then identifies what it calls "hardcore restrictions" that can countervail the presumption of legality. These include restrictions on the parties' independent price-setting for products covered by the agreement; reciprocal output limitations; the delineation of exclusive product markets, geographic territories, or technical fields; obligations accepted not to license the technology to parties other than the agreement's active partners; and provisions allowing a licensee to produce a covered product only for its own use. Other restrictions that can nullify an exemption include mandates for a licensee to license or grant back to the licensor exclusive rights to any improvement inventions in the relevant field of technology. The regulation does not mention other restrictions that would make it fully consistent with the U.S. "nine no-nos" such as tying and resale price maintenance.

Japan

Japan's policies with respect to intellectual property also exhibit a considerable evolution over time. A competition law was imposed unilaterally upon Japan in 1947 by the post-World War II occupation authorities (notably, the United States). The intent of the occupation authorities was mainly twofold: to prevent Japanese firms' participation in international cartels and (consistent with sentiments current in the United States at the time) to limit the economic power of the Zaibatsu conglomerates dominating the Japanese economy. After that, the law was amended several times as Japan made spectacular progress toward becoming one of the world's most technologically adept nations.[51]

Japan's economic development strategy emphasized absorbing foreign technology as rapidly as possible and incorporating it into the capabilities of domestic enterprises, building those firms' export potential, and conserving the nation's initially scarce foreign exchange reserves through a system of payments controls implemented by the Ministry of Finance. As part of the technology absorption strategy, license agreements with foreign firms were encouraged, but the royalties paid under those agreements were kept down by the Finance Ministry's recalcitrant dispensation of foreign exchange allocations. At first, domestic companies were required to report to government authorities cross-border technology transfer agreements before they could be implemented. After 1968, such agreements only had to be reported after-the-fact,

---

50   . The block exemption approach follows earlier United Kingdom precedents with respect to price fixing and similar agreements.

51   . This discussion relies heavily upon Hiroka Yamane, "Competition Analysis of Licensing Agreements: Japan's Developmental Perspectives and Micromanagent of License Protection," manuscript (2012).

and when they came into conflict with competition rules, the Fair Trade Commission could intervene to limit or repeal them.

With a focus on building their nation's technological capabilities, the Japanese authorities placed special emphasis on two main kinds of patent or know-how license restrictions: clauses that required the Japanese license recipients to grant back to the licensors licenses to any improvement inventions that might subsequently be made; and clauses that prevented the Japanese licencees from competing through exports in the licensor's home markets or export markets. The rationale of the grantback constraints was this: If Japanese companies were required to concede rights to any technological improvements they made, their incentives to make those improvements might be limited. And of course, preventing them from competing with licensors would also inhibit demand-pull incentives and their progress toward becoming world-class suppliers. Among the approximately 315 cases in which the Japanese authorities intervened (i.e., provided "administrative guidance") concerning international technology transfer agreements between 1975 and 1990, 64 percent of the objections were raised against one-way rights grantback provisions (i.e., from Japanese licensee to foreign licensor but not vice versa) and 27 percent against agreements not to compete in the licensors' markets.[52] Other interventions against nine practices singled out for scrutiny in a 1968 statement by the Japanese Fair Trade Commission (anticipating the U.S. "nine no-nos") were much less frequent -- e.g., against tie-in sales, resale price maintenance, and other limitations concerning distribution channels. From a 1982 survey, it appears that 39 percent of the international license interventions pertained to patents, 47 percent to know-how, and 44 to technical assistance agreements.

Policies in Noteworthy Industries

Although one could extend our analysis at length by examining the relevant competition policies of other countries, we proceed best by exploring in some detail the precedents evolved in two particularly patent-sensitive fields of commerce: pharmaceuticals and information technology. From them we can see what has been accomplished, what has failed, and what major challenges still exist.

Pharmaceuticals

Patents were a key element in one of the most closely contested antitrust actions in U.S. history, the so-called tetracycline cases.[53] During the 1960s tetracycline was the most widely-prescribed of the so-called broad-spectrum "wonder drugs" invented to fill therapeutic gaps left by the pioneering antibiotic penicillin (introduced during World War II). In separate antitrust complaints pursued in parallel by the U.S. Federal Trade

---

52   . Computed from Yamane, Tables I and II.
53   . For a more extensive discussion of the cases with legal citations, see F. M. Scherer, "The F.T.C., Oligopoly, and Shared Monopoly," forthcoming in the Review of Industrial Organization (2014).

Commission and (with criminal charges) the Department of Justice, it was alleged that drug-makers Pfizer, American Cyanamid, and Bristol-Myers had conspired to ensure that a patent priority dispute in which they were immersed was settled amicably in favor of Pfizer, that they collusively suppressed information which would have prevented issuance of the product patent on tetracycline, and that they colluded to set uniformly high and non-competitive prices (e.g., of $30.60 per 100 capsules at wholesale) when their production costs averaged approximately $2.50.

In the Department of Justice case, these charges were presented before a jury in New York City. Prosecuters implied inter alia that the "unreasonable" prices charged by defendants were evidence of collusion. Company executives denied under oath that they had colluded to fix prices or agreed to limit the number of patent licensees. Instructing the jury, Judge Frankel stated:

> I think you will find it helpful to translate the word "unreasonable" to mean "unusual" or "artificial" or "extra-ordinary." By these suggested definitions I am trying to convey the thought that the idea of unreasonableness in the present context is meaningful only if it is understood to refer to kinds of price behavior or price levels which appear to be divorced from variations and differences in available supply or demand or cost or other economic factors that may normally be expected to cause variations or changes in the prices charged in a competitive market. To put the thought in another and slightly shorter way, the charge of unreasonableness in this case is material only insofar as it poses the issue of whether the prices involved exhibited qualities or peculiarities of a type that could be deemed evidence that such prices resulted from agreement rather than competition.

The jury voted for conviction on all counts, but on appeal, the judgment was reversed in a 2-1 split decision, largely because in devoting substantial attention to such "inflammatory issues" as patents, pricing, and profits, Judge Frankel had failed to focus the jury's attention on the key issue of what agreements, if any, were reached among company executives. The Supreme Court divided 3-3 on whether to overturn the appellate court reversal. A new trial, held six years after the original trial, led to a bench judgment that the prosecution had not conclusively shown collusive restraints.

Meanwhile the Federal Trade Commission case was experiencing similar reverses. The hearing officer ruled that collusion had not been proven, but the Commission as a whole reversed his decision and ordered that the tetracycline patent and two tetracycline salt patents be licensed at a royalty rate of 2.5 percent. The Commission's decision was voided on procedural grounds, and a new hearing was ordered. It focused only on the question of whether the companies suppressed information that tetracycline had emerged by natural causes as a co-product in the manufacture of a predecessor antibiotic, chlortetracycline (Aureomycin). The hearing officer concluded that information which would have invalidated the patent was in fact suppressed, and in 1972 the Commission as a whole again ordered compulsory licensing, this time only of the key tetracycline patent. But the decree probably had little direct effect, because several other companies had entered without licenses into tetracycline production, and prices had fallen substantially. The new entrants presumably inferred that they could enter the market without fear of infringement suits because the patent holder -- in this case, Pfizer -- knew from the wide publicity about alleged suppression of co-production that it could not succeed in legal efforts to sustain its patent and block entrants' sales.

In the early 1970s, the tranquilizer Valium (diazapoxide) was the most frequently prescribed drug in West Germany.[54] It and a molecularly similar drug Librium were developed in the U.S. laboratories of Switzerland's Hoffmann-LaRoche Company during the late 1950s. The two drugs' combined peak share of the market for benzodiazepine tranquilizers in Germany was 91.6 percent in 1965, with the earlier of the two, Librium, holding a majority position at first but losing its favored position during the 1970s to Valium. Both molecules were patented, and both were sold in Germany (as in many other nations) at prices far in excess of production costs, even when average company R&D costs were considered. As part of a multi-pronged effort to combat inflation, the German Federal Cartel Office (Bundeskartellamt) brought an action against Hoffmann-LaRoche in 1974. It did not attack Roche's patents per se, but sought to curb the company's monopoly power by compelling price reductions -- in it first 1974 order, by 60 percent for Valium and 65 percent for Librium. As in the tetracycline case, the case bounced back and forth among judicial authorities for six years -- twice to the Berlin Court of Appeals (Kammergericht) and twice to the German Republic's supreme court. In the end, the Cartel Office's attempts failed. The key issue was the definition of an "as if" price, i.e., the price that would be charged if the markets for Valium and Librium were effectively competitive, but taking account also the existence of patent protection. At first the Cartel Office attempted to use prices in Italy as a benchmark, but that approach was rejected by higher courts because in Italy, unlike Germany, drugs could not be patented, and because Italy had pervasive price controls even for its unpatented drugs. The focus then turned to prices charged by Centrafarm, a generic supplier in Netherlands. This comparison was rejected by the Federal Supreme Court, in part because Centrafarm obtained its supplies in bulk from Italy (where they were unpatented) and England, and in the end mainly because Centrafarm's Valium sales were so small, even at home in the Netherlands, that they provided an insufficient basis for competitive comparison. As a result, according to Erich Kaufer,[55] "... the zealous efforts of the FCA to use Sec. 22 as an instrument of price control in order to fight inflation, or to lower the general level of drug prices, have been halted." Instead of using competition laws as a price control mechanism, nations have attempted to limit

---

54   . This account relies upon Erich Kaufer, "The Control of the Abuse of Market Power by Market-Dominant Firms under the German Law Against Restraints of Competition," Zeitschrift fuer die gesamte Staatswissenschaft, September 1980, pp. 510-531; and Ingo Schmidt, "Different Approaches and Problems in Dealing with Control of Market Power," Antitrust Bulletin, Summer 1983, pp. 417-460.

55   . Supra note 54 at p. 529.

monopoly pricing power through price controls implemented as part of a more general pharmaceutical regulation system[56] or by invoking the more flexible compulsory licensing provisions of TRIPS Agreement Section 31.

South Africa was a pioneer in combining the TRIPS provisions with its own competition laws to improve the supply of retrovirals effective against HIV/AIDS, with which it was severely afflicted.[57] By 2003, it had become known that a so-called "triple therapy," including three different anti-retroviral drugs, was the most effective way to treat AIDS. Three-drug therapy was more effective in abetting the frequent mutations that could render individual therapeutic molecules impotent, and combining three molecules in one twice-daily pill was a superior way to ensure daily compliance, again reducing the danger of mutation. But patents covering one of the drugs (AZT) were held by GlaxoSmithKline (successor to Burroughs-Wellcome) and those for two other key ingredients were held by the German firm Boehringer-Ingelheim. All three drugs were sold by those firms in South Africa at prices far above their production costs. The two firms declined to cross-license each other, so no single-pill therapy was available. An action by the South African Competition Commission aided by CPTECH, an offspring of Ralph Nader's U.S. consumer advocacy organization, induced the firms to offer compulsory licenses, first to a South African generic supplier, Aspen Pharmacare, and then to foreign (e.g. Indian) suppliers.[58] New triple therapies became available at unprecedentedly low prices.

A dispute over when applicable patent rights have expired, allowing the generic production of the broad-spectrum antibiotic cefaclor, provided a key test of Canada's Intellectual Property Enforcement Guidelines, issued in 2000. On p. 8, the Guidelines state that "A transfer of IP rights that lessens or prevents competition is a further example of a situation in which competitive harm results from something more than the mere exercise of the IP right to refuse." And on pp. 6-7, the Guidelines assert that "In assessing whether a particular licensing arrangement raises a competition issue, the Bureau examines whether the terms of the license serve to create, enhance or maintain the market power of either the licensor or the licensee. The Bureau will not consider licensing agreements involving IP to be anti-competitive unless they reduce competition substantially or unduly relative to that which would have likely existed in the absence of the license."

56　. See Patricia Danzon, Pharmaceutical Price Regulation (AEI Press, 1997).

57　. This paragraph is drawn from F. M. Scherer, "Patents, Monopoly Power, and the Pricing of Pharmaceuticals in Low-Income Nations," in Daniele Archibugi and Andrea Filipetti, eds. The Handbook of Global Science, Technology and Innovation (forthcoming in 2014 from Wiley-Blackwell). We are indebted to Jamie Love, who led the CPTECH effort, for background materials.

58　. The settlement was essentially by consent, with no formal judicial decision. But see Competition Commission of South Africa, "GSK and BI Issue Anti-retroviral Licenses," Competition News, March 2004, pp. 1-2; and "Agreement Expands Generic Drugs in South Africa to Fight AIDS," New York Times, December 11, 2003, p. A24.

A challenge soon emerged. By April 27, 1995, the main product patent covering Eli Lilly's highly profitable cefaclor antibiotic, brand-named Ceclor, had expired. On that day, two important events occurred.[59] The U.S. Food and Drug Agency approved the generic production of cefaclor, and Lilly purchased from a Japanese company, Shiongi, that company's U.S. and Canadian rights to two patents covering the principal alternative process (not encompassed by Lilly patents) for manufacturing the drug. Apotex of Canada imported bulk generic cefaclor from an Indian supplier allegedly using the Shionogi technology (although the facts on its use were disputed). Lilly sued Apotex for infringement, and Apotex countered by arguing that the exclusive agreement with Shionogi was an illegal conspiracy to monopolize the Canadian market. Apotex' appeal to the Federal Court of Appeals against a negative lower court decision was joined by the Canada Competition Bureau, which argued that the assignment of patents like Shionogi's could "have the potential to increase Lilly's market power beyond what was contemplated under [Canada's] Patent Act."[60] The Appeals Court ruled that such patent assignment agreements were not exempted from Canada's cartel law and noted that the Lilly-Shionogi transfer was inconsistent with Canada's Intellectual Property Guidelines. On remand to consider the facts, the court of first instance observed that many factual issues remained unresolved and that "The Court could not really do justice to all the issues raised."[61] Ruling against the plea of Apotex to deny Lilly's claims for infringement damages because of the monopoly-sustaining Lilly-Shionogi agreement, Federal Court Judge Gauthier concluded that "Put plainly, the anticompetitive consequences of an assignment of patent rights do not in and of themselves undermine or undo a lawful assignment of rights.[62] The Court found no reason to apply the Competition Bureau's Guidelines (para. 717) and said that if the Competition Bureau objected to the Shionogi-Lilly transfer, it should have brought its own Competition Act enforcement action (para. 724). Damages to be determined subsequently were ordered. Further appeals to the Appeals Court yielded no reversal.[63] Thus, in an extraordinarily long and profusely-contested case, the Competition Bureau's approach was in effect rejected.

The difficult question of when the generic production of a pharmaceutical can

---

59   . On the same day Lilly sued to enjoin three companies authorized by the U.S. Food and Drug Administration to sell generic cefaclor, alleging infringement of the Shionogi patents. Judge Barker of Indianapolis denied the injunction. Co-author Scherer testified in the July 1995 proceedings and also prepared in 2003 an affidavit (apparently not filed) in the later Canadian Apotex case.

60   . See OECD, Competition, Patents and Innovation II, report of a conference in Paris in June 2009, pp. 91-92.

61   . Eli Lilly and Co. et al. v. Apotex Ltd et al., opinion of Justice Gauthier, October 1, 2009, para. 6-9.

62   . Ibid., para. 640.

63   . Report by Scott Foster for the Association of Corporate Counsel on 2010 FCA 2400, http://www.lexology.com/library/detail. aspx?g=d5a6b72f-4396-a13a-a149aa86ef62.

begin has evoked a much wider-ranging debate. As in the Ceclor cases, key patents may have expired and regulatory approval for generic entry may be secured, but other more peripheral improvement patents may remain in force. The U.S. Hatch-Waxman Act allows regulators to approve generic entry when the generic firms claim that the remaining patents are not binding. Then an asymmetry of motives often emerges. To illustrate, suppose that before generic entry begins, the original patent holder is selling its product and realizing a gross margin of $200 million per year, i.e., 80 percent of its $250 million sales. Because they lack first-mover reputation advantages, the first generic entrants usually sell their products at a substantial discount relative to the branded first mover -- e.g., at a 50 percent discount that then increases as additional generic competitors appear.[64] In the first years of generic entry, the entrants capture much less than all sales of the relevant product. Assume it is 30 percent in the first year of generic sale. Then the sales of generic entrants are approximately $250 million x .30 (the generic share) x .50 (recognizing the price discount) = $37.5 million, from which must be deducted production costs of $15 million (assuming generics' unit costs to be the same as those of the incumbent), leading to a generic gross margin of $22.5 million. If some relevant but marginal patents remain in force, the incumbent has an incentive to use them as the basis for a patent infringement suit, attempting to defend the $60 million gross margin it would lose because of entry. There is an asymmetry, however; the generic entrants stand to gain at most $22.5 million if they are successful. And they (like the incumbent) face substantial litigation costs with uncertain outcome. So there are incentives for a deal. The incumbent can offer the generic entrants $25 million per year for remaining out of its market, retaining on sales that otherwise would be ceded to generic competitors a gross margin of $35 million. The would-be generic entrants are at least as well off accepting this "pay for delay" offer as compared to entering at reduced margins and incurring litigation costs. The only losers are the consumers, who otherwise would have saved $37.5 million buying lower-priced generic drugs, and the lawyers who would have profited from costly litigation.

Many such "pay for delay" schemes, less pejoratively called "reverse payment" agreements, materialized during the 1990s, inducing the U.S. Federal Trade Commission to issue a report emphasizing their anti-competitive consequences.[65] Numerous Federal and private class action lawsuits alleging antitrust law violations were brought, and diverse lower courts disagreed in their posture toward reverse payments and the principles for judging their legality. In the first such case to reach the U.S. Supreme Court, the Court divided by five-to-three, but in the end the majority rejected the Federal Trade Commission's argument that such agreements be ruled "presumptively illegal," calling instead for a rule of reason analysis weighing anticompetitive effects against the possibility that the settlement was primarily a means

---

64   . See F. M. Scherer, "Pharmaceutical Innovation," in A. P. Cuyler and J. P. Newhouse, eds, Handbook of Health Economics (North-Holland, 2000), AROUND p. 1225.

65   . U.S. Federal Trade Commission, staff report, Generic Entry Prior to Patent Expiration (Washington: 2002).

of avoiding complex and costly patent validity litigation.[66] The Court's majority recognized that the U.S. Congress intended in passing generic drug legislation to promote competition, but it observed also that reverse payments might approximate the litigation expenses saved through settlement. The outcome of patent validity contests, both the majority and dissenting minority agreed, is uncertain.[67] The majority insisted that a rule of reason approach did not require the competition policy advocates to "litigate the patent's validity, empirically demonstrate the virtues or vices of the patent system, [or] present every possible supporting fact or refute every possible pro-defense theory."[68] But it left to the lower courts the task of "structuring the ... rule-of-reason antitrust litigation" to weigh conflicting theories and resolve the key issues. In other words, it dodged the hard question of determining whether reverse payments did or did not tend in the typical case to be anti-competitive.

Startlingly absent from the Supreme Court's analysis was any recognition of evidence published nearly two month's before the Court's decision in what is widely considered the leading journal of the physical sciences.[69] From a study of 277 challenges between original drug patent holders and would-be generic producers, authors Hemphill and Sampat found a striking difference between the cases focusing on patents covering main active ingredients and the so-called "secondary" patents, involving "ancillary aspects of drug innovation -- such as particular drug formulations and compositions -- beyond the core ... patent on a novel active ingredient." In the primary patent cases litigated to completion, patent holders won against alleged infringers by a ratio of 12 to 1. In the fully litigated and much more numerous secondary patent cases, however, the alleged infringers prevailed by a ratio of 2 to 1.[70] Such evidence could have suggested that at least in cases where the original chemical composition patents had expired and only later, secondary patents were at issue, a presumption might be endorsed viewing "pay for delay" payments as anticompetitive. But what is clear is that further costly litigation will follow.

---

66   . Federal Trade Commission v. Actavis, Inc. et al., slip opinion, decided June 17, 2013, p. 20.

67   . As Chief Justice Roberts wrote in the dissent,
"[W]e're not quite certain if the patent is actually valid, or if the competitor is actually infringing it. But that is always the case, and is plainly a question of patent law."

68   . Majority opinion, slip opinion p. 21.

69   . C. Scott Hemphill and Bhaveen Sampat, "Drug Patents at the Supreme Court," Science, March 200, 2013, pp. 1886-1387.

70   . Out-of-court settlements not included in these ratios were more prevalent for secondary than for primary patents. The primary vs. secondary issue was also crucial in the Indian Supreme Court's decision in 2013 to reject a Novartis application for patent protection on Gleevec, an anti-cancer drug. The broad primary claim covering the molecular structure of Gleevec (U.S. patent 5521184) was ineligible for patenting at the time under India's pre-TRIPS patent law, and the claim rejected by the Indian Supreme court (U.S. patent 6894051) was clearly secondary and confined mainly to formulation variations.

"Pay for delay" agreements have also attracted the intense attention of European Union competition policy enforcers. In June 2013 the European Commission assessed fines of 94 million Euros against a Danish company, Lundbeck, and 52 million Euros on several generic producers as penalties for payments to delay or in one case rescind the marketing of generic substitutes for Lundbeck's Citalopram antidepressant. Lundbeck's basic product patent had expired, and several process patents provided only "more limited protection." Announcing the action, European competition policy head Joaquin Almunia stated flatly:[71]

> It is unacceptable that a company pays off its competitors to stay out of its market and delay the entry of cheaper medicines. Agreements of this type directly harm patients and national health systems, which are already under tight budgetary constraints. The Commission will not tolerate such anticompetitive practices.

Assuming no reversal on appeal to the European High Court, it appears that the European Commission has chosen to come much closer to a per se approach than the U.S. Supreme Court. In December 2013 a further decision concerning Novartis and Johnson & Johnson is expected.

Information Technology

Especially in the realm of information technology, standards must be established allowing devices such as computers and cellular telephones to encode, transmit, and interpret data in a form compatible with devices at all stages of the interoperating network. At first, for telegraph and telephone communications, the standard-setting body was quasi-governmental, notably, the eventually was called the International Telecommunication Union, located in Geneva. More recently standards have been set by committees representing interested parties. Problems can arise when a participant in the standard-setting process successfully advocates standard details that require the use of patented technology, e.g., in the form of integrated circuit layouts or software, without revealing that it controls relevant essential patents, and, once need is established through standard adoption, can demand high royalties to license the patents. The OECD staff has called such behavior a "patent ambush."[72]

The so-called Rambus case illustrates a prominent example.[73] A private committee set standards for computer memory chips. Representatives of Rambus, Inc. participated in committee meetings and advocated certain designs while deliberately concealing the fact that their employer had patents pending that covered those designs. Rambus then brought patent infringement suits against several producers of dynamic random access memory (DRAM) chips, demanding substantial royalties. Both the U.S.

---

71   . European Commission Press Release, 19 June 2013.
72   . See Jeremy West, "Background Note," OECD document DAF/COMP(2009)22 (2009), pp. 16 ff.
73   . See West, loc. cit., pp. 35-36.

Federal Trade Commission and the European Commission filed challenges to Rambus' actions. The Federal Trade Commission found on appeal that "Rambus was able to distort the standard-setting process and engage in anticompetitive 'hold-up' of the computer memory industry" and found Rambus' conduct to contribute to the acquisition of unacceptable monopoly power.[74] It ordered Rambus to license the relevant patents for a royalty rate not exceeding 0.5 percent, dropping to zero after three years for standards-essential patents. In 2007 the European Commission filed its own statement of objections to Rambus' behavior, asserting that the company was demanding unreasonable royalties following its successful patent ambush.[75]

The problems in these and other standards patent ambush cases have led the European Community, the United States, and other jurisdictions to insist that companies holding standards-critical patents disclose their patent positions fully before standards are established (so that standards committees can circumvent the patents if the royalties demanded are too high) and that they commit in advance during the standards-setting process to license these patents to all applicants on "fair, reasonable, and non-discriminatory" terms. This has come to be known as the FRAND doctrine or (omitting the "fair") in the United States as the RAND doctrine. This position is not without controversy. Agreeing in industry-based committee proceedings to charge a particular royalty rate comes close to the coordinated setting of prices, which under other conditions is a clear violation against national and European price-fixing prohibitions.[76] A consensus appears to have emerged, however, that it is better to avoid patent ambushes when standards are necessary than to follow traditional competition policy doctrine rigidly -- in other words, to apply a rule of reason.

Acceptance of FRAND still requires that there be a means of establishing what royalty rate is "fair" or "reasonable."[77] This, U.S. appellate court Judge Richard Posner makes clear, is not easily accomplished and can be led astray by biased or incompetent

---

74   . In the matter of Rambus, Inc., FTC docket 9302 (2006 and 2007). For additional cases, see Jeremy West, supra note 74; and Richard Gilbert and Alan Weinschel, "Competition Policy for Intellectual Property: Balancing Competition and Reward," in American Bar Association, Issues in Competition Law and Policy, supra note 14, vol. III, at pp. 2031-2033.

75   . West, supra note 74, at p. 36.

76   . See e.g. the statement of the American Antitrust Institute underlying testimony before the U.S. Senate Judiciary Committee in hearings on standard-essential patents, July 11, 2012.

77   . For some history and theory, see F. M. Scherer, The Economic Effects of Compulsory Patent Licensing, New York University Monograph Series in Finance and Economics, 1977, pp. 43-50; and F. M. Scherer and Jayashree Watal, "Post-TRIPS Options for Access to Patented Medicines in Developing Nations," Journal of International Law, December 2002, pp. 920-924.

In 2013, the Competition Commission of India was reported to be investigating excessive royalty demands by Ericsson of Sweden for the licensing of mobile phone patents -- i.e., applying royalty rates to the prices of whole telephones rather than to the value of the narrow patents licensed. "India: Patent Wars Head to India," Competition Policy International internet report, December 2, 2013.

expert witnesses.[78] At maximum, he observed, the royalty in such cases should not exceed the cost of inventing around the subject patent, which is also not readily ascertained. Arraying 15 alternatives proposed in an earlier U.S. royalty-setting case, Judge Posner agonizes, "[C]ould a judge or jury really balance 15 or more factors and come up with anything resembling an objective assessment?"[79] How FRAND royalties are set will continue to be a focus of controversy.

Implicit in the FRAND approach is the assumption that patent holders will license their patents for royalties and not seek to enjoin the sale of allegedly infringing products altogether. This assumption is widely accepted in all patent cases, not only standards cases, and consistent with a precedent-altering decision by the U.S. Supreme Court in 2006.[80] However, disputes continue, leading to both U.S. presidential and European Commission intervention into running patent claims and counter-claims advanced by Samsung, Apple, Google, and other internationally prominent enterprises in 2013.[81]

Information technology, perhaps more than other fields, has lent itself to the proliferation of many thousands of patents covering details of integrated circuits, microwave tubes, compression codes, transmission methods, and much else. A Fordham University study found that on "smart phones" alone, the number of U.S. patents issued was averaging nearly 3,000 per month in 2012.[82] With so many patents in force, most of them not deemed standard-essential, the risk of inadvertently infringing some is great. Developing new products has come to be like walking through a mine field, with a constant risk of serious consequences when one steps on an unobserved patent. An ambitious quantitative analysis of the U.S. patent experience suggests that in most fields, chemicals and pharmaceuticals excepted, the legal, infringement damage, and related costs associated with patent law suits began in the 1990s to exceed by increasing amounts the patents' worldwide incremental economic value to U.S. publicly-listed corporations.[83]

---

78   . Opinion and order in Apple Inc. et al. v. Motorola Inc. et al., U.S. District Court for the Northern District of Illinois, Case no. 1:11-cv-08540 (June 22, 2012). As Judge Posner observed, inept testimony "invites guesswork. It won't do."

79   . Ibid., slip opinion p. 14. Judge Posner cites Georgia Pacific v. United States Plywood, 318 F. Supp. 1116, 1120 (1970).

80   . I.e., in eBay v. Merc Exchange, 547 U.S. 388 (2006). It stressed that injunctions should be issued only when irreparable injury from infringement has been proven, remedies such as the payment of damages are insufficient to compensate for the injury, and crucially, when the public interest is served by an injunction.

81   . See "Samsung in Talks To Settle EU Antitrust Case," Reuters dispatch by Foo Yunchee, June 25, 2013; Robert D. Stoner, "USTR Disapproves USITC 337 Ruling on Apple v. Samsung," Economists Ink, Fall 2013; and "A President Steps Between Apple and Samsung," Bloomberg Business Week, August 8, 2013, p. 14.

82   . Joel P. Reidenberg et al., "The Impact of the Acquisition and Use of Patents on the Smartphone Industry," draft report to the World Industrial Property Organisation, October 2012.

83   . James Bessen and Michael Meurer, Patent Failure: How Judges, Bureaucrats, and

A specialized facet of the patent accumulation problem deserves further consideration. Although the phenomenon has historical precedents, in recent years some companies, called "patent assertion entities" or more pejoratively, "patent trolls," have as their primary business model acquiring the patents assigned to other individuals and corporations and then finding deep-pocketed infringers against whom infringement suits can be launched. If the suit is successful, substantial damages may be obtained. But more likely, the costs of a law suit are so great that the target company will arrange a settlement by paying less than the expected litigation costs, taking into account also the not-insubstantial probability that error-prone trials will lead to a damages award. Joel Reidenberg and colleagues found that among 267 identifiable U.S. patent infringement suits involving cellular "smart phone" technology, at least 50 were brought by assertion entities, i.e., those that did not perform research and development or produce hardware themselves.[84] Assertion companies also represented from 30 to 40 percent of the most frequent litigants by number. Although one might argue that such companies help perfect markets for patents, in the main, their activities appear to have little redeeming social value.

The U.S. Federal Trade Commission began an investigation of the competitive consequences of patent troll activity in 2013, the results of which have not yet been released.[85] A task force operating directly under U.S. President Barack Obama focused attention on the issue in June 2013, suggesting mainly reforms at the U.S. Patent Office to issue patents of higher quality.[86] Draft bills before the U.S. Congress in 2013 would among other things allow presiding judges more scope in ordering patent suit plaintiffs to pay the legal fees of their targets when the plaintiffs lose.[87] Substantial companies have attempted to defend themselves from blackmail by asking the U.S. Patent Office to reconsider administratively on an accelerated schedule the validity of patents with which they have been attacked.[88] Not suggested by any official source, but also within the

---

Lawyers Put Innovators at Risk (Princeton University Press: 2008), especially p. 138. Litigation costs were estimated by the change in stock market value occurring when patent law suits are announced. They include both legal costs and expected wealth transfers contingent upon successful judgments in favor of plaintiffs. The value of patents was estimated mainly through studies of how much companies are willing to pay to renew their patents.

84 . Supra note 84 at pp. 40-42.
85 . "F.T.C. Is Said to Plan Inquiry of Frivolous Patent Lawsuits," New York Times, June 20, 2013, p. 1.
86 . Brian Kahin, "Troll Economics: The White House Weighs In," www.patentprogress.org/2013/06/14/troll-economics-the-white-house-weighs-in (June 2013).
87 . "Congress Takes on Abusive Patent Suits," New York Times, editorial, Sunday Review, p. 10. See also Randall R. Rader et al., "Make Patent Trolls Pay in Court," op. ed. column, New York Times, June 5, 2013. The authors report that targets' legal costs were shifted to plaintiffs in only 20 out of roughly 3,000 patent cases filed in 2011. Rader was chief judge of the special U.S. appellate court hearing patent appeals.
88 . "A Cheaper Way to Defuse Patent Claims," Bloomberg Business Week, October 24, 2013, p. 41.

realm of possibility, would be retroactively applying the laws prohibiting anticompetitive mergers and acquisitions to challenge large-scale patent acquisitions by non-practicing entities that lead to law suits jeopardizing continued technological progress by enterprises actually producing goods and services.

Conclusion

In this paper we have surveyed the interface between competition policy and the use of patents and other intellectual property across an array of technologically advanced nations. It is clear that widely varying policy tradeoffs have been made. One must assume that national decision-makers were responding reasonably to the changing economic circumstances with which they were confronted and the diverse ideological beliefs they carried into their policy deliberations. Our analysis was conducted to inform developing countries faced with implementing TRIPS Articles 40 and 31 with respect to how intellectual property is used in their home jurisdictions. What our findings suggest is that developing countries, like the developed nations on which we have mainly focused, can reasonably choose among a broad menu of policy alternatives as their national interests dictate. Like Japan in its early postwar economic development phase, the developing countries need precedents that enable their firms to absorb on reasonable terms the technologies that will facilitate their growth. And they might be well advised to favor *per se* rules distilled from the experience of technologically advanced nations rather than adopting a rule of reason approach, with the attendant attorney and expert consultant costs and delays required to balance complex conflicting facts and values.